Scale Aircraft Drawings

Volume 1—World War I

Published by Air Age Inc.
100 East Ridge
Ridgefield, CT 06877-4606 USA.

Manufactured in the United States of America
This book was designed by Alan J. Palermo.

Publishers: Dr. Louis V. DeFrancesco, Yvonne M. DeFrancesco and Louis V. DeFrancesco, Jr.
Editor: Dan Santich
Cover photos by Budd Davisson.

ACKNOWLEDGEMENT: The publishers wish to express their sincere gratitude to
the following: *Jane's All the World's Aircraft; Jane's Encyclopedia of Aviation;* The
American Aviation Historical Society; The Smithsonian Institute; Leonard Opdycke,
WW I Aeroplanes, Inc.; Acme Photo Service; Garden City Press; Arco Publishing Co.
Inc.; The Society of World War I Aero Historians; The Wright Bros. Historical Foun-
dation; Silver Hill Aviation Museum; Air Force Museum; Naval Air Museum; Boeing
Aircraft Corp.; The Curtiss-Wright Aircraft Corp. and Curtiss Museum; Paris Air and
Space Museum.

Contents

INTRODUCTION

by DAN SANTICH

The time-scale of this book represents the period in history when aviation was born. There were no rules. In many cases pilots were self-taught and their airplanes were handmade creations of fabric, wood, and dreams. Pilot comfort was not a pressing issue, and airports to operate from were a long time in coming.

Most of the aircraft presented in this book are only memories: scraps of fabric and wire that one time filled the sky with ambition and heroics. The photographs are all authentic; they represent a relatively new idea for the era—aviation photography.

A scale model is only as good as the effort that went into the research of it. There is, in absolute terms for scale modelers, no substitute for a dimension. A measurement of a given dimension of a given part of an aircraft is one of the most valuable aids to a scale project. With that dimension, a conversion to inches is a simple matter of mathematics. If it isn't given, it's only a guess.

These drawings are of both historical and artistic interest, and are what are generally referred to as Master Drawings.

This book is dedicated to the doer and the dreamer, the armchair pilot and the Captain of tomorrow's spaceship. It's history in black and white. The drawings presented herein are the works of master illustrators, such as Wylam, Nye, Larsen, Karlstrom, and others. It was a massive effort, and the drawings reflect countless hours of research and digging through the halls of history. In some cases, measurements were taken from the actual aircraft. In many cases there were no remaining examples of the aircraft. Obtaining the accurate dimensions of these aircraft was difficult, if not impossible. Where factory drawings and sketches were available, many differences in dimensions were found. To resolve this dilemma, a best-guess approach was used. But it was an educated guess.

Some errors, a few major and some minor, are noted in the text. Modelers and enthusiasts should check them carefully against available photographs before undertaking major projects. A lot of technical material has been uncovered in the last 30 years that was not available to these draftsmen.

It should be noted that the scale reference given in the title block of each drawing does not reflect the scale size of that drawing. All of the drawings in this book have been reduced for presentation and are available from us in their full-size to the appropriate scale. These Master Drawings were rendered in varying scales.

For the scale modeler, this book is invaluable. For the historian, it's a collector's dream. For the aviation-minded, modeler or not, it's a fascinating collection of winged history. We hope you enjoy it.

Albatros D.I to D.VI

drawings by WILLIAM WYLAM

Front view of the Albatros D.V. "Jane's All the World's Aircraft" photo.

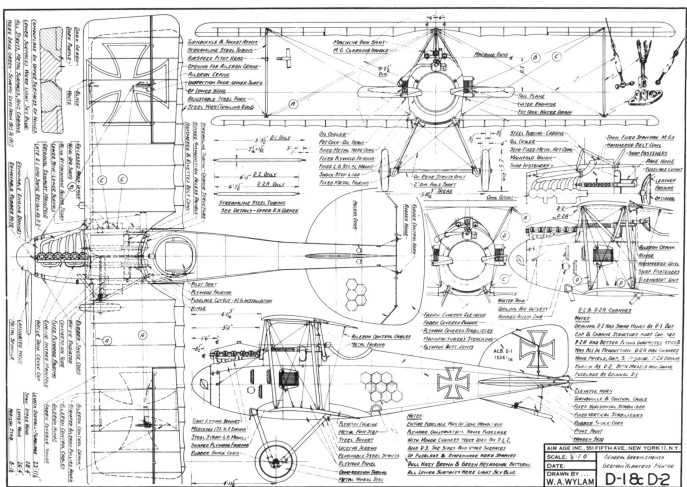

Albatros D.I to D.VI

THE ALBATROS was introduced in
April 1916 by the Albatros Werke, a
manufacturing plant and civil flying
school with excellent aero credentials, in
the town of Johannisthal near Berlin.
The Albatros was the mainstay of
German airpower during the entire first
world war, although it was outclassed by
faster British and French aircraft later in
the war. The Albatros D.I made its
combat debut on September 17, 1916,
against an ill-fated flight of seven British
F.E.2b pushers, resulting in the loss of
five of the pushers and no loss to the
Germans.

The D.1 immediately made every other
fighter aircraft at the front obsolete.
Development continued, however, which
ended with the D.XII. The combat career
of the Albatros did not end with the
closing of WW I, but went into Polish
and Czechoslovakian units. Two survive,
both D.Va's; one at the National Air &
Space Museum, the other in Australia.

□

*Above: A D.Va. The Albatros was a departure from the typical WW I fabric-and-stick fuselage
and utilized advanced streamlining techniques for the times. "Jane's All the World's Aircraft"
photo. Below: A captured Albatros D.III bearing RAF markings is another example of German
streamlining attempts. Squadron/Signal Publications photo.*

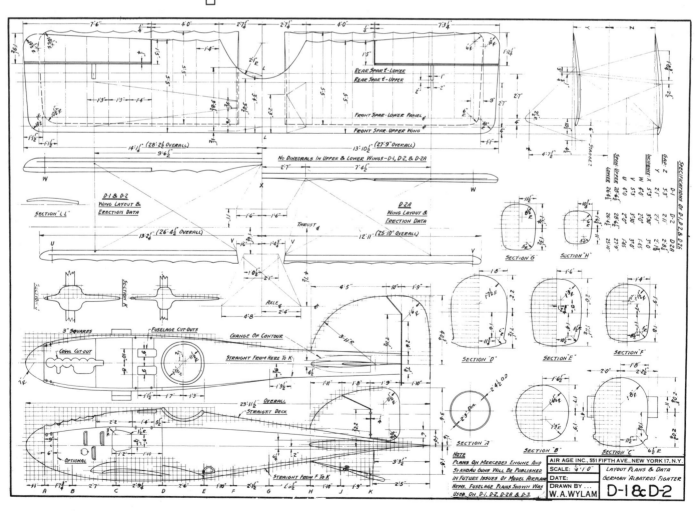

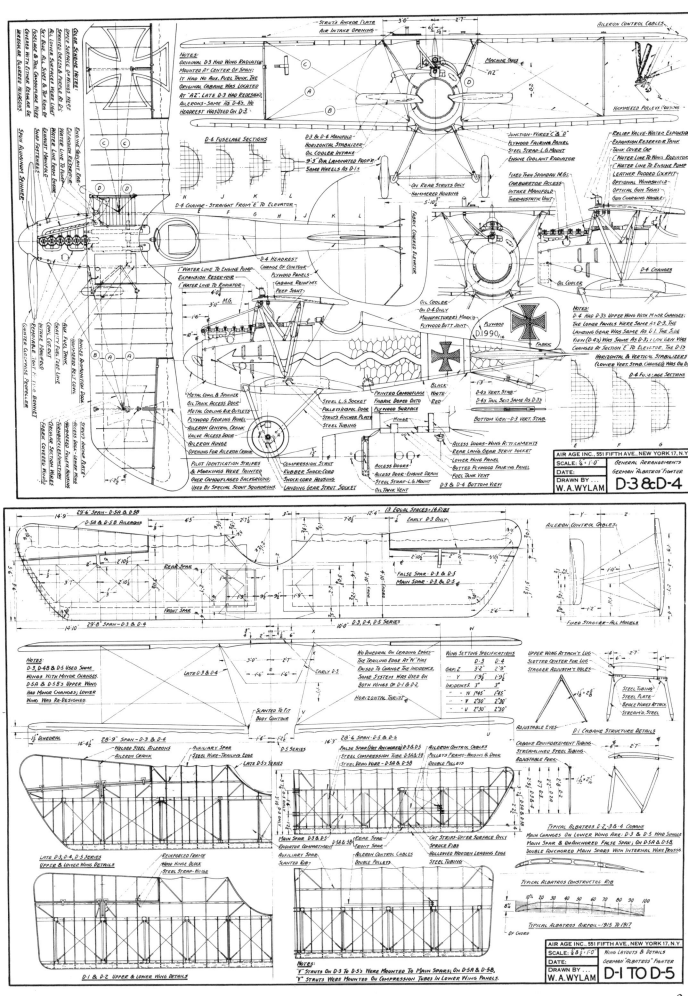

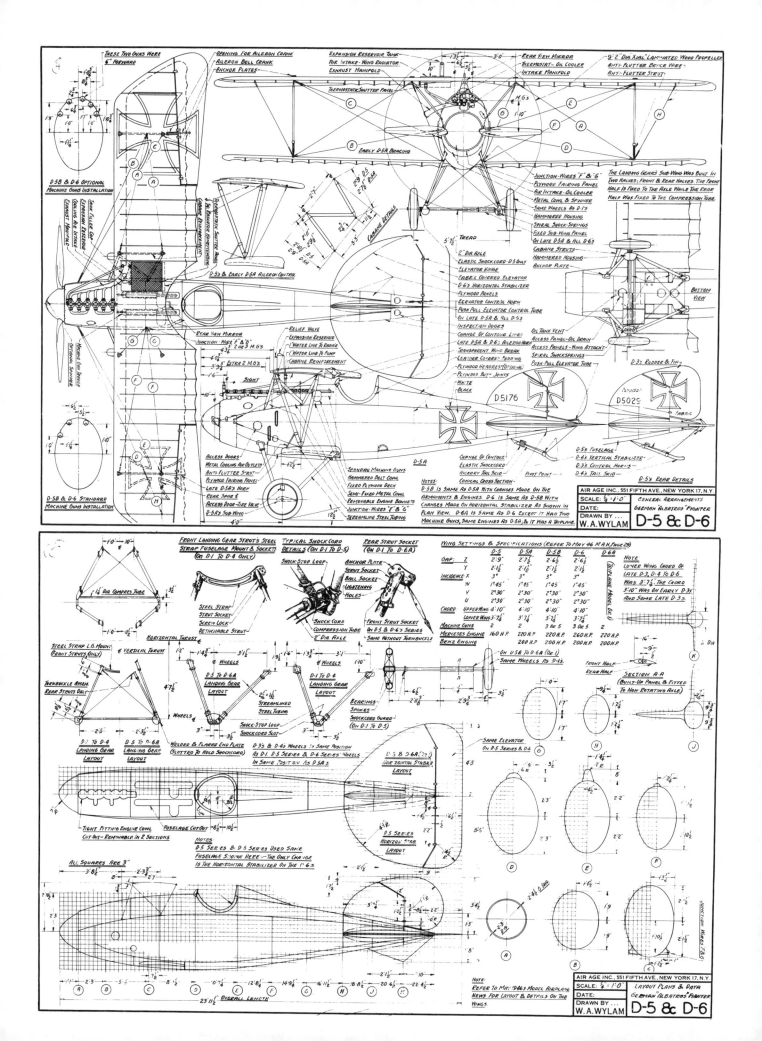

AIR AGE INC., 551 FIFTH AVE., NEW YORK 17, N.Y.
SCALE: ⅜"=1'·0" GENERAL ARRANGEMENTS
DATE: GERMAN ALBATROS FIGHTER
DRAWN BY ...
W. A. WYLAM D-5 & D-6

AIR AGE INC., 551 FIFTH AVE., NEW YORK 17, N.Y.
SCALE: ½"=1'·0" LAYOUT PLANS & DATA
DATE: GERMAN ALBATROS FIGHTER
DRAWN BY ...
W. A. WYLAM D-5 & D-6

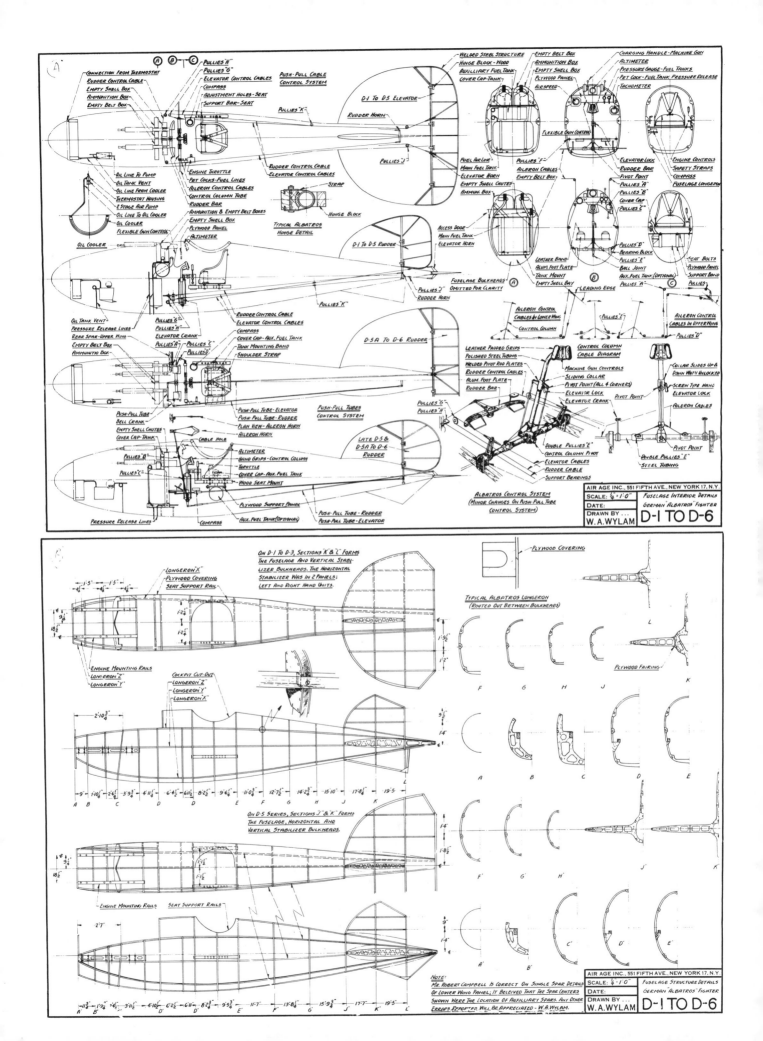

Ansaldo SVA-1

drawing by WILLIS NYE

Ansaldo SVA-4 was nearly identical to SVA-1. Note extra strut in center section bracing. Robert Hare photos from Air Age file.

ALTHOUGH little has been written of Italy's contributions during the first world war, the record is an amazing one. Italy's aerodynamicists were numbered among the world's finest, her factories were efficient, and Italian designs were definitely first class.

One of the largest companies was a firm known as "Societa Gio Ansaldo" of Genoa. To guarantee consistent quality, the firm established a testing program virtually unheard of during that period. In-plant testing and inspections were more critical than any contemporary manufacturer had even thought of. From these facilities came the famous S.V.A. series of fighter and bomber aircraft.

Fitted with a six-cylinder, water-cooled vertical-type engine that developed 225 hp at 1,700 rpm, the aircraft was suited to roles of both fighter and bomber. Altogether six models of the basic S.V.A. design are known to have been built, and of these three were exclusively single-seat fighters, two were listed as "escort" types, and one was fitted out as a single-seat bomber. Only the S.V.A.-4 and -5 reached true production status.

Operationally, the S.V.A.-4 and -5 were a distinct success. Nearly all Italian pursuit squadrons were fitted with the fighter version toward the war's end, while four bomber squadrons were entirely -4 equipped. They regularly took on missions of up to 700 miles round trip, which were completed in less than seven hours. Because of their versatility, the -5 fighters were often fitted with bombs for shorter range work and with extra fuel to escort the bombers.

A curious feature of Ansaldo aircraft, as well as other Italian aircraft up through WW II, was that the left-hand wings were *longer* than the right-hand wings to help overcome torque. Most drawings, including Nye's, do not show this.

The S.V.A. team was a formidable weapon deserving of an everlasting place in aviation's Hall of Fame. Seven survive, five in Italy and two in the U.S. □

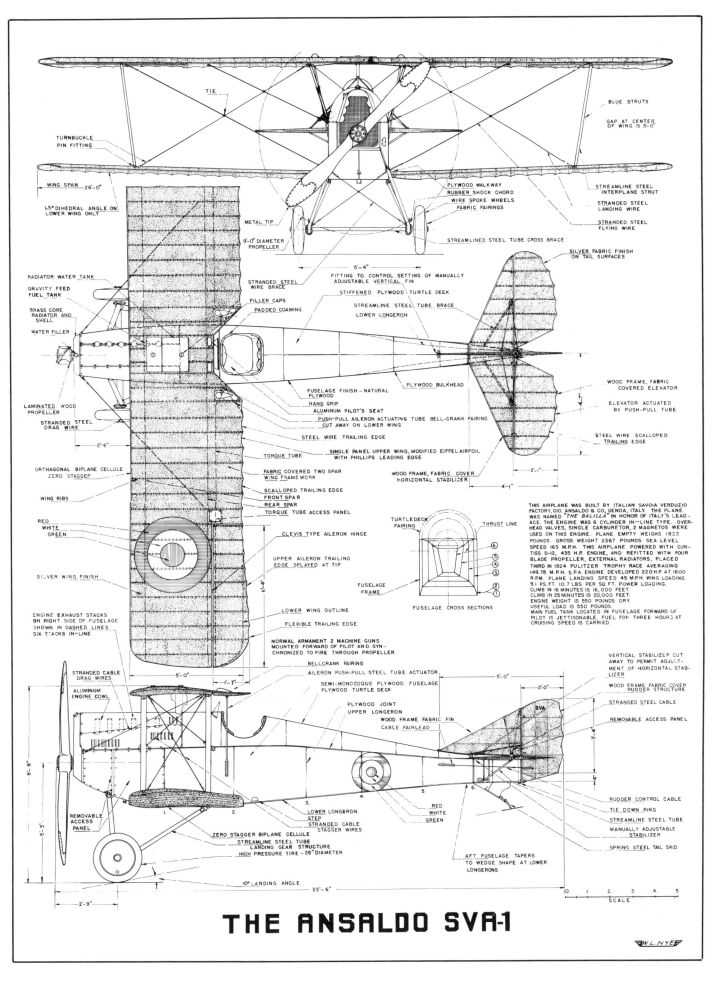

TIE

TURNBUCKLE
PIN FITTING

WING SPAN — 26'-0"

1.5° DIHEDRAL ANGLE ON
LOWER WING ONLY

RADIATOR WATER TANK

GRAVITY FEED
FUEL TANK

BRASS CORE
RADIATOR AND
SHELL

WATER FILLER

LAMINATED WOOD
PROPELLER

STRANDED STEEL
DRAG WIRE

2'-6"

ORTHOGONAL BIPLANE CELLULE
ZERO STAGGER

WING RIBS

RED
WHITE
GREEN

SILVER WING FINISH

ENGINE EXHAUST STACKS
ON RIGHT SIDE OF FUSELAGE.
SHOWN IN DASHED LINES
SIX STACKS IN-LINE

STRANDED CABLE
DRAG WIRES

ALUMINUM
ENGINE COWL

8'-8"

5'-3"

REMOVABLE
ACCESS
PANEL

2'-9"

BLUE STRUTS

GAP AT CENTER
OF WING IS 5-0

PLYWOOD WALKWAY
RUBBER SHOCK CHORD
WIRE SPOKE WHEELS
FABRIC FAIRINGS

STREAMLINE STEEL
INTERPLANE STRUT

STRANDED STEEL
LANDING WIRE

STRANDED STEEL
FLYING WIRE

METAL TIP

9'-0" DIAMETER
PROPELLER

5'-4"

STREAMLINED STEEL TUBE CROSS BRACE

SILVER FABRIC FINISH
ON TAIL SURFACES

STRANDED STEEL
WIRE BRACE

FILLER CAPS

PADDED COAMING

FITTING TO CONTROL SETTING OF MANUALLY
ADJUSTABLE VERTICAL FIN

STIFFENED PLYWOOD TURTLE DECK

STREAMLINE STEEL TUBE BRACE

LOWER LONGERON

FUSELAGE FINISH — NATURAL
PLYWOOD

HAND GRIP

ALUMINUM PILOT'S SEAT

PUSH-PULL AILERON ACTUATING TUBE BELL-CRANK FAIRING
CUT AWAY ON LOWER WING

STEEL WIRE TRAILING EDGE

SINGLE PANEL UPPER WING, MODIFIED EIFFEL AIRFOIL
WITH PHILLIPS LEADING EDGE

FABRIC COVERED TWO SPAR
WING FRAMEWORK

SCALLOPED TRAILING EDGE
FRONT SPAR
REAR SPAR
TORQUE TUBE ACCESS PANEL

CLEVIS TYPE AILERON HINGE

UPPER AILERON TRAILING
EDGE SPLAYED AT TIP

TORQUE TUBE

PLYWOOD BULKHEAD

WOOD FRAME, FABRIC
COVERED ELEVATOR

ELEVATOR ACTUATED
BY PUSH-PULL TUBE

STEEL WIRE SCALLOPED
TRAILING EDGE

2'-1"

4'-1"

WOOD FRAME, FABRIC COVER
HORIZONTAL STABILIZER

TURTLE DECK
FAIRING

THRUST LINE

6
5
4
3

FUSELAGE
FRAME

2
1

FUSELAGE CROSS SECTIONS

THIS AIRPLANE WAS BUILT BY ITALIAN SAVOIA VERDUZIO
FACTORY, GIO. ANSALDO & CO, GENOA, ITALY. THE PLANE
WAS NAMED "THE BALILLA" IN HONOR OF ITALY'S LEAD-
AGE. THE ENGINE WAS 6 CYLINDER IN-LINE TYPE. OVER-
HEAD VALVES, SINGLE CARBURETOR, 2 MAGNETOS WERE
USED ON THIS ENGINE. PLANE EMPTY WEIGHS 1823
POUNDS. GROSS WEIGHT 2367 POUNDS. SEA LEVEL
SPEED 165 M.P.H. THIS AIRPLANE POWERED WITH CUR-
TISS D-12, 435 H.P. ENGINE, AND REFITTED WITH FOUR
BLADE PROPELLER, EXTERNAL RADIATORS, PLACED
THIRD IN 1924 PULITZER TROPHY RACE AVERAGING
149.78 M.P.H. S.P.A. ENGINE DEVELOPED 220 H.P. AT 1600
R.P.M. PLANE LANDING SPEED 45 M.P.H. WING LOADING
9.1 P.S. FT. 10.7 LBS PER SQ. FT. POWER LOADING.
CLIMB IN 16 MINUTES IS 16,000 FEET.
CLIMB IN 25 MINUTES IS 20,000 FEET.
ENGINE WEIGHT IS 550 POUNDS DRY.
USEFUL LOAD IS 550 POUNDS.
MAIN FUEL TANK LOCATED IN FUSELAGE FORWARD OF
PILOT IS JETTISONABLE. FUEL FOR THREE HOURS AT
CRUISING SPEED IS CARRIED.

LOWER WING OUTLINE

FLEXIBLE TRAILING EDGE

NORMAL ARMAMENT 2 MACHINE GUNS
MOUNTED FORWARD OF PILOT AND SYN-
CHRONIZED TO FIRE THROUGH PROPELLER

BELLCRANK FAIRING

AILERON PUSH-PULL STEEL TUBE ACTUATOR

SEMI-MONOCOQUE PLYWOOD FUSELAGE
PLYWOOD TURTLE DECK

PLYWOOD JOINT
UPPER LONGERON

WOOD FRAME FABRIC FIN
CABLE FAIRLEAD

VERTICAL STABILIZER CUT
AWAY TO PERMIT ADJUST-
MENT OF HORIZONTAL STAB-
ILIZER

WOOD FRAME FABRIC COVER
RUDDER STRUCTURE

STRANDED STEEL CABLE

REMOVABLE ACCESS PANEL

RUDDER CONTROL CABLE

TIE DOWN RING

STREAMLINE STEEL TUBE

MANUALLY ADJUSTABLE
STABILIZER

SPRING STEEL TAIL SKID

LOWER LONGERON
STEP
STRANDED CABLE
STAGGER WIRES

RED
WHITE
GREEN

ZERO STAGGER BIPLANE CELLULE
STREAMLINE STEEL TUBE
LANDING GEAR STRUCTURE
HIGH PRESSURE TIRE — 26" DIAMETER

AFT FUSELAGE TAPERS
TO WEDGE SHAPE AT LOWER
LONGERONS

10° LANDING ANGLE

22'-6"

5'-0"

2'-0"

5'-0"

1'-7"

SVA

0 1 2 3 4 5
SCALE

THE ANSALDO SVA-1

W.L. NYE

13

Antoinette VII

drawing by WILLIS NYE

FROM their motorboat engine factory, Leon Levavasseur and Jules Gastambide began building airplanes in 1903; the first successful design, Model IV, flew in 1908. Herbert Latham used it, much modified, in his first cross-Channel attempt, and the Model VII on his second: both efforts ended in the water. Most of the Antoinette designs were heavily modified: the two photographs on this page, and Nye's drawing, are all of the same machine.

The designs were fast and stable: Latham later flew his Model VII, repaired and dried out, over the Golden Gate Bridge in San Francisco in 1911. He was observed on the occasion by Willis L. Nye, our draftsman.

The firm also built the Monobloc, the first internally-braced low-wing monoplane, in 1910: it was too heavy to fly. Three Model VIIs were lent to the U.S. Navy by Harry Harkness, and two of them appear in photographs of the Curtiss training school at North Island, in California.

Three Antoinettes are left, one in London, one in Paris, and one in Krakow, in Poland. □

The advancement in aircraft design exhibited here in 1908 was quite revolutionary. Note rudder and elevator control surfaces. The entire wing panels were moved for lateral control. Photos courtesy of Leonard Opdycke, WW I Aeroplanes.

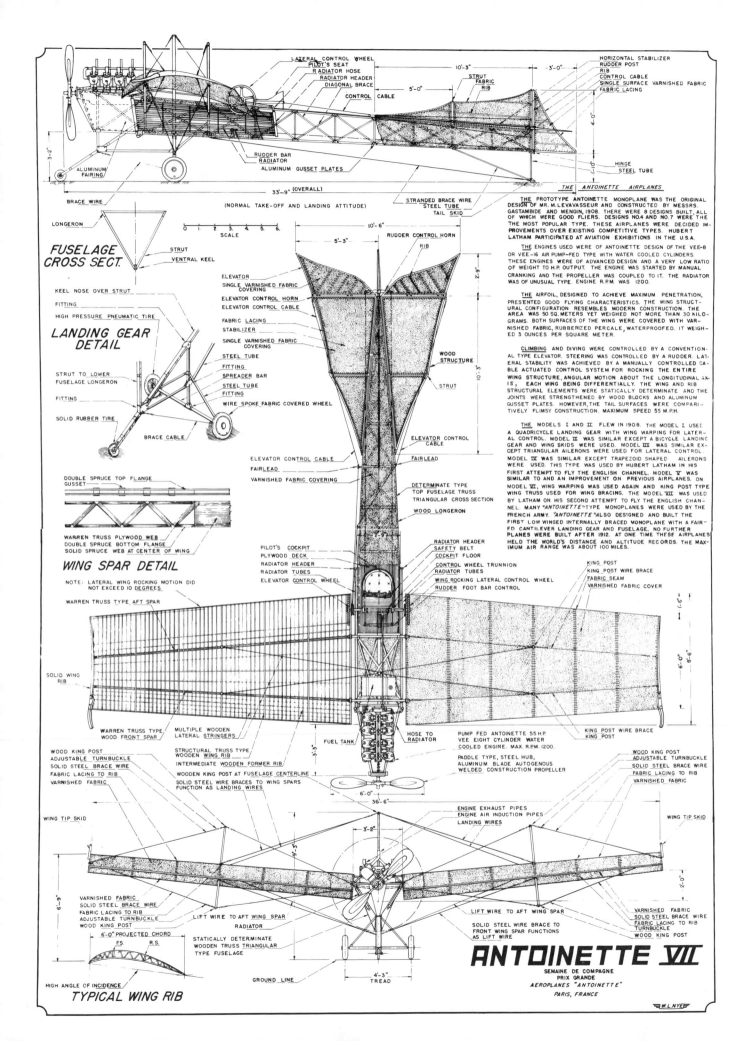

FUSELAGE CROSS SECT.

LONGERON
BRACE WIRE
STRUT
VENTRAL KEEL

LANDING GEAR DETAIL

KEEL NOSE OVER STRUT
FITTING
HIGH PRESSURE PNEUMATIC TIRE
STRUT TO LOWER FUSELAGE LONGERON
FITTING
SOLID RUBBER TIRE
BRACE CABLE

WING SPAR DETAIL

DOUBLE SPRUCE TOP FLANGE
GUSSET
WARREN TRUSS PLYWOOD WEB
DOUBLE SPRUCE BOTTOM FLANGE
SOLID SPRUCE WEB AT CENTER OF WING

NOTE: LATERAL WING ROCKING MOTION DID NOT EXCEED 10 DEGREES

WARREN TRUSS TYPE AFT SPAR

SOLID WING RIB

WARREN TRUSS TYPE WOOD FRONT SPAR
MULTIPLE WOODEN LATERAL STRINGERS
STRUCTURAL TRUSS TYPE WOODEN WING RIB
INTERMEDIATE WOODEN FORMER RIB
WOODEN KING POST AT FUSELAGE CENTERLINE
SOLID STEEL WIRE BRACES TO WING SPARS FUNCTION AS LANDING WIRES

WOOD KING POST
ADJUSTABLE TURNBUCKLE
SOLID STEEL BRACE WIRE
FABRIC LACING TO RIB
VARNISHED FABRIC

WING TIP SKID

VARNISHED FABRIC
SOLID STEEL BRACE WIRE
FABRIC LACING TO RIB
ADJUSTABLE TURNBUCKLE
WOOD KING POST

6'-0" PROJECTED CHORD
FS   R.S.
HIGH ANGLE OF INCIDENCE

TYPICAL WING RIB

STATICALLY DETERMINATE WOODEN TRUSS TRIANGULAR TYPE FUSELAGE
LIFT WIRE TO AFT WING SPAR
RADIATOR
GROUND LINE

LATERAL CONTROL WHEEL
PILOT'S SEAT
R.RADIATOR HOSE
RADIATOR HEADER
DIAGONAL BRACE
CONTROL CABLE

HORIZONTAL STABILIZER
RUDDER POST
RIB
CONTROL CABLE
SINGLE SURFACE VARNISHED FABRIC
FABRIC LACING

STRUT
FABRIC
RIB

RUDDER BAR
RADIATOR
ALUMINUM GUSSET PLATES

ALUMINUM FAIRING

33'-9" (OVERALL)

(NORMAL TAKE-OFF AND LANDING ATTITUDE)

HINGE
STEEL TUBE

STRANDED BRACE WIRE
STEEL TUBE
TAIL SKID

SCALE 0 1 2 3 4 5 6

RUDDER CONTROL HORN
RIB

ELEVATOR
SINGLE VARNISHED FABRIC COVERING
ELEVATOR CONTROL HORN
ELEVATOR CONTROL CABLE
FABRIC LACING
STABILIZER
SINGLE VARNISHED FABRIC COVERING
STEEL TUBE
FITTING
SPREADER BAR
STEEL TUBE
FITTING
WIRE SPOKE FABRIC COVERED WHEEL

WOOD STRUCTURE

STRUT

ELEVATOR CONTROL CABLE

ELEVATOR CONTROL CABLE
FAIRLEAD
VARNISHED FABRIC COVERING

FAIRLEAD

DETERMINATE TYPE TOP FUSELAGE TRUSS TRIANGULAR CROSS SECTION

WOOD LONGERON

PILOT'S COCKPIT
PLYWOOD DECK
RADIATOR HEADER
RADIATOR TUBES
ELEVATOR CONTROL WHEEL

RADIATOR HEADER
SAFETY BELT
COCKPIT FLOOR
CONTROL WHEEL TRUNNION
RADIATOR TUBES
WING ROCKING LATERAL CONTROL WHEEL
RUDDER FOOT BAR CONTROL

KING POST
KING POST WIRE BRACE
FABRIC SEAM
VARNISHED FABRIC COVER

KING POST WIRE BRACE
KING POST

WOOD KING POST
ADJUSTABLE TURNBUCKLE
SOLID STEEL BRACE WIRE
FABRIC LACING TO RIB
VARNISHED FABRIC

FUEL TANK
HOSE TO RADIATOR

PUMP FED ANTOINETTE 55 H.P. VEE EIGHT CYLINDER WATER COOLED ENGINE. MAX. R.P.M. 1200.

PADDLE TYPE, STEEL HUB, ALUMINUM BLADE AUTOGENOUS WELDED CONSTRUCTION PROPELLER

36'-6"

ENGINE EXHAUST PIPES
ENGINE AIR INDUCTION PIPES
LANDING WIRES

WING TIP SKID

LIFT WIRE TO AFT WING SPAR
SOLID STEEL WIRE BRACE TO FRONT WING SPAR FUNCTIONS AS LIFT WIRE

VARNISHED FABRIC
SOLID STEEL BRACE WIRE
FABRIC LACING TO RIB
TURNBUCKLE
WOOD KING POST

4'-3" TREAD

THE ANTOINETTE AIRPLANES

THE PROTOTYPE ANTOINETTE MONOPLANE WAS THE ORIGINAL DESIGN OF MR. M. LEVAVASSEUR AND CONSTRUCTED BY MESSRS. GASTAMBIDE AND MENGIN, 1908. THERE WERE 8 DESIGNS BUILT, ALL OF WHICH WERE GOOD FLIERS. DESIGNS NO.4 AND NO.7 WERE THE THE MOST POPULAR TYPE. THESE AIRPLANES WERE IMPROVEMENTS OVER EXISTING COMPETITIVE TYPES. HUBERT LATHAM PARTICIPATED AT AVIATION EXHIBITIONS IN THE U.S.A.

THE ENGINES USED WERE OF ANTOINETTE DESIGN OF THE VEE-8 OR VEE-16 AIR PUMP-FED TYPE WITH WATER COOLED CYLINDERS. THESE ENGINES WERE OF ADVANCED DESIGN AND A VERY LOW RATIO OF WEIGHT TO H.P. OUTPUT. THE ENGINE WAS STARTED BY MANUAL CRANKING AND THE PROPELLER WAS COUPLED TO IT. THE RADIATOR WAS OF UNUSUAL TYPE. ENGINE R.P.M. WAS 1200.

THE AIRFOIL, DESIGNED TO ACHIEVE MAXIMUM PENETRATION, PRESENTED GOOD FLYING CHARACTERISTICS. THE WING STRUCTURAL CONFIGURATION RESEMBLES MODERN CONSTRUCTION. THE AREA WAS 50 SQ. METERS YET WEIGHED NOT MORE THAN 30 KILOGRAMS. BOTH SURFACES OF THE WING WERE COVERED WITH VARNISHED FABRIC, RUBBERIZED PERCALE, WATERPROOFED. IT WEIGHED 3 OUNCES PER SQUARE METER.

CLIMBING AND DIVING WERE CONTROLLED BY A CONVENTIONAL TYPE ELEVATOR. STEERING WAS CONTROLLED BY A RUDDER. LATERAL STABILITY WAS ACHIEVED BY A MANUALLY CONTROLLED CABLE ACTUATED CONTROL SYSTEM FOR ROCKING THE ENTIRE WING STRUCTURE, ANGULAR MOTION ABOUT THE LONGITUDINAL AXIS, EACH WING BEING DIFFERENTIALLY. THE WING AND RIB STRUCTURAL ELEMENTS WERE STATICALLY DETERMINATE AND THE JOINTS WERE STRENGTHENED BY WOOD BLOCKS AND ALUMINUM GUSSET PLATES. HOWEVER, THE TAIL SURFACES WERE COMPARITIVELY FLIMSY CONSTRUCTION. MAXIMUM SPEED 55 M.P.H.

THE MODELS I AND II FLEW IN 1908. THE MODEL I USED A QUADRICYCLE LANDING GEAR WITH WING WARPING FOR LATERAL CONTROL. MODEL II WAS SIMILAR EXCEPT A BICYCLE LANDING GEAR AND WING SKIDS WERE USED. MODEL III WAS SIMILAR EXCEPT TRIANGULAR AILERONS WERE USED FOR LATERAL CONTROL. MODEL IV WAS SIMILAR EXCEPT TRAPEZOID SHAPED AILERONS WERE USED. THIS TYPE WAS USED BY HUBERT LATHAM IN HIS FIRST ATTEMPT TO FLY THE ENGLISH CHANNEL. MODEL V WAS SIMILAR TO AND AN IMPROVEMENT ON PREVIOUS AIRPLANES. ON MODEL VI, WING WARPING WAS USED AGAIN AND KING POST TYPE WING TRUSS USED FOR WING BRACING. THE MODEL VII WAS USED BY LATHAM ON HIS SECOND ATTEMPT TO FLY THE ENGLISH CHANNEL. MANY "ANTOINETTE"-TYPE MONOPLANES WERE USED BY THE FRENCH ARMY. "ANTOINETTE" ALSO DESIGNED AND BUILT THE FIRST LOW WINGED INTERNALLY BRACED MONOPLANE WITH A FAIRED CANTILEVER LANDING GEAR AND FUSELAGE. NO FURTHER PLANES WERE BUILT AFTER 1912. AT ONE TIME THESE AIRPLANES HELD THE WORLD'S DISTANCE AND ALTITUDE RECORDS. THE MAXIMUM AIR RANGE WAS ABOUT 100 MILES.

ANTOINETTE VII

SEMAINE DE COMPAGNE
PRIX GRANDE
AEROPLANES "ANTOINETTE"
PARIS, FRANCE

W.L. NYE

Armstrong-Whitw

drawing by BJORN KARLSTROM

THE Armstrong-Whitworth F.K.8, designed by Mr. Frederick Koolhoven, was a heavier and an improved version of the F.K.3. It had a deeper fuselage, a slimmer type of undercarriage except that the central skid was cut short in front of the front V, and a 160-hp Beardmore engine. This machine was used to a large extent on various fronts of WW I for contact patrols, artillery spotting, light bombing, photography, and reconnaisance work up to the signing of the Armistice.

About halfway through its active service life, the F.K.8 was slightly modified by having a V-type undercarriage fitted (at first from Bristol fighters, and when the stock ran low, from B.E.2c's, finally from Armstrong-Whitworth), and smaller radiators of improved efficiency installed. A long exhaust pipe was also added to carry the exhaust fumes well clear of the crew.

None survive. □

With 120-hp Beardmore engine, the F.K.8 had a top speed of 85 mph. Developed by the British, this aircraft served notably throughout WW I. "Jane's All the World's Aircraft" photos.

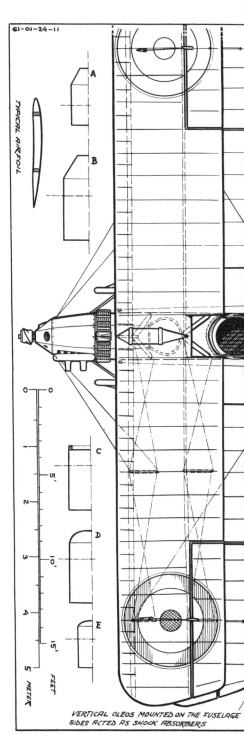

VERTICAL OLEOS MOUNTED ON THE FUSELAGE SIDES ACTED AS SHOCK ABSORBERS

Specification.

Type of machine	Two-seater Biplane.
Name or type No. of machine ..	Armstrong-Whitworth F.K.3.
Purpose for which intended ..	Sport and Training.
Span	40 ft.
Overall length	28 ft. 8 in.
Maximum height.. ..	10 ft. 2½ in.
Engine type and h.p. ..	90 h.p. R.A.F.
Weight of machine empty ..	1,900 lbs.
Tank capacity in hours ..	3½ hours.

Performance.

Speed at 1,000 feet	85 m.p.h.
Landing speed..	38 m.p.h.

Climb.

To 10,000 feet in minutes ..	23 minutes.

orth F.K.8

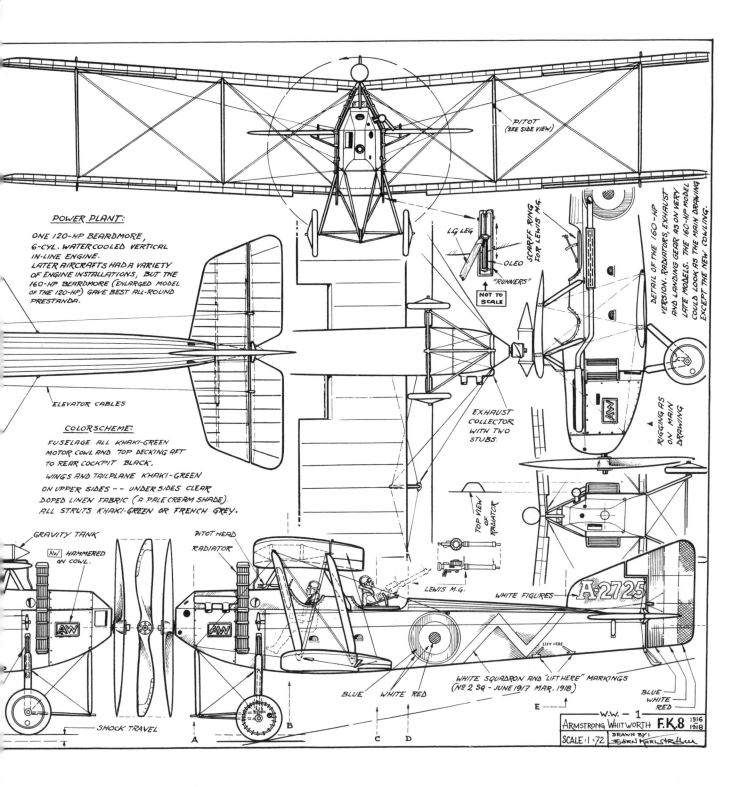

POWER PLANT:

ONE 120-HP BEARDMORE,
6-CYL. WATERCOOLED VERTICAL
IN-LINE ENGINE.
LATER AIRCRAFTS HAD A VARIETY
OF ENGINE INSTALLATIONS, BUT THE
160-HP BEARDMORE (ENLARGED MODEL
OF THE 120-HP) GAVE BEST ALL-ROUND
PRESTANDA.

ELEVATOR CABLES

COLORSCHEME:

FUSELAGE ALL KHAKI-GREEN
MOTOR COWL AND TOP DECKING AFT
TO REAR COCKPIT BLACK.
WINGS AND TAILPLANE KHAKI-GREEN
ON UPPER SIDES -- UNDER SIDES CLEAR
DOPED LINEN FABRIC (A PALE CREAM SHADE).
ALL STRUTS KHAKI-GREEN OR FRENCH GREY.

PITOT
(SEE SIDE VIEW)

LG LEG

OLEO

"RUNNERS"

NOT TO
SCALE

SCARFF RING
FOR LEWIS M.G.

DETAIL OF THE 160-HP
VERSION. RADIATORS, EXHAUST
AND LANDING GEAR AS ON VERY
LATE MODELS. THE 160-HP MODEL
COULD LOOK AS THE MAIN DRAWING
EXCEPT THE NEW COWLING.

RIGGING AS
ON MAIN
DRAWING

AW

EXHAUST
COLLECTOR
WITH TWO
STUBS.

TOP VIEW
OF RADIATOR

GRAVITY TANK

AW HAMMERED
ON COWL.

AW

PITOT HEAD

RADIATOR

LEWIS M.G.

WHITE FIGURES

A·2725

LIFT HERE

WHITE SQUADRON AND "LIFT HERE" MARKINGS
(No 2 SQ - JUNE 1917 MAR. 1918)

BLUE   WHITE RED

BLUE
WHITE
RED

SHOCK TRAVEL

A

B

C   D

E

W.W. — 1

ARMSTRONG WHITWORTH F.K.8 1916/1918

SCALE: 1:72   DRAWN BY: BJÖRN KARLSTRÖM

Bleriot XI

drawing by WILLIAM WYLAM

ONE of the epic flights of aviation history, probably equal in importance and impact to Lindbergh's flight, was Louis Bleriot's 22-mile flight across the English Channel in 1909. With this amazing feat, the French pioneer created a worldwide sensation and focused the attention of all civilization on the potential use of the airplane as a transportation vehicle.

The Bleriot XI was small and weighed only 660 pounds. Power was a three-cylinder Y-type Anzani air-cooled engine that developed about 20 hp. The airframe was wood, with rubberized fabric covering. Lateral control was attained by warping the wings.

Sparked by an award of $5,000 by the *London Daily Mail* for the first flight across the Channel, Bleriot was challenged for the award by Hubert Latham, a famous record-smashing pilot of that period. On Sunday, July 25, 1909, Louis Bleriot landed his plane near Dover Castle, England, after crossing the Channel in less than one hour, a feat which garnered him over $15,000 in prize money.

Many variants of the XI design were built by the Bleriot firm, including parasols and two-seaters. The photograph and Wylam's drawing show the aircraft Bleriot used to fly the Channel. Note the inflated bladder inside the fuselage.

Many Bleriot XIs are still around, in museums or privately owned. □

An extremely rare photograph, this shot taken as Bleriot commenced his journey into history crossing the English Channel on Sunday, July 25, 1909. Air Age file photo.

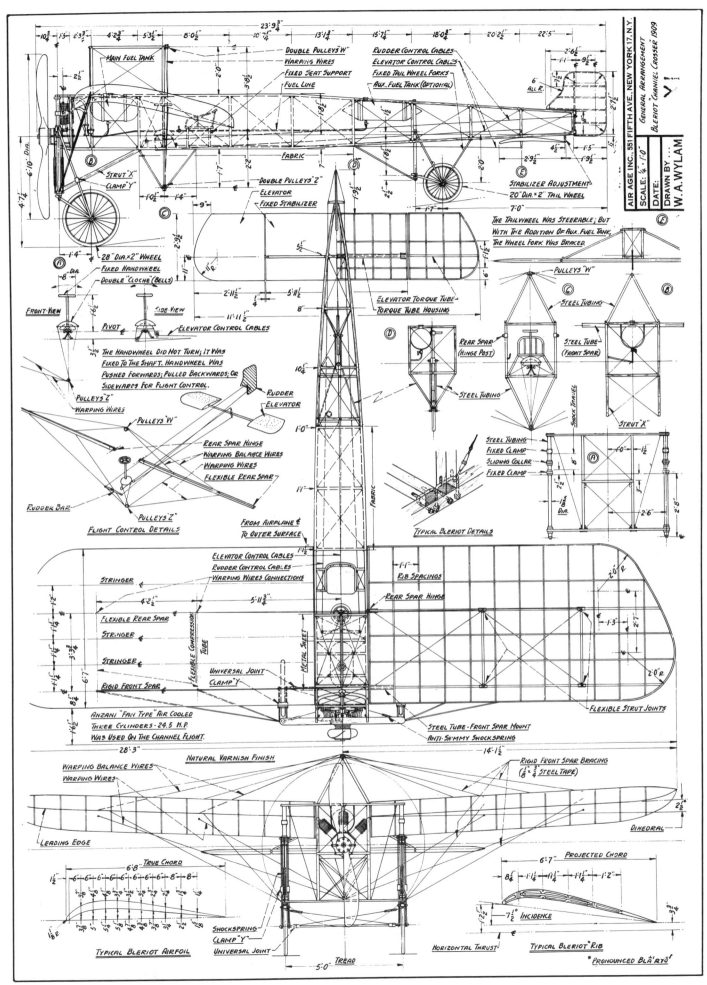

Typical Bleriot Airfoil

Typical Bleriot "Rib"

*Pronounced Blā'ryŌ

AIR AGE INC., 551 FIFTH AVE. NEW YORK 17, N.Y.
SCALE: ¼" = 1'-0"
DATE:
DRAWN BY.....
W. A. WYLAM
GENERAL ARRANGEMENT
Bleriot "Channel Crosser" 1909

19

Boeing MB-3A

drawing by JOSEPH NIETO

"IF THE WAR had lasted..." That was a common speculation among aircraft engineers and enthusiasts following the Armistice of WW I. Of course, no sane person of the period was genuinely in favor of continuing the European holocaust, but there was, after the fracas was all over, a somewhat nostalgic—and disappointed—feeling that swept over the American aircraft industry. The Thomas Morse Aircraft Co. had but one thing in mind with the MB-3: to equal, and possibly outperform any European plane of the same type. Designed in 1918, and not flown until February 1919, it was too late to see service in the war.

Boeing was contracted, along with Thomas Morse, to build the Thomas Morse design and the versions produced by Boeing were the MB-3A, which featured modifications to the control surfaces and empennage, among other changes to cowling and engine. The result was an airplane that, in its time, was equal to or better than anything in the air. Serving up until 1929, the MB-3A established Boeing as a quality craft builder at a time when the aviation business was really tough. □

Top photo, "Pedigree of Champions, Boeing Since 1916." Left photo, "Chronicle of Aviation History in America."

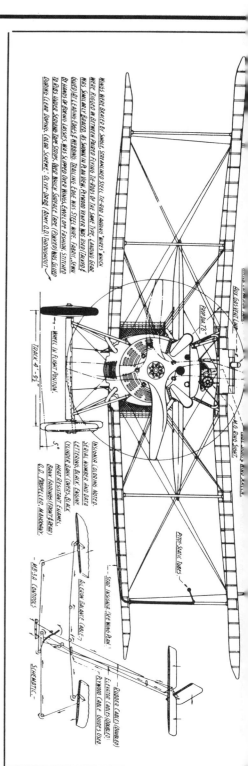

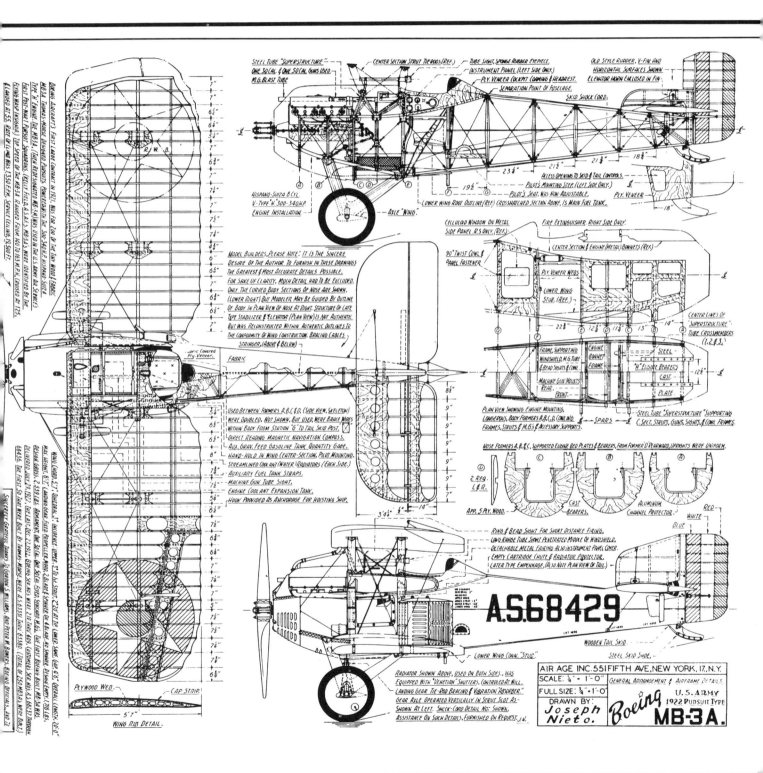

AIR AGE. INC. 551 FIFTH AVE., NEW YORK, 17, N.Y.
SCALE: ¼" = 1'-0"   General Arrangement & Airframe Details.
FULL SIZE: ¾" = 1'-0"   U.S. ARMY
DRAWN BY: 1922 Pursuit Type
Joseph   Boeing
Nieto.   MB-3A.

Bristol F.2B

drawings by WILLIAM WYLAM

AN OUTSTANDING success in every role it was to play in WW I, the Bristol fighter, affectionately known as the "Brisfit," was described as a "pilot's airplane" by all accounts on file with the British Air Ministry. But its first appearance over the Front—six F.2A's—ended with four of them shot down, because their pilots had not yet learned to fly them like fighters instead of observation planes. When they did learn, in the middle of 1917, the Fighter began to replace the then-staged S.E.5. It didn't take long for stories about the F.2B's fighting ability to get around. A two-place airplane, the F.2B was a departure from pilots' prior experience and the acceptance of it was initially slow. The training methods, however, stressed the remarkable features of the airplane itself and the pilot-observer teamwork necessary to obtain the greatest possible effect. The result was to fulfill a specific function—fighting in the air.

The engine selection varied from 190 to 280 hp, depending on the job expected of the plane and its date of manufacture. Radiators were fitted accordingly and differed in shape and size. The F-2B was probably the only two-seater built during WW I that handled like a single-seater. It was maneuverable and as fast as the Fokker D.VII. These features made it possible for pilots such as Capt. Andrew McKeever to gain 23 of his 30 victories. And McKeever had only one eye!

As many as ten F.2B's survive, all in

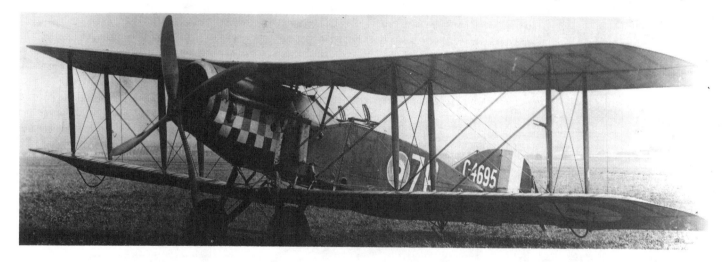

England; two of them in museums, the rest fragments being restored.

Wylam's drawings of the F.2B are among his most beautiful and least accurate. Modelers should check especially carefully against good photographs the shape of the oval radiator, the tapering rear fuselage, vertical tail, and underline of engine cowling. □

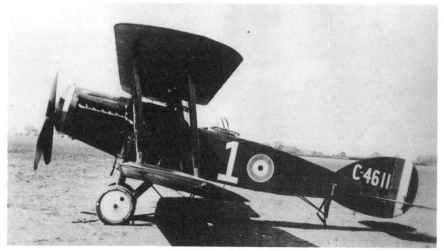

The highly successful British Bristol Brisfit was very maneuverable and as fast as the Fokker D.VII. Air Age file photos.

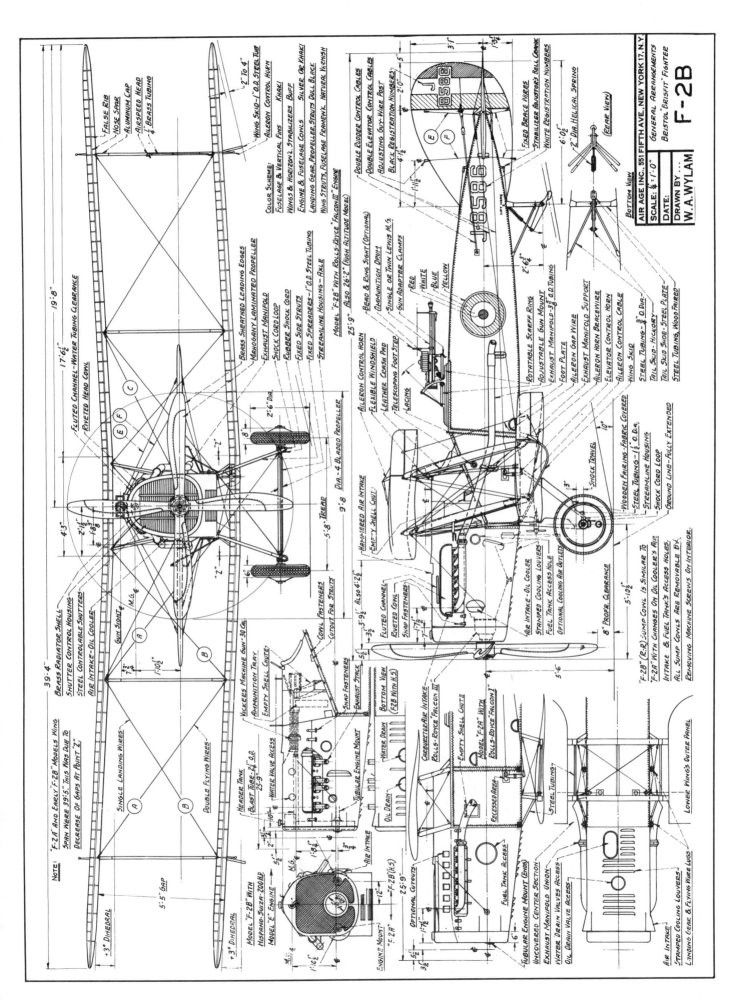

F-2B

Bristol "Brisfit" Fighter

General Arrangements

AIR AGE INC.... 551 FIFTH AVE., NEW YORK 17, N.Y.

SCALE: ¼" = 1'-0"

DATE:

DRAWN BY .... W. A. WYLAM

Bottom View

(Rear View)

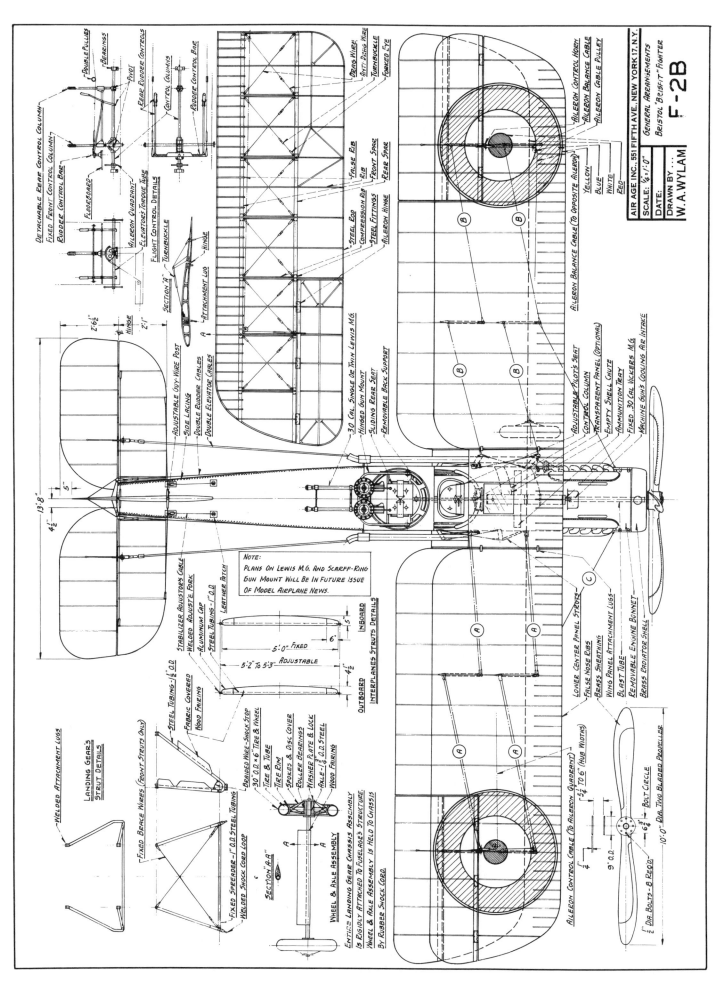

F-2B

AIR AGE INC., 551 FIFTH AVE., NEW YORK 17, N.Y.
GENERAL ARRANGEMENTS
BRISTOL "BRISFIT" FIGHTER
SCALE: ¼"=1'-0"
DATE:
DRAWN BY ....
W. A. WYLAM

NOTE:
PLANS ON LEWIS M.G. AND SCARFF-RING GUN MOUNT WILL BE IN FUTURE ISSUE OF MODEL AIRPLANE NEWS.

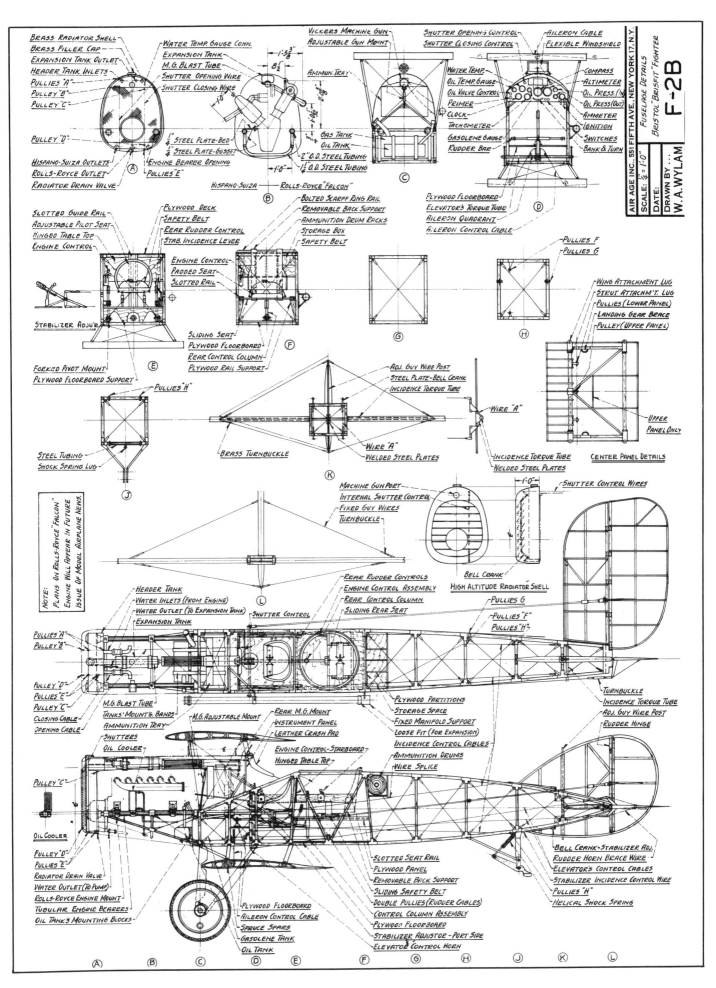

VICKERS MACHINE GUN
ADJUSTABLE GUN MOUNT

SHUTTER OPENING CONTROL
SHUTTER CLOSING CONTROL

AILERON CABLE
FLEXIBLE WINDSHIELD

AIR AGE INC., 551 FIFTH AVE., NEW YORK 17, N.Y.
FUSELAGE DETAILS
BRISTOL "BRISFIT" FIGHTER
F-2B
SCALE: ¾" = 1'-0"
DATE:
DRAWN BY —
W. A. WYLAM

BRASS RADIATOR SHELL
BRASS FILLER CAP
EXPANSION TANK OUTLET
HEADER TANK INLETS
PULLIES "A"
PULLEY "B"
PULLEY "C"

WATER TEMP. GAUGE CONN.
EXPANSION TANK
M.G. BLAST TUBE
SHUTTER OPENING WIRE
SHUTTER CLOSING WIRE

AMMUN. TRAY

WATER TEMP.
OIL TEMP. GAUGE
OIL VALVE CONTROL
PRIMER
CLOCK
TACHOMETER
GASOLENE GAUGE
RUDDER BAR

COMPASS
ALTIMETER
OIL PRESS.(IN)
OIL PRESS (OUT)
AMMETER
IGNITION
SWITCHES
BANK & TURN

PULLEY "D"

HISPANO-SUIZA OUTLETS
ROLLS-ROYCE OUTLET
RADIATOR DRAIN VALVE

¼" STEEL PLATE-BED
¼" STEEL PLATE-GUSSET
ENGINE BEARER OPENING
PULLIES "E"

GAS TANK
OIL TANK
2" O.D. STEEL TUBING
1½" O.D. STEEL TUBING

PLYWOOD FLOORBOARD
ELEVATOR'S TORQUE TUBE
AILERON QUADRANT
AILERON CONTROL CABLE

HISPANO-SUIZA   ROLLS-ROYCE "FALCON"

Ⓐ

Ⓑ

Ⓒ

Ⓓ

SLOTTED GUIDE RAIL
ADJUSTABLE PILOT SEAT
HINGED TABLE TOP
ENGINE CONTROL

PLYWOOD DECK
SAFETY BELT
REAR RUDDER CONTROL
STAB. INCIDENCE LEVER

BOLTED SCARFF RING RAIL
REMOVABLE BACK SUPPORT
AMMUNITION DRUM RACKS
STORAGE BOX
SAFETY BELT

PULLIES F
PULLIES G

WING ATTACHMENT LUG
STRUT ATTACHM'T. LUG
PULLIES (LOWER PANEL)
LANDING GEAR BRACE
PULLEY (UPPER PANEL)

ENGINE CONTROL
PADDED SEAT
SLOTTED RAIL

STABILIZER ADJU'R.

SLIDING SEAT
PLYWOOD FLOORBOARD
REAR CONTROL COLUMN
PLYWOOD RAIL SUPPORT

Ⓖ

Ⓗ

FORKED PIVOT MOUNT
PLYWOOD FLOORBOARD SUPPORT

Ⓔ

ADJ. GUY WIRE POST
STEEL PLATE-BELL CRANK
INCIDENCE TORQUE TUBE

WIRE "A"

UPPER
PANEL ONLY

PULLIES "H"

STEEL TUBING
SHOCK SPRING LUG

Ⓙ

BRASS TURNBUCKLE

WIRE "A"
WELDED STEEL PLATES

Ⓚ

INCIDENCE TORQUE TUBE
WELDED STEEL PLATES

CENTER PANEL DETAILS

MACHINE GUN PORT
INTERNAL SHUTTER CONTROL
FIXED GUY WIRES
TURNBUCKLE

SHUTTER CONTROL WIRES

NOTE:
PLANS ON ROLLS-ROYCE "FALCON"
ENGINE WILL APPEAR IN FUTURE
ISSUE OF MODEL AIRPLANE NEWS.

Ⓛ

BELL CRANK

HIGH ALTITUDE RADIATOR SHELL

REAR RUDDER CONTROLS
ENGINE CONTROL ASSEMBLY
REAR CONTROL COLUMN
SLIDING REAR SEAT

PULLIES G

HEADER TANK
WATER INLETS (FROM ENGINE)
WATER OUTLET (TO EXPANSION TANK)
EXPANSION TANK

SHUTTER CONTROL

PULLIES "F"
PULLIES "H"

PULLIES "A"
PULLEY "B"

PLYWOOD PARTITIONS
STORAGE SPACE
FIXED MANIFOLD SUPPORT
LOOSE FIT (FOR EXPANSION)
INCIDENCE CONTROL CABLES
AMMUNITION DRUMS
WIRE SPLICE

TURNBUCKLE
INCIDENCE TORQUE TUBE
ADJ. GUY WIRE POST
RUDDER HINGE

PULLEY "D"
PULLIES "E"
PULLEY "C"
CLOSING CABLE
OPENING CABLE

M.G. BLAST TUBE
TANKS' MOUNT'G. BANDS
AMMUNITION TRAY

M.G. ADJUSTABLE MOUNT

REAR M.G. MOUNT
INSTRUMENT PANEL
LEATHER CRASH PAD

ENGINE CONTROL-STARBOARD
HINGED TABLE TOP

SHUTTERS
OIL COOLER

PULLEY "C"

OIL COOLER

PULLEY "D"
PULLIES "E"
RADIATOR DRAIN VALVE
WATER OUTLET (TO PUMP)
ROLLS-ROYCE ENGINE MOUNT
TUBULAR ENGINE BEARERS
OIL TANK'S MOUNTING BLOCKS

PLYWOOD FLOORBOARD
AILERON CONTROL CABLE
SPRUCE SPARS
GASOLENE TANK
OIL TANK

SLOTTED SEAT RAIL
PLYWOOD PANEL
REMOVABLE BACK SUPPORT
SLIDING SAFETY BELT
DOUBLE PULLIES (RUDDER CABLES)
CONTROL COLUMN ASSEMBLY
PLYWOOD FLOORBOARD
STABILIZER ADJUSTOR - PORT SIDE
ELEVATOR CONTROL HORN

BELL CRANK-STABILIZER ADJ.
RUDDER HORN BRACE WIRE
ELEVATOR'S CONTROL CABLES
STABILIZER INCIDENCE CONTROL WIRE
PULLIES "H"
HELICAL SHOCK SPRING

Ⓐ   Ⓑ   Ⓒ   Ⓓ   Ⓔ   Ⓕ   Ⓖ   Ⓗ   Ⓙ   Ⓚ   Ⓛ

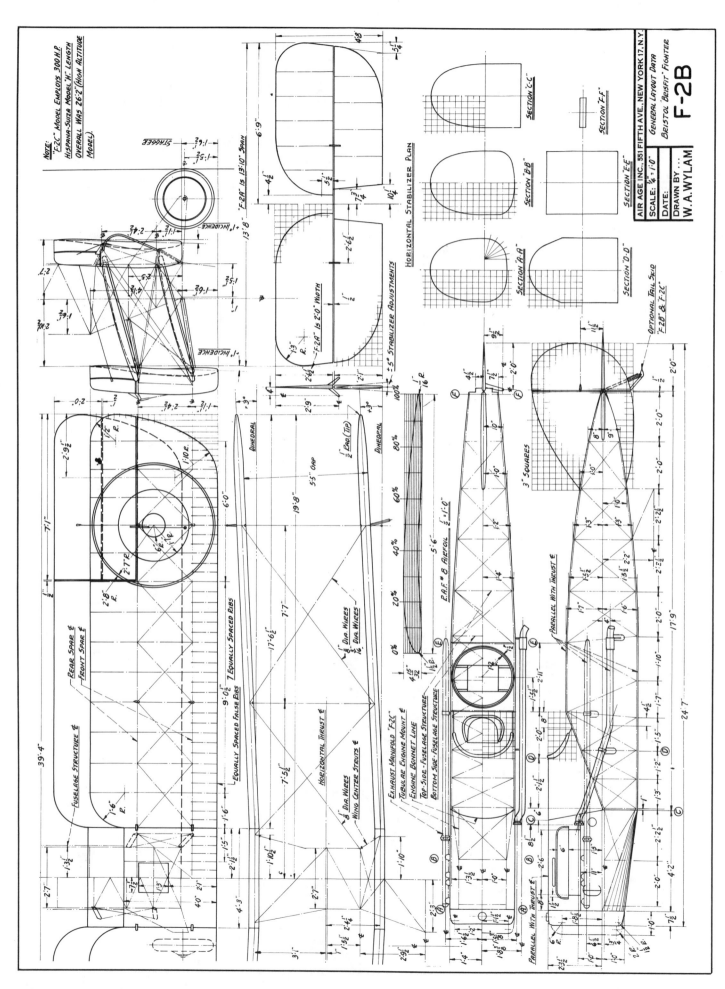

F-2B

General Layout Data

Bristol "Brisfit" Fighter

AIR AGE INC., 551 FIFTH AVE., NEW YORK 17, N.Y.	
SCALE: ¼" = 1'-0"	
DATE:	
DRAWN BY ... W. A. WYLAM	

NOTE:
"F-2C" MODEL EMPLOYS 300 H.P.
HISPANA-SUIZA MODEL "H" LENGTH
OVERALL WAS 26'2" (HIGH ALTITUDE
MODEL).

HORIZONTAL STABILIZER PLAN

±5° STABILIZER ADJUSTMENTS

SECTION "C-C"

SECTION "F-F"

SECTION "B-B"

SECTION "E-E"

SECTION "A-A"

SECTION "D-D"

R.A.F. "B" AIRFOIL ½" = 1'-0"

OPTIONAL TAIL SKID "F-2B" & F-2C"

3" SQUARES

PARALLEL WITH THRUST ₵

DINEDRAL

5'3" GAP

Chance Vought

drawings by WILLIS NYE

VE-7, VE-9, & UO-1

THE CHANCE-Vought VE-7 was designed as an entrant in the U.S. Army advanced trainer competition held in 1917, and the first experimental airplane was submitted for testing to Army authorities in 1918. The VE-7 won the competition and was ordered into production by the parent company and two licensees, the Springfield Aircraft Co. and the B.F. Sturtevant Co. Twenty VE-7's were delivered by the end of WW I, and in 1922 to 1923 twenty-seven VE-9 airplanes were procured by the U.S. Army Air Service.

The VE-9 was an improved version of the VE-7, and was the first American-designed ship-board airplane that could be launched from a catapult. The service time of this version was one of the longest of that era, spanning over 10 years, which gave credibility to the company that was to remain a main provider of aircraft for the U.S. armed forces for many years. □

Their association with Naval aircraft design is legendary. Air Age file photos of VE-7.

CHANCE VOUGHT VE-7 & UO-1

(DRAWN FOR MODEL AIRPLANE NEWS BY WILLIS L. NYE)

VE-7 (U.S.ARMY)

U.S.NAVY

U.S.S. TENNESSEE

UO-1 (U.S.NAVY)

A.S.6 4713

VE-7 (U.S.ARMY) (FIRST FLIGHT TESTED FEB? 1918)

GAP 4'-8"

TIE

6'-7"

4'-9"

2'-6"

AILERON CABLE

BLUE, WHITE, RED

3'-6"

3'-9"

2'-4"

N-6646

203

RED, WHITE, BLUE

1.25° DIHEDRAL

1.75° INCIDENCE

2.25° INCIDENCE

.125° DIHEDRAL

INSIGNIA

DRAG WIRE

SHOCK ABSORBER FAIRING

DOUBLE FLYING WIRES

SINGLE FLYING WIRES

IDENTIFICATION INSIGNIA

AILERON CONTROL HORN

SUBMERGED WING STRUT FITTING

WALKWAY

AIR DRIVEN SINGLE BLADE RADIO D.C. GENERATOR

MAGNETIC COMPASS SUSPENDED FROM WING CENTER SECTION

45 LBS INFLATION PRESSURE

BLACK LEATHER, ALUMINUM ALLOY STORAGE COMPARTMENT

BUAER SERIAL NO.

BLACK LETTERING

SHIPBOARD PLANE NAME

FAIRING STRIP

TRAILING WIRE ANTENNA LEAD-IN

FABRIC COVERED FUSELAGE

DRAIN PLUG RING

ENTIRE AIRPLANE FINISHED IN ALUMINUM LACQUER. FLOATS IN GRAY ENAMEL

ON SHIPBOARD AIRCRAFT THE ARRESTING GEAR WAS DELETED SEE SHEET NO.2. VE-3.

2 PLY LAMINATED PLYWOOD PONTOON SKIN

WATER LINE

SEE SHEET 2 FOR RIGGING DATA

DURALUMIN WING TIP PONTOON

AERODYNAMIC BALANCE

STATION NO.

LENGTH SCALE

FUEL QUANTITY GAUGE

CARBURETOR AIR INDUCTION

AILERON LINK CABLE

INSTRUMENT PANEL ACCESS

FAIRED TURTLE DECK

ALUMINUM FAIRING

CONTROL STICK ACCESS PANEL

AILERON CONTROL HORN

U.S.A.S. MARKING

1" WING STAGGER

ENGINE OIL COOLER

REMOVABLE TAIL SKID SHOE

TAIL SKID ACCESS PANEL

POLISHED ALUMINUM RADIATOR SHELL

HIGH PRESSURE TIRE INFLATION VALVE

HEIGHT SCALE

THIS AIRPLANE HAD GOOD FLIGHT AND MANEUVERING CHARACTERISTICS BUT WAS RESTRICTED AGAINST SNAP ROLLS.

RADIATOR CAP

BRACE CABLE

STEEL PROPELLER HUB

FUEL TANK

ALUMINUM ALLOY COWLING

WRIGHT J-4 AIRCOOLED 200 H.P. ENGINE

MAGNETO CONTROL

SCINTILLA MAGNETO

ENGINE EXHAUST MANIFOLD

WALKWAY

MOORING CHOCK

DRAIN PLUG

CHINE

DOUBLER

HEIGHT SCALE

LENGTH SCALE

DESIGN NOTES VE-7

① THE PROTOTYPE VOUGHT VE-7 WAS POWERED WITH THE WRIGHT-MARTIN HISPANO-SUIZA 8 CYLINDER WATERCOOLED 150 H.P. MODEL "A" ENGINE. THE AIR-PLANE WAS ALSO TESTED WITH THE 180 H.P. HISPA-NO-SUIZA ENGINE WITH AN IMPROVEMENT IN OVER-ALL PERFORMANCE. ANOTHER VERSION WAS POWER-ED WITH THE CURTISS OX-6 ENGINE.

② ON CERTAIN VE-7 AIRPLANES, THE LOUVRE CONFIG-URATION VARIED FROM WHAT IS SHOWN.

③ WHEN THE HISPANO-SUIZA ENGINE IS INSTALLED, IF FLIGHTS OVER 3 HOURS WERE UNDERTAKEN, THE USE OF AN OIL COOLER WAS MANDATORY AS WELL AS AN ENGINE OIL TANK. THIS WAS NECESSARY SO THAT A SUPPLY OF FRESH OIL WAS AVAILABLE TO REPLENISH OIL THAT WAS BURNED. (2 QUARTS PER HOUR)

④ THIS INSPECTION ACCESS PLATE (CLEAR PLASTIC SHEET) WAS NOT INSTALLED ON ALL VE-7S.

⑤ THE RUDDER CONFIGURATION SHOWN IS THAT USED ON THE PROTOTYPE AIRPLANE. THE RUDDER USED ON THE UO-1 WAS ALSO INSTALLED ON THE VE-7.

⑥ THIS DRAG WIRE WAS NOT INSTALLED ON ALL VE-7S.

⑦ SOME AIRPLANES HAD A CIRCULAR CUTOUT BE-TWEEN FORWARD AND AFT SPAR.

⑧ LENGTH THIS STREAMLINING VARIED ON EACH AIRPLANE OF THIS TYPE.

⑨ MANUALLY CONTROLLED RADIATOR SHUTTERS WERE FITTED ON ALL AIRPLANES PRODUCED AFTER THE PROTOTYPE.

⑩ ON THE PROTOTYPE AIRPLANE A FIN SIMILAR TO UO-1 WAS EXPERIMENTALLY INSTALLED.

⑪ AIRPLANE COULD BE FITTED FOR GUNNERY TRAIN-ING BY SEALING FORWARD COCKPIT, USING A .30-CALIBER M.G. AND TELESCOPIC SIGHT.

Vought VE-7

WINGS: CELLULE IS FOUR AILERON TYPE. TOP CENTER SECTION CUT AWAY FOR VISION. AIRFOIL R.A.F. 15. ANGLE OF INCI-DENCE IS DIFFERENTIAL BETWEEN WINGS. WING CELL-ULE CONSISTS OF FIVE PANELS ASSEMBLED WITH SUBMERGED FITTINGS. WING SPARS OF SOLID I-BEAM ROUTED SPRUCE, REIN-FORCED AT PANEL POINTS. WING RIBS ARE UNIT-ASSEMBLY TYPE. DOUBLE SWAGE WIRES IN INTERNAL DRAG TRUSS WITH ADJUST-ABLE END FITTINGS. MAIN WING ATTACHMENT AND INTER-PLANE STRUT FITTINGS ARE OF THE SUBMERGED TYPE. WINGS COVERED WITH LINEN, SEWED TO WING RIBS, AND TAPED. FIVE COATS ACETATE DOPE AND TWO COATS GRAY ENAMEL. INTER-PLANE STRUTS OF SOLID SPRUCE STREAMLINE CROSS SECTION. WIRE BRACING IS ROEBLING 19-STRAND, ADJUSTABLE TURN-BUCKLES. FLYING WIRES DOUBLE, LANDING WIRES SINGLE.

LANDING GEAR: VOUGHT VEE STRUT DUAL WHEEL TYPE. DE-TACHABLE BY REMOVAL OF PINS AT FUSELAGE FITTINGS. WHEELS 26 x 4 WIRE SPOKE TYPE. STEEL STUB AXLES OPERATE IN MET-AL GUIDES, FLOATING TYPE SHOCK ABSORBERS OPERATE IN STEEL GUIDE AXLES. SPREADER BAR AND SHOCK ABSORBERS STREAMLINED IN PRESSED METAL HOUSING. STRUTS OF ASH AND RUBBER CORD COTTON SHEATHED 5/16" DIAMETER. METAL PARTS FINISHED IN BLACK ENAMEL. WOOD STRUTS WITH THREE COATS CLEAR VARNISH. WHEELS STREAMLINED WITH FABRIC, DETACHABLE COVERS.

VOUGHT VE-7

ENGINE INSTALLATION: WRIGHT-MARTIN HISPANO-SUIZA, MODEL "A", 150 H.P. WATERCOOLED ENGINE.

PROPELLER: LIBERTY, 2-BLADE, 8'-4" DIAMETER OF LAMINATED WALNUT. PITCH 5-5½".

ENGINE EXHAUST MANIFOLD: TUBULAR WELDED SHEET SUPPORTED ON FORGED BRACKETS.

ENGINE STARTING: PILOT'S COCKPIT PROVIDED WITH BOOSTER MAGNETO AND LUNKENHEIMER FUEL PRIMER. ENGINE WAS HAND CRANKED.

ENGINE CONTROLS: EACH COCKPIT PROVIDED WITH THROTTLE, SPARK, AND FUEL MIXTURE LEVERS ON LEFT SIDE.

ENGINE RADIATOR: HONEYCOMB TYPE, 9½ GALLONS WATER SYSTEM CIRCULATION CAPACITY. DIS-TANCE TYPE TEMPERATURE INDICATOR. SHUT-TERS MANUALLY CONTROLLABLE.

FUEL SYSTEM: TWO FUEL TANKS, MAIN UNDER REAR SEAT, AUXILIARY UNDER COWL BETWEEN ENGINE AND INSTRUMENT PANEL. FUEL CAPACITY 32 GALLONS. FUEL PUMPED TO CARBURETOR BY AN ENGINE-DRIVEN FUEL PUMP. HAND AIR PUMP FOR STARTING IN PILOT'S COCKPIT. FUEL SHUT-OFF VALVES IN EACH COCKPIT.

FLIGHT CONTROLS: DUAL JOYSTICKS AND RUDDER BARS IN EACH COCKPIT. EACH ASSEMBLED AS A UNIT AND QUICKLY REMOVABLE.

INSTRUMENTS: CONSIST OF ALTIMETER, AIRSPEED INDICATOR, CLOCK, TACHOMETER, FUEL PRESSURE GAUGE, OIL PRESSURE GAUGE, WATER TEMPERATURE GAUGE, ETC.

DESIGN NOTES VE-7

⑫ VARIOUS MAKES AND TYPES OF LAMINATED PROP-ELLERS WERE USED WITH VARIATIONS IN PITCH.

⑬ INTERPLANE STRUTS OF CONSTANT OR VARIED STREAMLINE CROSS SECTION WERE USED.

⑭ ENTIRE FLIGHT CONTROLS ARE CABLE ACTUATED. ALL CABLES ARE DOUBLE, FLEXIBLE TYPE.

THE AMERICAN VERSION OF THE HISPANO-SUIZA ENGINE WAS MANUFACTURED UNDER FOREIGN LI-CENSE BY THE SIMPLEX AUTOMOBILE COMPANY. THIS COMPANY WAS LATER ABSORBED BY THE WRIGHT-MARTIN AIRCRAFT COMPANY OF NEW BRUNSWICK, N.J., THE PARENT COMPANY OF THE PRESENT CURTISS-WRIGHT CORPORATION.

Vought VE-7

FUSELAGE: ENGINE COWLS ARE PRESSED SHEET ALUMINUM. IN-SPECTION PLATES PROVIDED FOR ACCESS TO INSTRUMENTS, FLIGHT CONTROLS AND TAIL SKID. FRAME HAS SPRUCE LONGER-ONS AND STRUTS, STEEL CABLE BRACING, AND STEEL FITTINGS. RECTANGULAR CROSS SECTION. ENGINE SECTION IS DEMOUNT-ABLE AS A UNIT. ENGINE COWLINGS LIGHT BLUE ENAMEL, FAB-RIC GRAY ENAMEL. FUSELAGE TRUSS FAIRED TOP AND BOTTOM.

SEATING: EACH COCKPIT UPHOLSTERED WITH IMITATION LEATH-ER. PLYWOOD SEATS. LEATHER COCKPIT COAMING.

WINDSHIELDS: CLEAR REINFORCED PLASTIC SHEET.

EMPENNAGE: FIXED DOUBLE CAMBERED HORIZONTAL STAB-ILIZER. ELEVATORS DUAL CONNECTED. FIXED VERTICAL STAB-ILIZER. AERODYNAMICALLY BALANCED RUDDER. ALL FRAMES OF STEEL TUBES WELDED OR BRAZED TOGETHER. WOOD RIB FILLED OVER TUBULAR STEEL AND ROUTED SPRUCE SPARS. STRUCTURE INTERNALLY BRACED WITH SWAGED CABLES AND ADJUSTABLE STEEL FITTINGS. ENTIRE EMPENNAGE COVERED WITH APPROVED COTTON FABRIC, FINISHED TO MATCH FUSE-LAGE COVERING.

TAILSKID: PATENTED VOUGHT DESIGN, FLOATING TYPE, SEMI-UN-IVERSAL AND SELF-ALIGNING IN ACTION. FITTED WITH RUBBER SHOCK ABSORBERS AND RENEWABLE METAL SHOE.

FACTOR OF SAFETY: UNIFORM FACTOR OF SAFETY OF 9 PLUS AT HIGH INCIDENCE CONDITION IN STATIC TESTS.

WEIGHT (GROSS): 2000 POUNDS INCLUDING 525 POUNDS USEFUL LOAD AND 78 POUNDS ENGINE COOLING WATER.

(SHEET NO.1)

28

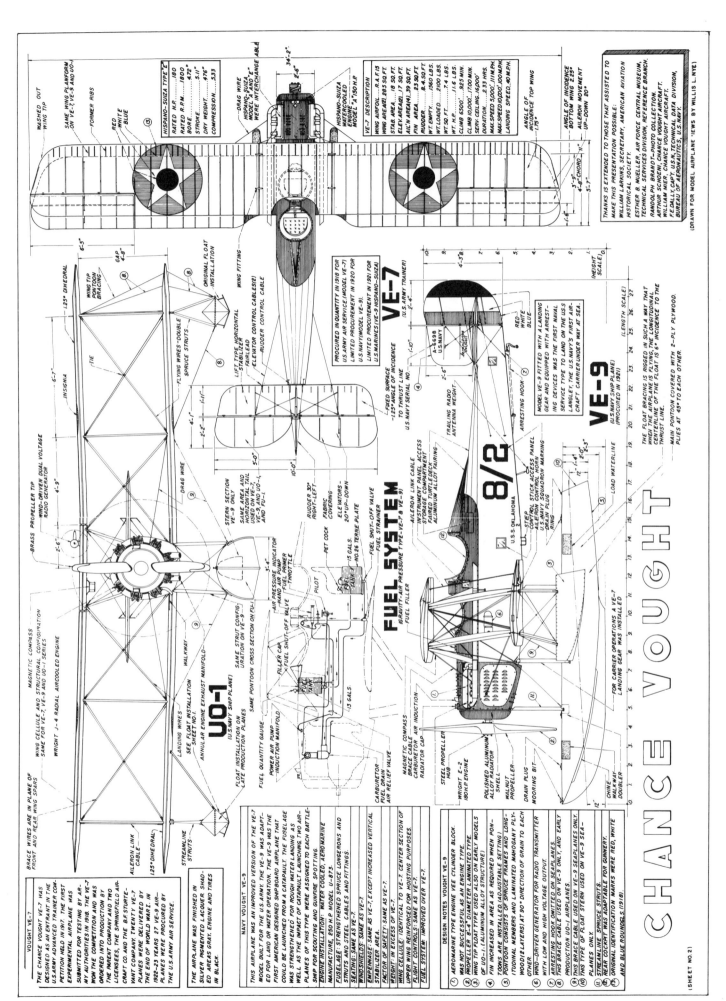

CHANCE VOUGHT

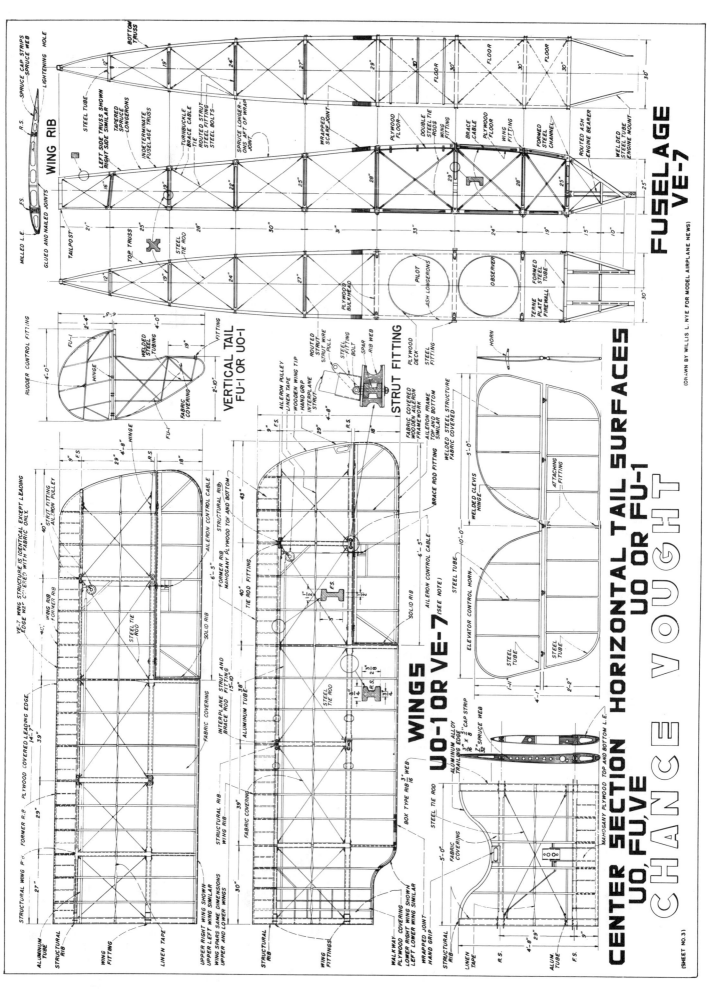

FUSELAGE VE-7

WING RIB

(DRAWN BY WILLIS L. NYE FOR MODEL AIRPLANE NEWS)

VERTICAL TAIL
FU-1 OR UO-1

STRUT FITTING

HORIZONTAL TAIL SURFACES
UO OR FU-1

WINGS
UO-1 OR VE-7

CENTER SECTION
UO, FU, VE

CHANCE VOUGHT

(SHEET NO. 3)

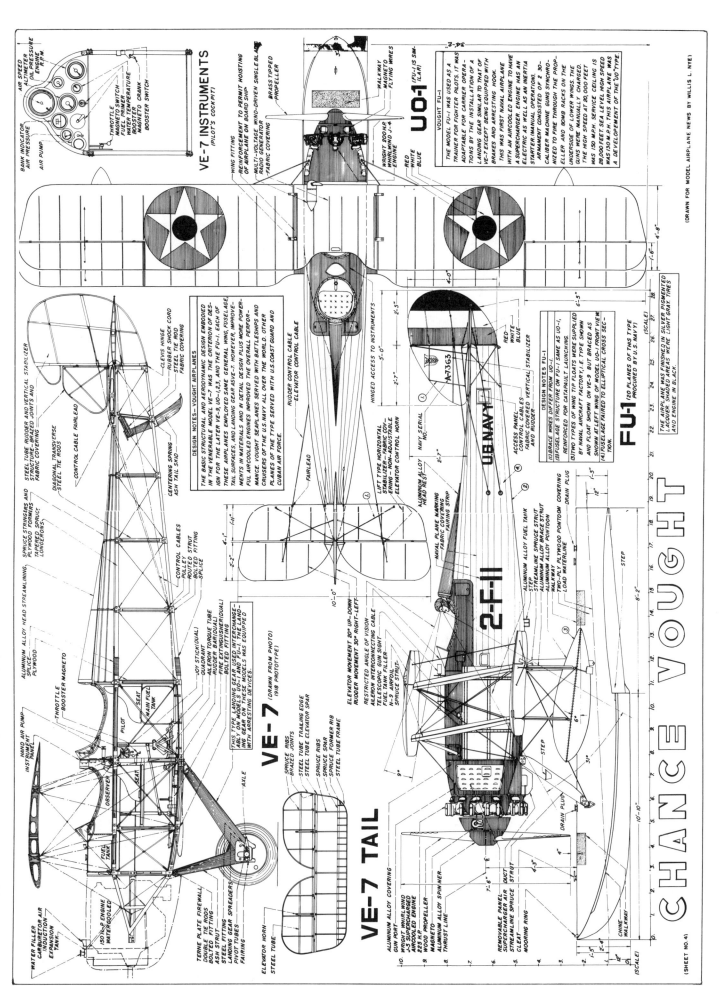

CHANCE VOUGHT

VE-7 INSTRUMENTS (PILOT'S COCKPIT)

UO-1

FU-1 (20 PLANES OF THIS TYPE PROCURED BY U.S. NAVY)

VE-7

VE-7 TAIL

DESIGN NOTES—VOUGHT AIRPLANES

THE BASIC STRUCTURAL AND AERODYNAMIC DESIGN EMBODIED IN THE VENERABLE MODEL VE-7 WAS THE CRITERION OF DESIGN FOR THE LATER VE-9, UO-1,2,3, AND THE FU-1. EACH OF THESE AIRPLANES EMPLOYED SAME GENERAL WING, FUSELAGE, TAIL SURFACES, AND LANDING GEAR AS VE-7. HOWEVER, IMPROVEMENTS IN MATERIALS AND IN DETAIL DESIGN PLUS MORE POWERFUL AIRCOOLED ENGINES IMPROVED THE OVERALL PERFORMANCE. VOUGHT SEAPLANES SERVED WITH BATTLESHIPS AND CRUISERS OF THE U.S. NAVY ALL OVER THE WORLD. OTHER PLANES OF THIS TYPE SERVED WITH U.S. COAST GUARD AND CUBAN AIR FORCE.

Vought FU-1

THE MODEL FU-1 WAS USED AS A TRAINER FOR FIGHTER PILOTS. IT WAS ADAPTABLE FOR CARRIER OPERATIONS BY THE INSTALLATION OF A LANDING GEAR SIMILAR TO THAT OF VE-7 EXCEPT BEING EQUIPPED WITH BRAKES AND ARRESTING HOOK. THIS WAS FIRST NAVAL AIRPLANE WITH AN AIRCOOLED ENGINE TO HAVE A SUPERCHARGER ENGINE HAS AN ELECTRIC AS WELL AS AN INERTIA STARTER (MANUAL OPERATION). ARMAMENT CONSISTED OF 2 .30-CALIBER MACHINE GUNS SYNCHRONIZED TO FIRE THROUGH THE PROPELLER AND BOMB RACKS ON THE UNDERSIDE OF LOWER WINGS. THE GUNS WERE MANUALLY CHARGED. THE HIGH SPEED AT 20,000 FEET WAS 130 M.P.H. SERVICE CEILING WAS 28,000 FEET. SEA LEVEL HIGH SPEED WAS 120 M.P.H. THIS AIRPLANE WAS A DEVELOPEMENT OF THE UO-TYPE.

Design Notes FU-1

1) BRACE WIRES DIFFER FROM UO-1.
2) FUSELAGE STRUCTURE ON FU-1 SAME AS UO-1.
3) TWO TYPES OF WING TIP FLOATS WERE SUPPLIED BY NAVAL AIRCRAFT FACTORY, I.E. TYPE SHOWN AND FLOAT SHOWN ON VE-9 BUT BRACED AS SHOWN AT LEFT WING OF MODEL UO-1 FRONT VIEW.
4) FUSELAGE FAIRED TO ELLIPTICAL CROSS SECTION.

THE AIRPLANE WAS FINISHED IN SILVER PIGMENTED LACQUER SHADED AREAS WERE LIGHT GRAY. TIRES AND ENGINE IN BLACK.

(DRAWN FOR MODEL AIRPLANE NEWS BY WILLIS L. NYE)

(SHEET NO. 4)

31

Curtiss Jenny JN-4—JN-6H.

drawings by JOSEPH NIETO

Photo courtesy of UPI.

"Flying the World's Great Aircraft" photo.

The Jenny was purely American. Produced in great quantities (over 4,500) for that period, Curtiss was helped in the effort by many subcontractors in Canada and the British Empire.

There used to be a saying, "If you can fly a Jenny, you can fly anything." She had her shortcomings, yet she would give novice pilots more than an even break. She was designed to teach men to fly and nothing more was ever expected of her.

However clear-cut the Jenny's wartime purpose may have been, her greatest fame actually came in the post-war years of the 1920s. By sheer numbers she invaded—and took over—the initial phases of American aviation. She flew the first regular airmail schedule and became the first readily available private plane.

To those who teethed on a Jenny there is something magical in recalling the feel of air pressure on her elevators or rudder, of the throbbing of her OX-5 engine pulling her out of a dirt field, of every rib, strut, and wire vibrating in unison, of fabric dancing to the same beat as she bored her way to history. There is no pilot who has put in time in a Jenny who will not admit, "Verily, *there* was an airplane!"

Many survive—several are still flying.□

The Curtiss Jenny served as a trainer, a barn stormer, a mailplane, and was used extensively in early Hollywood films.

"U.S. Airmail Service" photo.

U.S. Navy photo.

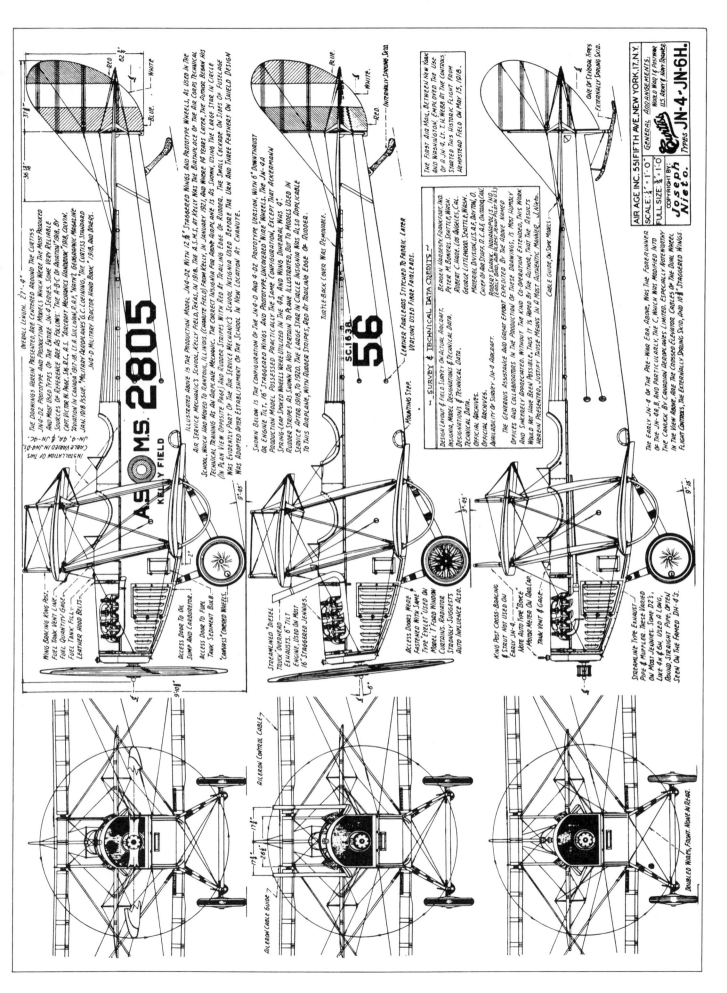

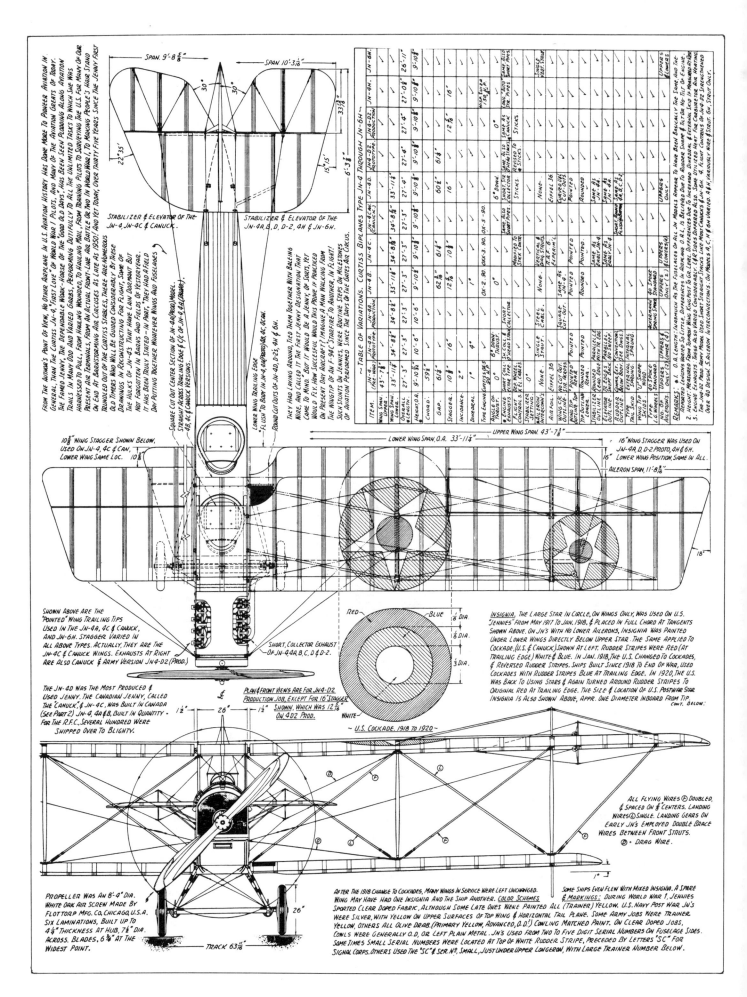

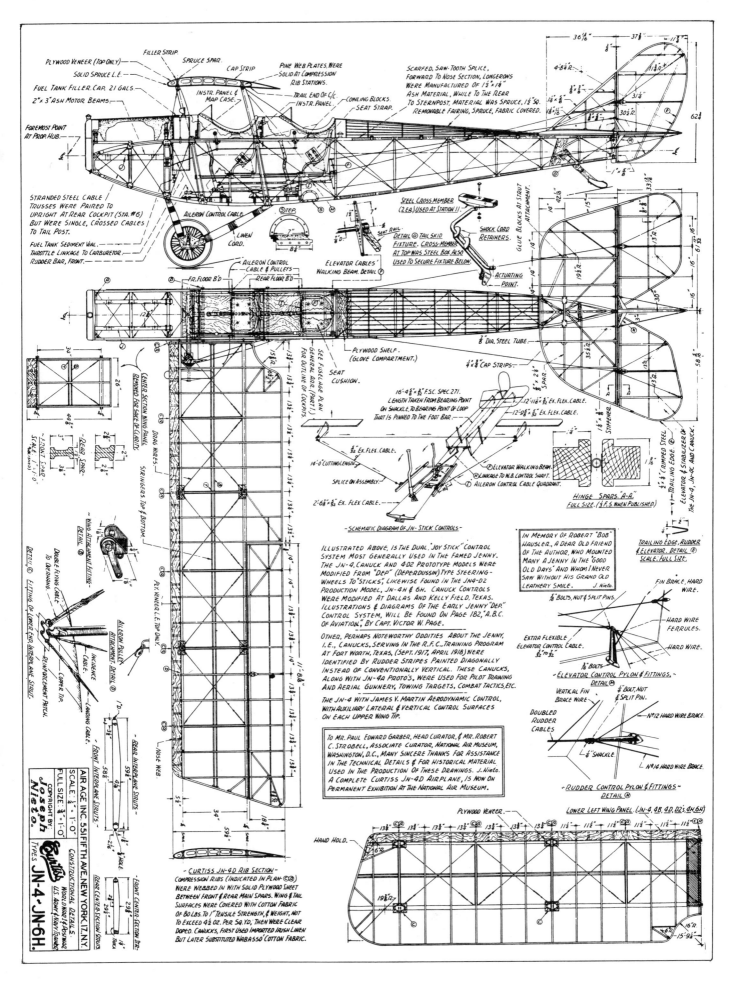

- SCHEMATIC DIAGRAM OF JN- STICK CONTROLS -

ILLUSTRATED ABOVE, IS THE DUAL "JOY STICK" CONTROL SYSTEM MOST GENERALLY USED IN THE FAMED JENNY. THE JN-4, CANUCK AND 4-D2 PROTOTYPE MODELS WERE MODIFIED FROM "DEP" (DEPERDUSSIN) TYPE STEERING-WHEELS TO "STICKS", LIKEWISE FOUND IN THE JN4-D2 PRODUCTION MODEL, JN-4H & 6H. CANUCK CONTROLS WERE MODIFIED AT DALLAS AND KELLY FIELD, TEXAS. ILLUSTRATIONS & DIAGRAMS OF THE EARLY JENNY "DEP." CONTROL SYSTEM, WILL BE FOUND ON PAGE 182, "A.B.C. OF AVIATION", BY CAPT. VICTOR W. PAGE.

OTHER, PERHAPS NOTEWORTHY ODDITIES ABOUT THE JENNY, I.E., CANUCKS, SERVING IN THE R.F.C., TRAINING PROGRAM AT FORT WORTH, TEXAS, (SEPT. 1917, APRIL 1918) WERE IDENTIFIED BY RUDDER STRIPES PAINTED DIAGONALLY INSTEAD OF CONVENTIONALLY VERTICAL. THESE CANUCKS, ALONG WITH JN-4A PROTO'S, WERE USED FOR PILOT TRAINING AND AERIAL GUNNERY, TOWING TARGETS, COMBAT TACTICS, ETC.

THE JN-4 WITH JAMES V. MARTIN AERODYNAMIC CONTROL, WITH AUXILIARY LATERAL & VERTICAL CONTROL SURFACES ON EACH UPPER WING TIP.

In Memory Of Robert "Bob" Hausler.. A Dear Old Friend Of The Author, Who Mounted Many A Jenny In The "Good Old Days" And Whom I Never Saw Without His Grand Old Leathery Smile.   J. Nieto.

To Mr. Paul Edward Garber, Head Curator, & Mr. Robert C. Strobell, Associate Curator, National Air Museum, Washington, D.C., Many Sincere Thanks For Assistance In The Technical Details & For Historical Material Used In The Production Of These Drawings. J. Nieto. A Complete Curtiss JN-4D Airplane, Is Now On Permanent Exhibition At The National Air Museum.

- CURTISS JN-4D RIB SECTION -
COMPRESSION RIBS (INDICATED IN PLAN-C12) WERE WEBBED IN WITH SOLID PLYWOOD SHEET BETWEEN FRONT & REAR MAIN SPARS. WING & TAIL SURFACES WERE COVERED WITH COTTON FABRIC OF 80 LBS. TO 1" TENSILE STRENGTH, & WEIGHT, NOT TO EXCEED 4½ OZ. PER SQ. YD. THEN WERE CLEAR DOPED. CANUCK'S, FIRST USED IMPORTED IRISH LINEN BUT LATER SUBSTITUTED WABASSO COTTON FABRIC.

- ELEVATOR CONTROL PYLON & FITTINGS - DETAIL ⊗

- RUDDER CONTROL PYLON & FITTINGS - DETAIL ⊗

TRAILING EDGE, RUDDER & ELEVATOR. DETAIL Ⓕ
SCALE: FULL SIZE.

LOWER LEFT WING PANEL. (JN-4, 4B, 4D, D2's, 4H, 6H)

COPYRIGHT BY Joseph Nieto.

Curtiss Types JN-4 · JN-6H.

AIR AGE INC. 55 FIFTH AVE. NEW YORK 17, N.Y.
CONSTRUCTIONAL DETAILS 5.
WORLD WAR I AIRPOWER
U.S. ARMY & NAVY TRAINER

SCALE ¾" = 1'-0"

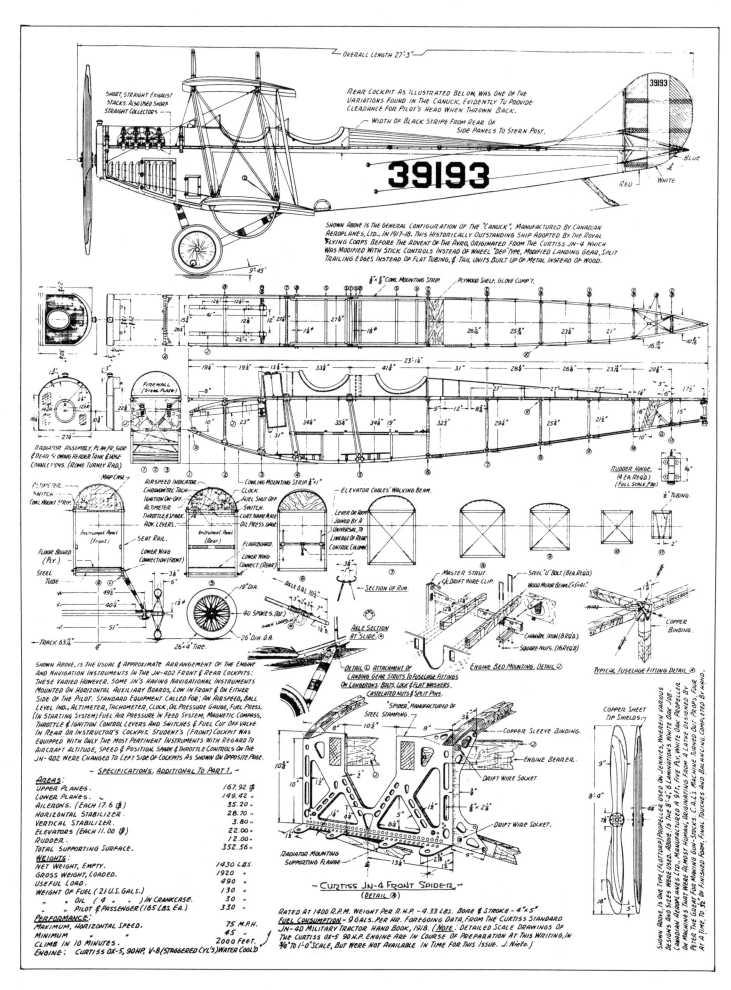

OVERALL LENGTH 27'-3"

SHORT, STRAIGHT EXHAUST STACKS. ALSO USED SHORT STRAIGHT COLLECTORS.

REAR COCKPIT AS ILLUSTRATED BELOW, WAS ONE OF THE VARIATIONS FOUND IN THE CANUCK, EVIDENTLY TO PROVIDE CLEARANCE FOR PILOT'S HEAD WHEN THROWN BACK.

WIDTH OF BLACK STRIPE FROM REAR OF SIDE PANELS TO STERN POST.

39193

BLUE
RED
WHITE

9'-45'

SHOWN ABOVE IS THE GENERAL CONFIGURATION OF THE "CANUCK", MANUFACTURED BY CANADIAN AEROPLANES, LTD., IN 1917-18. THIS HISTORICALLY OUTSTANDING SHIP ADOPTED BY THE ROYAL FLYING CORPS BEFORE THE ADVENT OF THE AVRO, ORIGINATED FROM THE CURTISS JN-4 WHICH WAS MODIFIED WITH STICK CONTROLS INSTEAD OF WHEEL "DEP" TYPE, MODIFIED LANDING GEAR, SPLIT TRAILING EDGES INSTEAD OF FLAT TUBING, & TAIL UNITS BUILT UP OF METAL INSTEAD OF WOOD.

RADIATOR ASSEMBLY, PLAN, FR, SIDE & REAR. SHOWING HEADER TANK & HOSE CONNECTIONS. (ROME TURNEY RAD.)

FIREWALL (STEEL PLATE)

RUDDER HINGE. (4 EA. REQ'D) (FULL SCALE, PBD)

½" TUBING.

ALTIMETER. SWITCH. COM. MOUNT STRIP.

MAP CASE

AIRSPEED INDICATOR. CHRONOMETRIC TACH. IGNITION ON-OFF. ALTIMETER. THROTTLE & SPARK. ADV. LEVERS.

COWLING MOUNTING STRIP. ⅛"×1".
CLOCK.
FUEL SHUT OFF SWITCH.
CURT. NAME PLATE
OIL PRESS. GAGE.

ELEVATOR CABLES' WALKING BEAM.

LEVER OR ARM JOINED BY A UNIVERSAL, TO LINKAGE OF REAR CONTROL COLUMN.

INSTRUMENT PANEL (FRONT)
SEAT RAIL.
LOWER WING CONNECTION (FRONT)

INSTRUMENT PANEL (REAR)
FLOORBOARD.
LOWER WING CONNECT. (REAR)

FLOOR BOARD (PLY.)
STEEL TUBE

SECTION OF RIM.

AXLE O.A.L. 70½"
AXLE SECTION AT SLIDE.

MASTER STRUT. C/& DRIFT WIRE CLIP.
STEEL "U" BOLT. (8 EA. REQ'D.)
WOOD MOTOR BEAM 2⅛"×41"

TYPICAL FUSELAGE FITTING. DETAIL Ⓧ
COPPER BINDING.

19" DIA.
40 SPOKES. (1 ot.)
SHOCK LOOPS (4)

26" DIA. O.A.
26"×4" TIRE.

TRACK 63 11/16"

CHANNEL IRON (8 REQ'D.)
SQUARE NUTS. (16 REQ'D.)

DETAIL Ⓒ ATTACHMENT OF LANDING GEAR STRUTS TO FUSELAGE FITTINGS ON LONGERONS: BOLTS, LOCK & FLAT WASHERS. CASTELLATED NUTS & SPLIT PINS.

ENGINE BED MOUNTING. DETAIL Ⓓ

"SPIDER" MANUFACTURED OF STEEL STAMPING.
COPPER SLEEVE BINDING.
ENGINE BEARER.
DRIFT WIRE SOCKET.
DRIFT WIRE SOCKET.
RADIATOR MOUNTING SUPPORTING FLANGE

COPPER SHEET TIP SHIELDS.

CURTISS JN-4 FRONT SPIDER
(DETAIL Ⓐ)

SHOWN ABOVE, IS THE USUAL & APPROXIMATE ARRANGEMENT OF THE ENGINE AND NAVIGATION INSTRUMENTS IN THE JN-4D2 FRONT & REAR COCKPITS: THESE VARIED HOWEVER, SOME JN'S HAVING NAVIGATIONAL INSTRUMENTS MOUNTED ON HORIZONTAL AUXILIARY BOARDS, LOW IN FRONT & ON EITHER SIDE OF THE PILOT. STANDARD EQUIPMENT CALLED FOR; AN AIRSPEED, BALL LEVEL IND., ALTIMETER, TACHOMETER, CLOCK, OIL PRESSURE GAUGE, FUEL PRESS. (IN STARTING SYSTEM) FUEL AIR PRESSURE IN FEED SYSTEM, MAGNETIC COMPASS, THROTTLE & IGNITION CONTROL LEVERS AND SWITCHES & FUEL CUT OFF VALVE IN REAR OR INSTRUCTOR'S COCKPIT. STUDENT'S (FRONT) COCKPIT WAS EQUIPPED WITH ONLY THE MOST PERTINENT INSTRUMENTS WITH REGARD TO AIRCRAFT ALTITUDE, SPEED & POSITION. SPARK & THROTTLE CONTROLS ON THE JN-4D2 WERE CHANGED TO LEFT SIDE OF COCKPITS AS SHOWN ON OPPOSITE PAGE.

~ SPECIFICATIONS, ADDITIONAL TO PART 1. ~

AREAS:
UPPER PLANES. 167.92 ☐'
LOWER PLANES. 149.42 "
AILERONS. (EACH 17.6 ☐) 35.20 "
HORIZONTAL STABILIZER. 28.70 "
VERTICAL STABILIZER. 3.80 "
ELEVATORS (EACH 11.00 ☐) 22.00 "
RUDDER. 12.00 "
TOTAL SUPPORTING SURFACE. 352.56 "
WEIGHTS:
NET WEIGHT, EMPTY. 1430 LBS.
GROSS WEIGHT, LOADED. 1920 "
USEFUL LOAD. 490 "
WEIGHT OF FUEL (21 U.S. GALS.) 130 "
" " OIL (4 ") IN CRANKCASE. 30 "
" " PILOT & PASSENGER (165 LBS. EA.) 330 "
PERFORMANCE:
MAXIMUM, HORIZONTAL SPEED. 75 M.P.H.
MINIMUM 45 "
CLIMB IN 10 MINUTES. 2000 FEET.
ENGINE: CURTISS OX-5, 90HP, V-8 (STAGGERED CYL'S) WATER COOL'D.

RATED AT 1400 R.P.M. WEIGHT PER R.H.P. -4.33 LBS. BORE & STROKE -4"×5" FUEL CONSUMPTION -9 GALS. PER HR. FOREGOING DATA, FROM THE CURTISS STANDARD JN-4D MILITARY TRACTOR HAND BOOK, 1918. (NOTE: DETAILED SCALE DRAWINGS OF THE CURTISS OX-5 90 H.P. ENGINE ARE IN COURSE OF PREPARATION AT THIS WRITING, IN ¾" TO 1'-0" SCALE, BUT WERE NOT AVAILABLE IN TIME FOR THIS ISSUE. J. NIETO.)

SHOWN ABOVE, IS ONE TYPE (FLAT OR PI) PROPELLER USED ON JENNIES, WHEREIN VARIOUS DESIGNS AND SIZES WERE USED. ABOVE, IS THE 8'-4", 6 GENUINE WHITE OAK JOB. CANADIAN AEROPLANES LTD. MANUFACTURED A 9FT., FIVE PLY, WHITE OAK PROPELLER ON MACHINES THAT WERE ALMOST HUMAN, ORIGINATING FROM A LATHE DESIGNED BY PETER THE GREAT FOR MAKING GUN-STOCKS. C.A.L'S MACHINE TURNED OUT PROPS, FOUR AT A TIME, TO 32 OF FINISHED FORM, FINAL TOUCHES AND BALANCING, COMPLETED BY HAND.

Curtiss Model D

drawing by WILLIAM WYLAM

THIS AIRCRAFT was the result of U.S. Signal Corps authorization by Congress to appropriate aircraft for the Army. After a 5-year struggle to prove the practicality of the airplane, the Wright Brothers' flight demonstration had opened the eyes of Army brass to a new spectrum of weaponry. In 1911 Congress approved the first allotment specifically for aeronautics, and the Wright Brothers and Glenn Curtiss received the first two such contracts.

Designated "Signal Corps" sequence numbers, S.C. 1, the first military aircraft of the Wright Brothers was retired to the Air Force Museum that year, and Curtiss' S.C. 2 was the second aircraft to enter testing at Fort Sam Houston in April 1911. G.E.M. Kelly flew the trials on the morning of April 10. He took it up and shortly came in for a landing, hit the ground hard, and bounced back in the air. Climbing slowly, Kelly banked the airplane away from the tent area, suddenly lost control, and plummeted to his death. The S.C. 2 was repaired, however, and was used as a trainer. It was removed from service on February 24, 1914.

Seven Pushers survive, and many reproductions. ☐

The Curtiss S.C. 2 was the second aircraft to enter the military inventory. "A.A.H.S." Journal photo.

Glen Curtiss at the controls of his June Bug was determined to prove the utility of the airplane to the military. "A.A.H.S. Journal" photo.

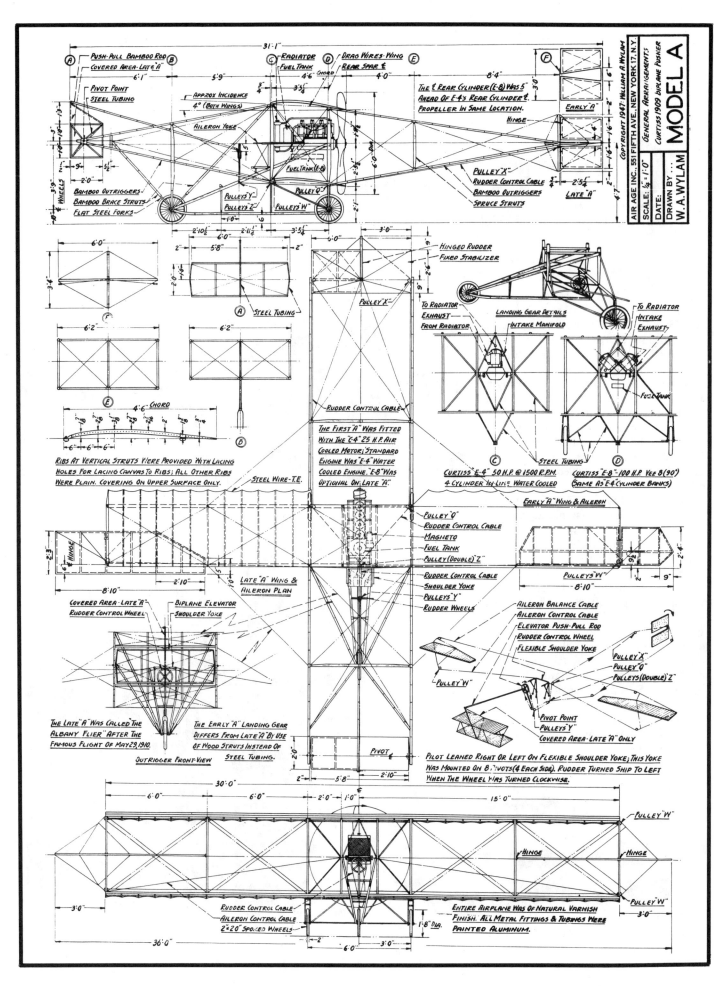

MODEL A

AIR AGE INC., 551 FIFTH AVE., NEW YORK 17, N.Y.
GENERAL ARRANGEMENTS
CURTISS 1909 BIPLANE PUSHER
COPYRIGHT 1947, WILLIAM R. WYLAM

SCALE: ¼"=1'-0"
DATE:
DRAWN BY ....
W. A. WYLAM

DeHavilland D.H.1

drawings by WILLIAM WYLAM

THE deHavilland D.H.1 was a two-bay pusher biplane designed by Geoffrey deHavilland in 1915 while he was with the Aircraft Manufacturing Company, producers of the plane. As simple as they were in those days, aircraft could be designed, built, and test-flown in a matter of just a few months. The D.H.1 was an immediate success and garnered much of that success from the 70-hp Renault V-type air-cooled engine. Its top speed at sea level was 78 mph, and its rate of climb was estimated at something less than 500 fpm.

DeHavilland himself did all the preliminary flight testing on the D.H.1. The lessons he had learned in the application of inherent stability theories to full-size aircraft were incorporated in his new pusher. He demonstrated these qualities very impressively by flying hands off during tests and on low passes.

Although the D.H.1 was never produced in quantity, it was a very good airplane both performance-wise and structurally.

With a good airplane on their hands but no orders, the makers decided to develop the D.H.1 into a more serviceable military design, thus the D.H.1A evolved, which did reach limited production. There are none left. □

Springboard for the deHavilland aircraft manufacturing firm, the D.H.1 was considered a fine aircraft in its time. Air Age file photos.

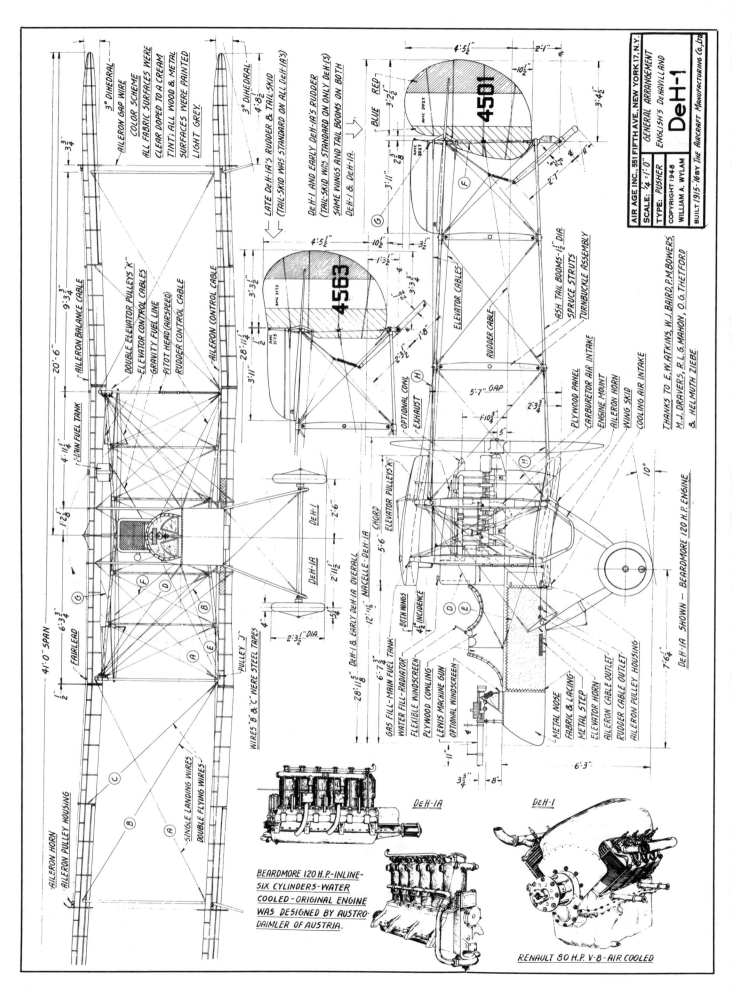

BEARDMORE 120 H.P.-INLINE-
SIX CYLINDERS-WATER
COOLED-ORIGINAL ENGINE
WAS DESIGNED BY AUSTRO-
DAIMLER OF AUSTRIA.

DEH-1A

DEH-1

RENAULT 80 H.P. V-8 AIR COOLED

AIR AGE INC., 551 FIFTH AVE., NEW YORK 17, N.Y.
SCALE: ¼″=1′-0″
TYPE: PUSHER
COPYRIGHT 1948
ENGLISH'S DeHAVILLAND
GENERAL ARRANGEMENT
DeH-1
WILLIAM A. WYLAM
BUILT 1915-'16 BY THE AIRCRAFT MANUFACTURING Co., Ltd.

THANKS TO E.W. ATKINS, W.J. BAIRD, P.M. BOWERS,
M.J. DRAVERS, R.L.G. MAHON, O.G. THETFORD
& HELMUTH ZIEBE.

DEH-1A SHOWN — BEARDMORE 120 H.P. ENGINE

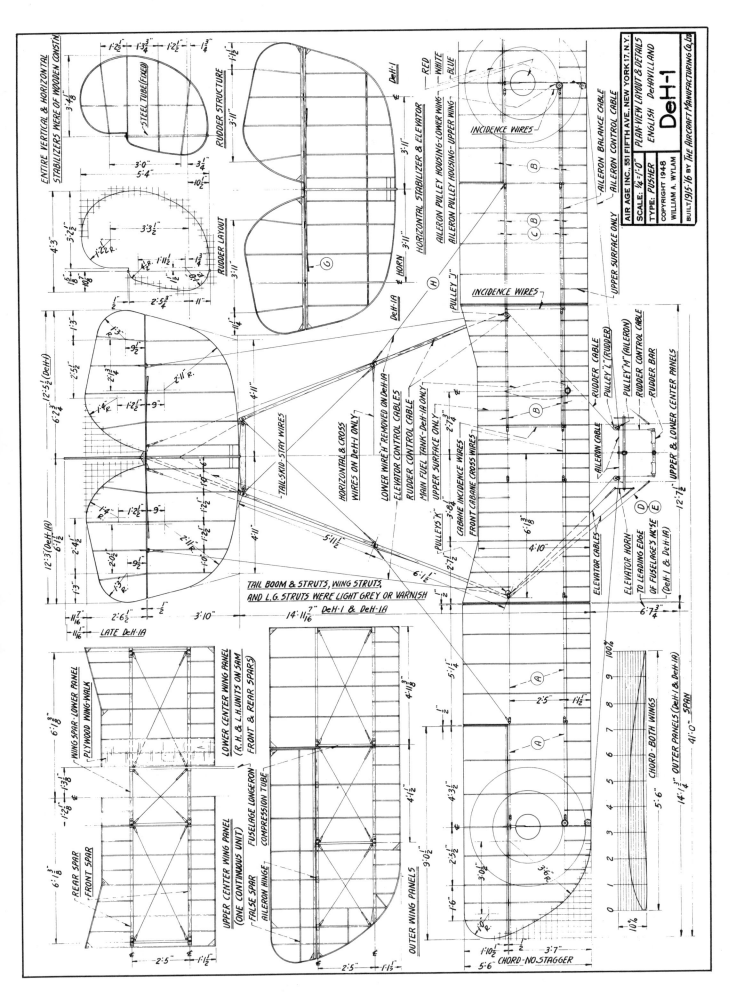

ENTIRE VERTICAL & HORIZONTAL
STABILIZERS WERE OF WOODEN CONSTR'N

STEEL TUBE (FIXED)

RUDDER STRUCTURE

RUDDER LAYOUT

INCIDENCE WIRES

AILERON BALANCE CABLE
AILERON CONTROL CABLE
UPPER SURFACE ONLY

AILERON PULLEY HOUSING—LOWER WING
AILERON PULLEY HOUSING—UPPER WING

HORIZONTAL STABILIZER & ELEVATOR

INCIDENCE WIRES

PULLEY "J"

TAIL-SKID STAY WIRES

HORIZONTAL & CROSS
WIRES ON DeH-1 ONLY

LOWER WIRE "H" REMOVED ON DeH-1A

ELEVATOR CONTROL CABLES
RUDDER CONTROL CABLE
MAIN FUEL TANK—DeH-1A ONLY
UPPER SURFACE ONLY

PULLEYS "X"
CABANE INCIDENCE WIRES
FRONT CABANE CROSS WIRES

RUDDER CABLE
PULLEY "L" (RUDDER)
PULLEY "M" (AILERON)
RUDDER CONTROL CABLE
RUDDER BAR

AILERON CABLE

UPPER & LOWER CENTER PANELS

ELEVATOR CABLES

ELEVATOR HORN
TO LEADING EDGE
OF FUSELAGE'S 1⅝"E
(DeH-1 & DeH-1A)

TAIL BOOM & STRUTS, WING STRUTS,
AND L.G. STRUTS WERE LIGHT GREY OR VARNISH

LATE DeH-1A

UPPER CENTER WING PANEL
(ONE CONTINUOUS UNIT)

WING SPAR—LOWER PANEL
PLYWOOD WING-WALK

LOWER CENTER WING PANEL
(R.H. & L.H. UNITS ON SAM)
FRONT & REAR SPARS

FUSELAGE LONGERON
FUSELAGE
COMPRESSION TUBE

REAR SPAR
FRONT SPAR
FALSE SPAR
AILERON HINGE

OUTER WING PANELS

CHORD—BOTH WINGS

SPAN

CHORD—NO-STAGGER

AIR AGE INC. 551 FIFTH AVE. NEW YORK 17. N.Y.
PLAN-VIEW LAYOUT & DETAILS
SCALE: ⅛"=1'-0"
ENGLISH DeHAVILLAND
TYPE: PUSHER
COPYRIGHT 1948
WILLIAM A. WYLAM
BUILT 1915-'16 BY THE AIRCRAFT MANUFACTURING Co., Ltd.

DeH-1

RED
WHITE
BLUE

DeH-1A

41

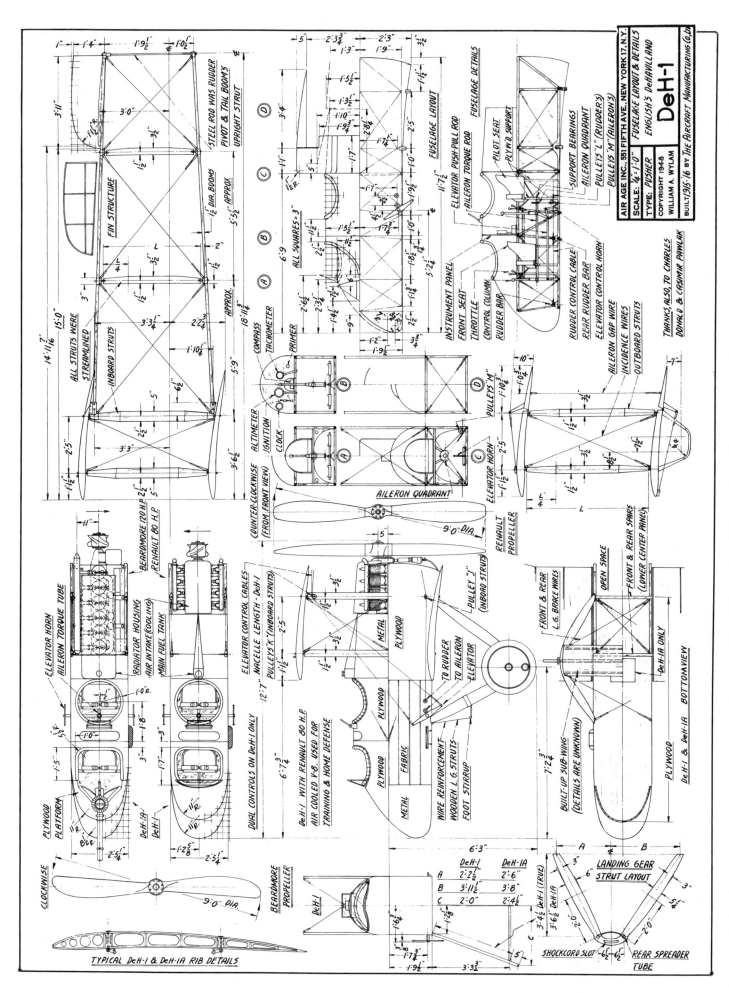

AILERON QUADRANT

RENAULT PROPELLER

9'-0" DIA.

TYPICAL DeH-1 & DeH-1A RIB DETAILS

BEARDMORE PROPELLER

9'-0" DIA.

CLOCKWISE

COUNTER-CLOCKWISE (FROM FRONT VIEW)

LANDING GEAR STRUT LAYOUT

	DeH-1	DeH-1A
A	2'-2½"	2'-6"
B	3'-11½"	3'-8"
C	2'-0"	2'-4½"

SHOCKCORD SLOT

REAR SPREADER TUBE

DeH-1 & DeH-1A BOTTOM VIEW

AIR AGE INC., 551 FIFTH AVE., NEW YORK 17, N.Y.
FUSELAGE LAYOUT & DETAILS
ENGLISH'S DeHAVILLAND
SCALE: ¼" = 1'-0"   TYPE: PUSHER
COPYRIGHT 1948   WILLIAM A. WYLAM
BUILT 1915-16 BY THE AIRCRAFT MANUFACTURING Co.Ltd

DeH-1

THANKS, ALSO, TO CHARLES DONALD & CASIMIR PAWLAK

42

DeHavilland D.H.4

drawings by WILLIAM WYLAM

THE BRITISH firm known as the Aircraft Manufacturing Company was founded by G. Holt Thomas in 1912, and among its talented designers was Geoffrey deHavilland. Credited with many successful designs, deHavilland was prolific. In June 1916 mechanics rolled out the prototype of the now famous D.H.4 biplane, which was later to be both condemned and praised for its characteristics and fighting abilities. The ship was big and beautiful, yet in some respects ungainly and unsafe.

The first production models to go into service in 1916 were fitted with a variety of engines from 200-260 hp. The completely enclosed fuselage with its occupants sitting in tandem was not new, but the fact that the gunner member of the crew sat in the rear seat was. The greatest influence in the change of crew positions was the advent of the synchronized gun on the cowling.

Later versions of the D.H.4 made use of the Rolls-Royce Falcon engine and later still the Eagle engine, which produced 375 hp.

Throughout the history of aviation, airplanes have been given nicknames, most of them of a complimentary nature, and which were supposed to describe the plane's most outstanding characteristics. "Flaming Coffin" was attached to the D.H.4 early in its career, because the fuel tank was positioned between the cockpits. Its excellent handling qualities and large speed range encouraged development, and in the DH-4B (American designation) the pilot was moved back and the tank forward.

Six D.H.4's are left, in various models in various conditions. □

Entered into service in 1916, the D.H.4 had a long and productive life despite its reputation as a "flying death trap." "Model Airplane News" photo.

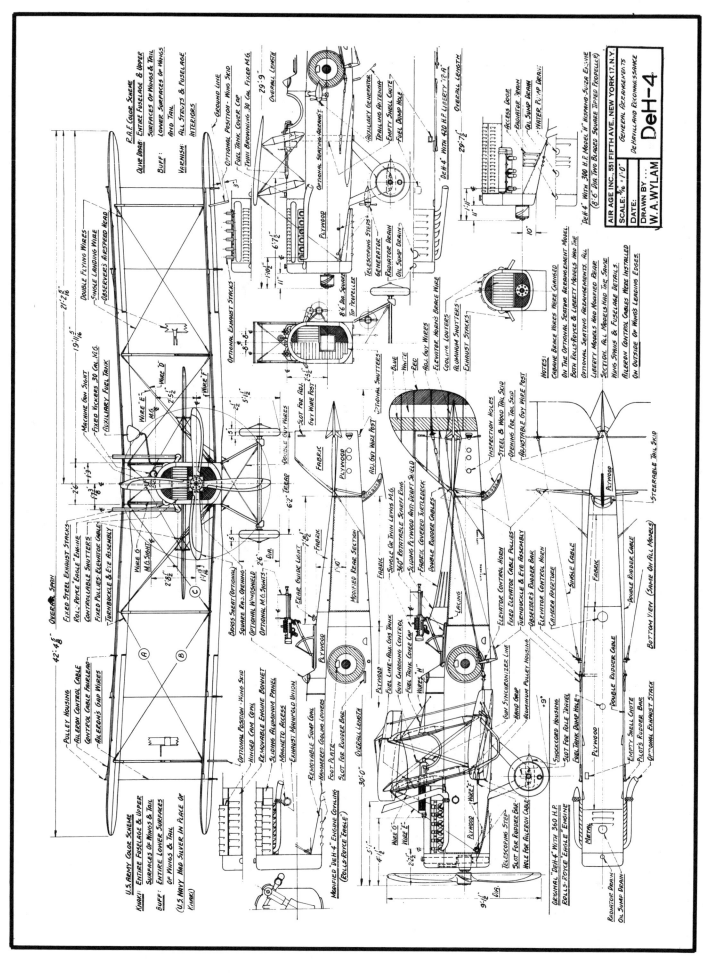

DeHavilland Reconnaissance
General Rearrangements

DeH-4

AIR AGE INC., 551 FIFTH AVE., NEW YORK 17, N.Y.
SCALE: 1/16" = 1'-0"
DATE:
DRAWN BY ... W. A. WYLAM

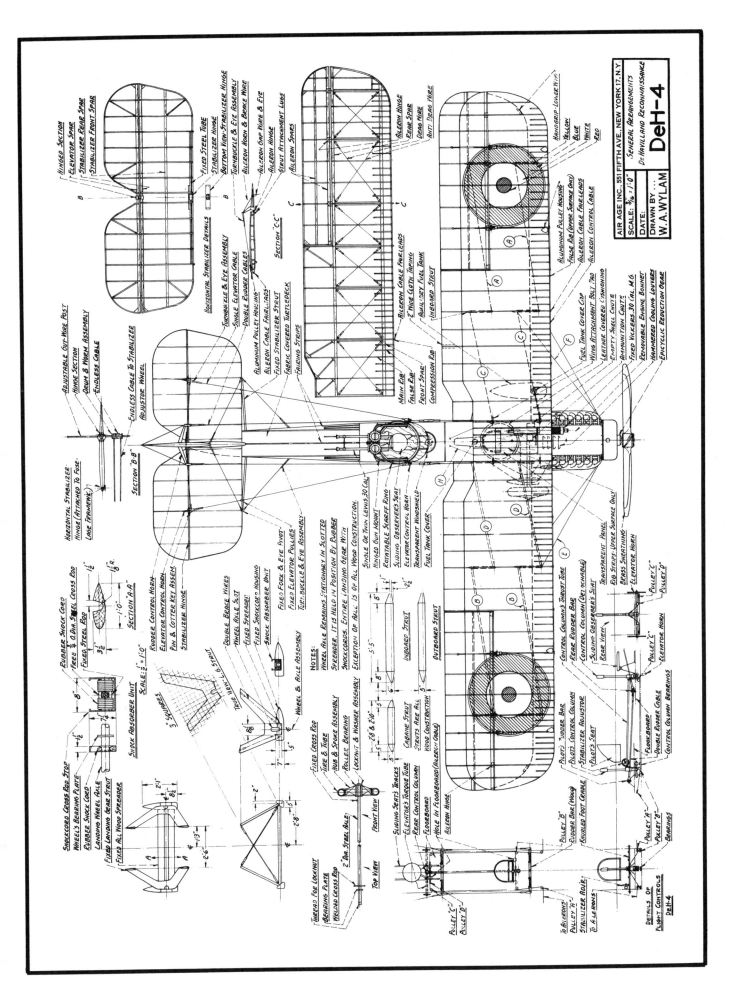

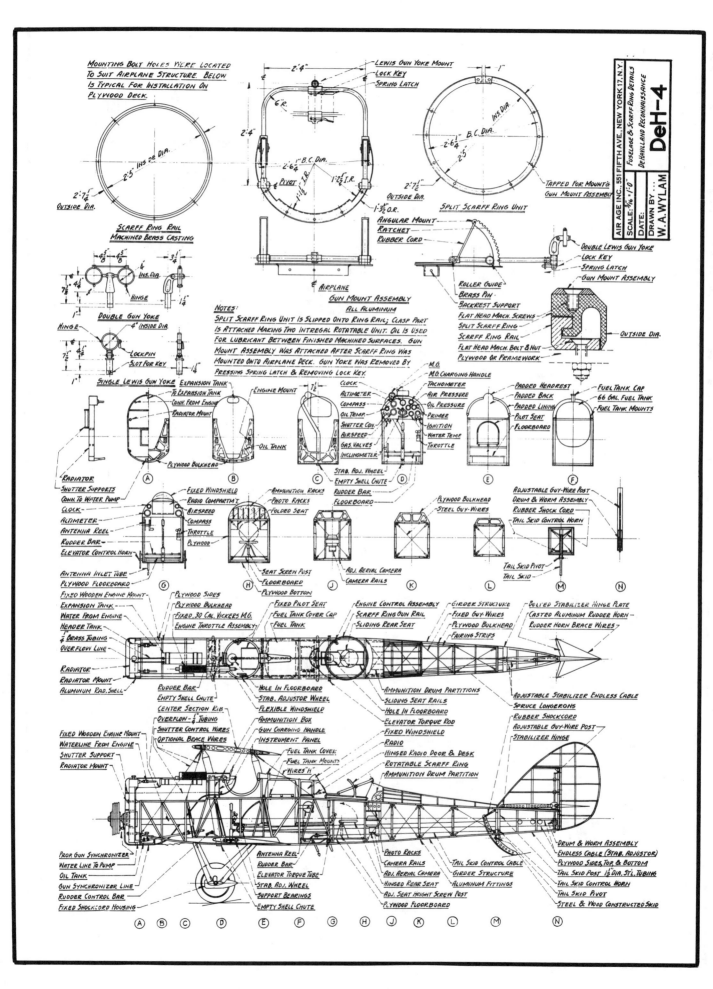

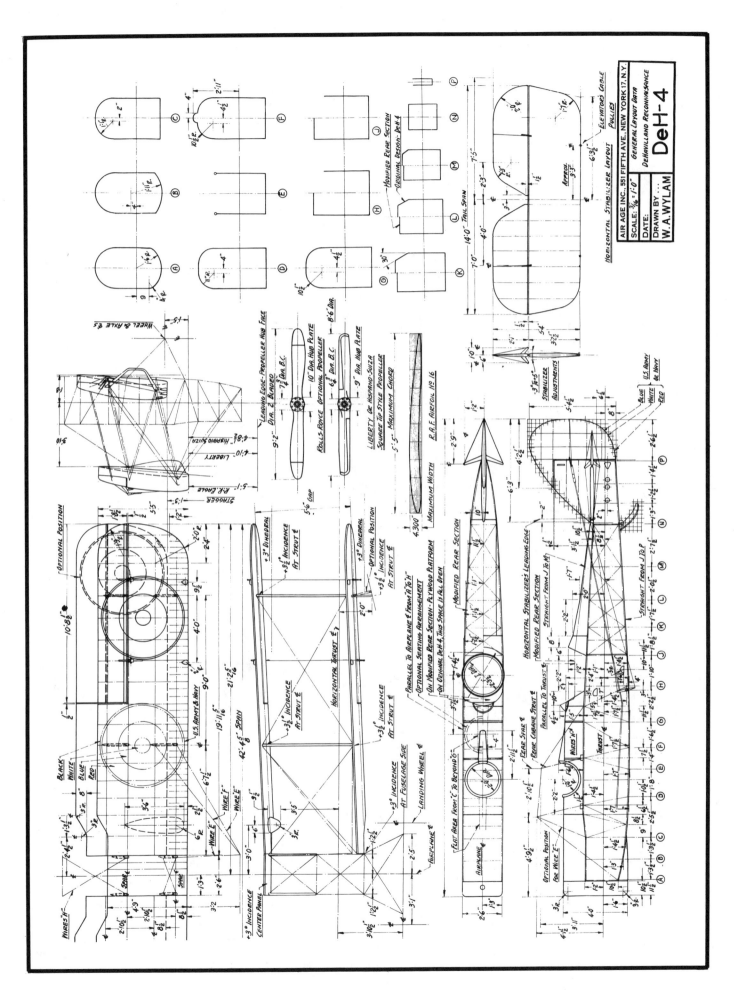

DeH-4

AIR AGE INC. 551 FIFTH AVE., NEW YORK 17, N.Y.

GENERAL LAYOUT DRAWN

SCALE: 3/16" = 1'-0"

DATE:

DRAWN BY W. A. WYLAM

DeHavilland Reconnaisance

Fokker Dr.1

drawings by JOSEPH NIETO

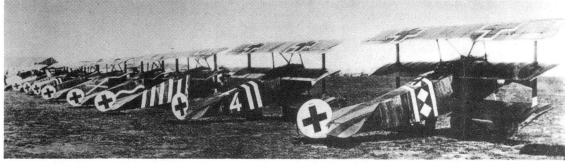

An airplane without flying wires, particularly a fighter, was unheard of in 1915. Anthony Fokker proved that self-supporting flying surfaces were not only practical but advantageous in his triplane. Air Age file photos.

ONE OF the most unusual fighters of WW I, the Fokker Triplane was also the most agile fighting machine during that period. Designed for dog fighting, the ship was unequaled in its ability to out-maneuver anything in the air. It quickly became apparent to German fighter pilots that the Dr.1 was the ship to fly when Manfred von Richthofen scored a victory on his first time out with the new design. The second time out he scored another. It also became apparent to British pilots that the Germans had something to reckon with.

One of the most unusual aspects of this design, other than its being a triplane, was that it had no wires. Today this seems academic, but in 1915 design engineers fully expected the wings to fold on any airplane that had non-supported flying surfaces. This airplane proved that a cantilever wing was not only possible, but practical.

Powered by the Oberursel rotary engine rated at 110 hp, the triplane had a top speed of 97 mph and a ceiling of 18,000 feet. The rate of climb was nearly 2,000 fpm and the landing speed in zero wind was only 30 mph. It was feather light on the controls and could literally turn on a dime, causing a near blackout to the pilot at the controls.

Von Richthofen was shot down in one.

Although the service period of the triplane was only seven months, it remains one of the most remembered aircraft of WW I. No original Triplane survived the war. ☐

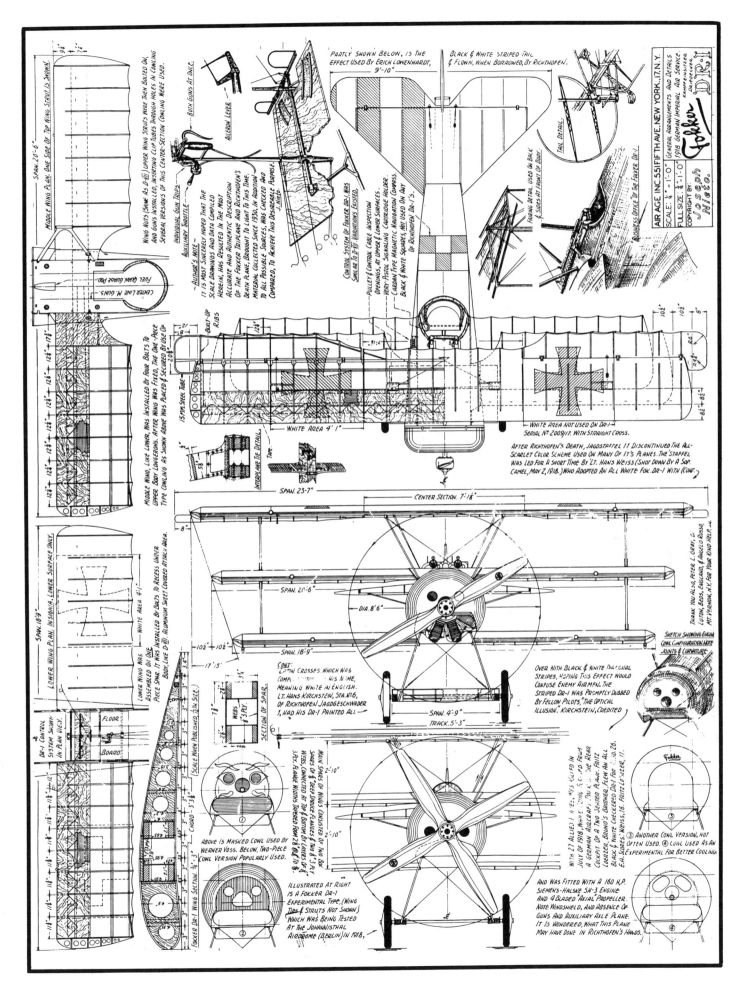

Fokker DR.I

AIR AGE INC. 55 IF FTH AVE. NEW YORK. 17. N.Y.
GENERAL ARRANGEMENTS AND DETAILS
1918 GERMAN IMPERIAL AIR SERVICE.
KAMPFEINSITZER DR. I DECKER.
BUSINESS OFFICE OF THE FOKKER DR-I.
COPYRIGHT BY: Joseph Nieto.
SCALE: ¾" = 1'-0"
FULL SIZE: ¾" = 1'-0"

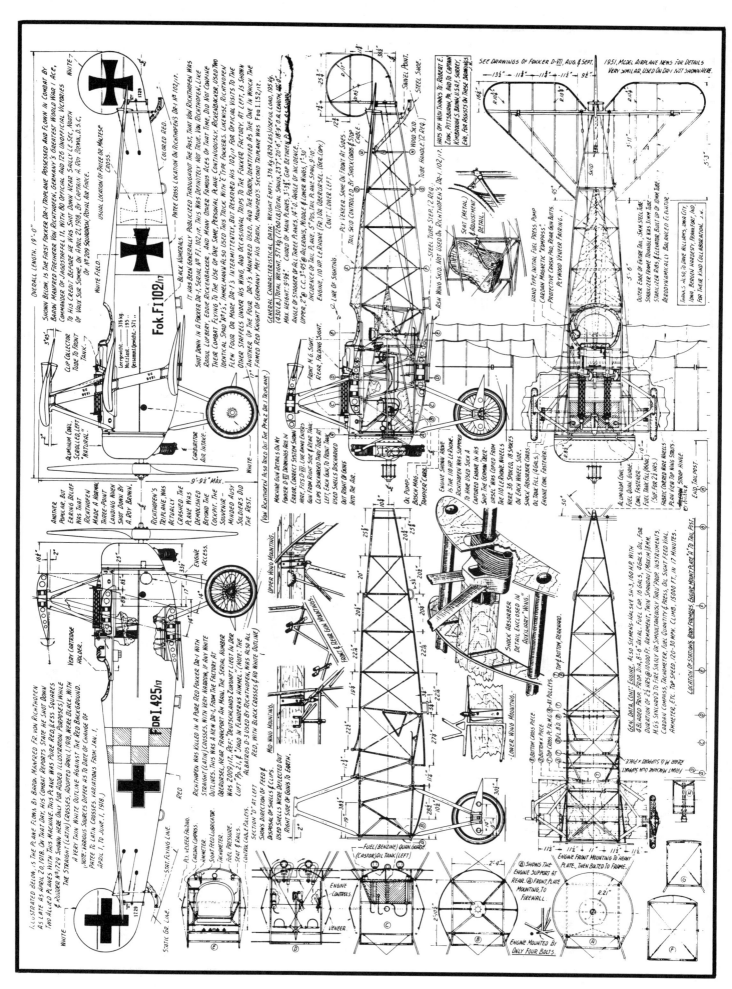

Fokker D.VII

drawings by JOSEPH NIETO

Probably the most famous of German WW I aircraft was the Fokker D.VII. Ernst Udet, shown below, was an advocate of the design, although he preferred the D.VIII. Air Age file photos.

EARLY in May 1918, pilots assigned to the French sector began to meet increasing numbers of a strange new German pursuit plane. They observed it flying with squadrons of Albatros and Pfalz single-seaters, perhaps two or three to a flight. The new ships stayed pretty well back and very seldom engaged in a dog fight, but they impressed Allied pilots by their ability to bound around in the air like a rubber ball. This new plane, the D.VII, was the shot in the arm the Germans were looking for.

Among modelers and WW I aviation enthusiasts, the question always arises as to which was the best plane of that period. The Fokker D.VII certainly will have its supporters in any such discussion. Simplicity was the keynote of the design. The fuselage was of wire-braced welded steel tubing (the Germans did not trust welds in tension); the tail was all-steel. The wings were each built on two massive wooden box-spars, and there was no wire rigging. Most examples

of the aircraft were powered by the Mercedes D.III engine, rated at 160 hp; however, later models were fitted with Daimler and B.M.W. engines for high altitude.

Two Spandau machine guns were mounted directly in front of the pilot, and the combination of pilot, machine, and firepower added up to a formidable

weapon for the Germans. From a historical standpoint, the Fokker D.VII will always hold a special significance as one of the most interesting airplanes ever built: it was the only German airplane by name to be mentioned in the Treaty of Versailles.

Seven original D.VIIs are in museums all over the world. □

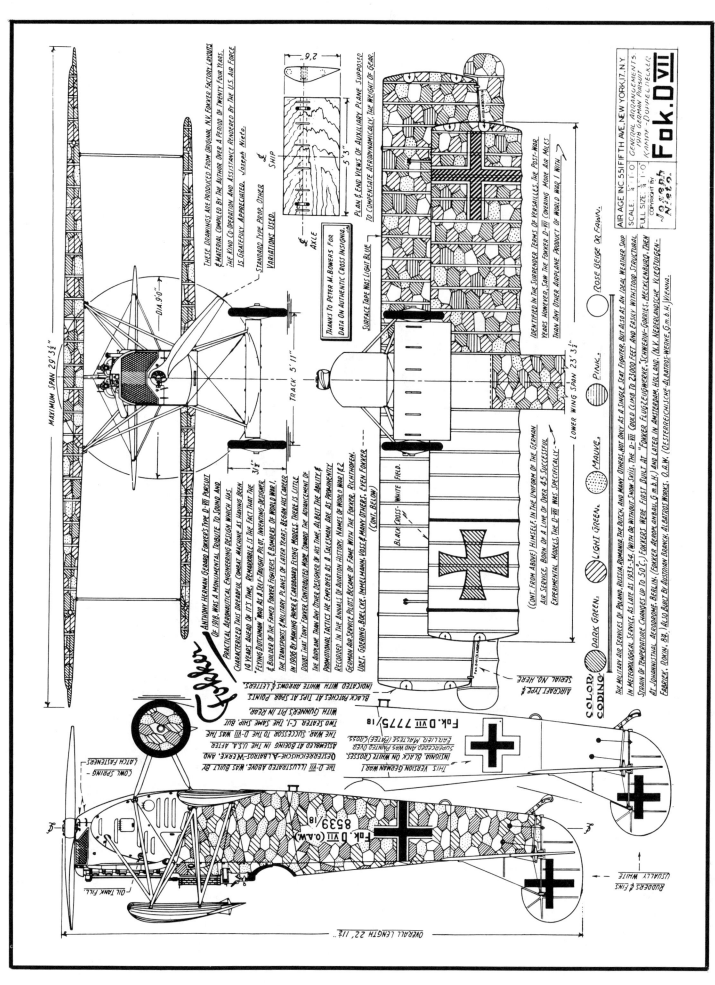

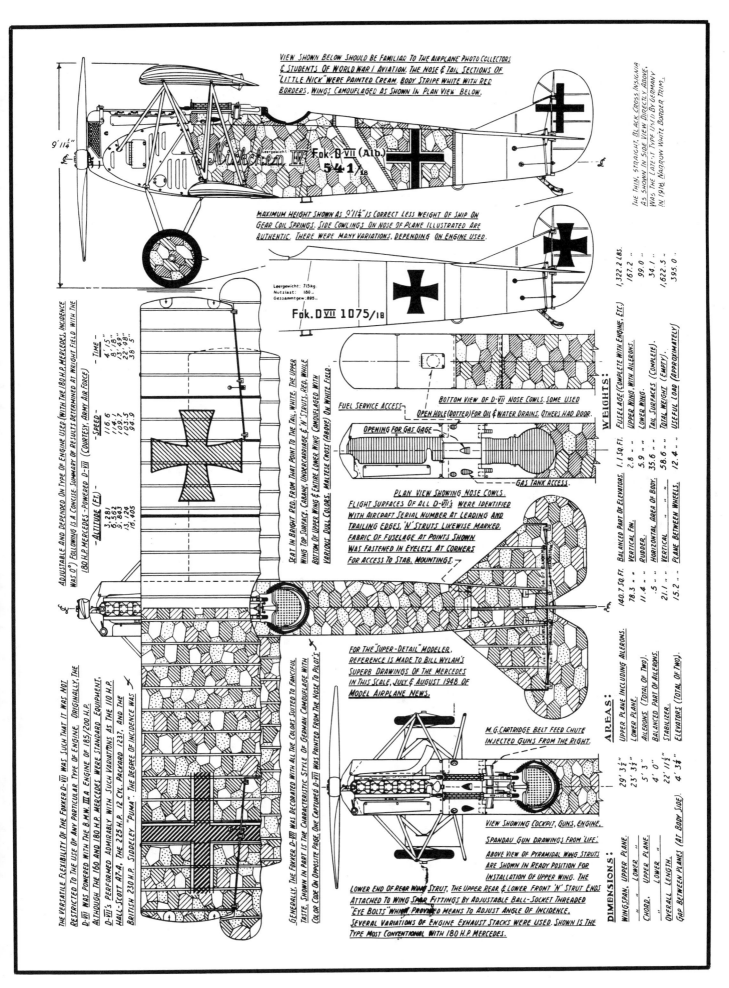

VIEW SHOWN BELOW SHOULD BE FAMILIAR TO THE AIRPLANE PHOTO COLLECTORS & STUDENTS OF WORLD WAR I AVIATION. THE NOSE & TAIL SECTIONS OF "LITTLE NICK" WERE PAINTED CREAM. BODY STRIPE WHITE WITH RED BORDERS. WINGS CAMOUFLAGED AS SHOWN IN PLAN VIEW BELOW.

9'11¼"

Mädchen IV Fok. Dⱽ'ᴵᴵ (Alb.)
Leergewicht 54 1/18

THE THIN, STRAIGHT, BLACK CROSS INSIGNIA AS SHOWN IN SIDE VIEW DIRECTLY ABOVE, WAS THE LATEST TYPE USED BY GERMANY IN 1918. NARROW WHITE BORDER TRIM.

MAXIMUM HEIGHT SHOWN AS 9'11¼" IS CORRECT LESS WEIGHT OF SHIP ON GEAR COIL SPRINGS. SIDE COWLINGS ON NOSE OF PLANE ILLUSTRATED ARE AUTHENTIC. THERE WERE MANY VARIATIONS, DEPENDING ON ENGINE USED.

Leergewicht: 715kg.
Nutzlast: 180 ..
Gessammtgew.: 895 ..

Fok. Dⱽ'ᴵᴵ 1075/18

WEIGHTS:

FUSELAGE (COMPLETE WITH ENGINE, ETC.)	1,322.2 LBS.
UPPER WING, WITH AILERONS.	167.2 ..
LOWER WING.	99.0 ..
TAIL SURFACES (COMPLETE).	34.1 ..
TOTAL WEIGHT (EMPTY).	1,622.5 ..
USEFUL LOAD (APPROXIMATELY)	395.0 ..

THE VERSATILE FLEXIBILITY OF THE FOKKER D-ⱽ'ᴵᴵ WAS SUCH THAT IT WAS NOT RESTRICTED TO THE USE OF ANY PARTICULAR TYPE OF ENGINE. ORIGINALLY, THE D-ⱽ'ᴵᴵ WAS POWERED WITH THE B.M.W. IIIᵃ ENGINE OF 185/200 H.P. ALTHOUGH THE 160 AND 180 H.P. MERCEDES WERE STANDARD EQUIPMENT, D-ⱽ'ᴵᴵ'S PERFORMED ADMIRABLY WITH SUCH VARIATIONS AS THE 110 H.P. HALL-SCOTT A7-A, THE 225 H.P. 12 CYL. PACKARD 1237, AND THE BRITISH 230 H.P. SIDDELEY "PUMA". THE DEGREE OF INCIDENCE WAS

ADJUSTABLE AND DEPENDED ON TYPE OF ENGINE USED (WITH THE 180 H.P. MERCEDES, INCIDENCE WAS 0°) FOLLOWING IS A CONCISE SUMMARY OF RESULTS DETERMINED AT WRIGHT FIELD WITH THE (180 H.P. MERCEDES—POWERED D-ⱽ'ᴵᴵ (COURTESY, ARMY AIR FORCE)

— SPEED —	— ALTITUDE (FT.) —	— TIME —
116.6	3,281	4' 15"
114.7	6,562	8' 18"
109.1	9,843	13' 49"
103.5	13,124	22' 28"
94.9	16,405	38' 5"

GENERALLY, THE FOKKER D-ⱽ'ᴵᴵ WAS DECORATED WITH ALL THE COLORS SUITED TO FANCIFUL TASTE. SHOWN IN PART IS THE CHARACTERISTIC STYLE OF GERMAN CAMOUFLAGE WITH COLOR CODE ON OPPOSITE PAGE. ONE CAPTURED D-ⱽ'ᴵᴵ WAS PAINTED FROM THE NOSE TO PILOT'S

FUEL SERVICE ACCESS —

BOTTOM VIEW OF D-ⱽ'ᴵᴵ NOSE COWLS. SOME USED OPEN HOLE (DOTTED) FOR OIL & WATER DRAINS. OTHERS HAD DOOR.

OPENING FOR GAS GAGE

GAS TANK ACCESS.

PLAN VIEW SHOWING NOSE COWLS.
FLIGHT SURFACES OF ALL D-ⱽ'ᴵᴵ'S WERE IDENTIFIED WITH AIRCRAFT SERIAL NUMBER AT LEADING AND TRAILING EDGES. 'N' STRUTS LIKEWISE MARKED. FABRIC OF FUSELAGE AT POINTS SHOWN WAS FASTENED IN EYELETS AT CORNERS FOR ACCESS TO STAB. MOUNTINGS. →

SEAT IN BRIGHT RED. FROM THAT POINT TO THE TAIL, WHITE. THE UPPER WING TOP SURFACE, CABANE, UNDERCARRIAGE & 'N' STRUTS, RED, WHILE BOTTOM OF UPPER WING & ENTIRE LOWER WING CAMOUFLAGED WITH VARIOUS DULL COLORS. MALTESE CROSS (ABOVE) ON WHITE FIELD.

FOR THE "SUPER-DETAIL" MODELER, REFERENCE IS MADE TO BILL WYLAM'S SUPERB DRAWINGS OF THE MERCEDES IN THIS SCALE, JULY & AUGUST 1948 OF MODEL AIRPLANE NEWS.

AREAS:

UPPER PLANE INCLUDING AILERONS.	140.7 SQ. FT.
LOWER PLANE.	78.3 ..
AILERONS (TOTAL OF TWO).	11.4 ..
BALANCED PART OF AILERONS.	.5 ..
STABILIZER.	21.1 ..
ELEVATORS (TOTAL OF TWO).	15.2 ..
BALANCED PART OF ELEVATORS.	1.1 SQ. FT.
VERTICAL FIN.	2.8 ..
RUDDER.	5.9 ..
HORIZONTAL AREA OF BODY.	35.6 ..
VERTICAL.	58.6 ..
PLANE BETWEEN WHEELS.	12.4 ..

M.G. CARTRIDGE BELT FEED CHUTE INJECTED GUNS FROM THE RIGHT.

VIEW SHOWING COCKPIT, GUNS, ENGINE.
SPANDAU GUN DRAWINGS FROM 'LIFE'. ABOVE VIEW OF PYRAMIDAL WING STRUTS ARE SHOWN IN READY POSITION FOR INSTALLATION OF UPPER WING. THE LOWER END OF REAR WING STRUT, THE UPPER REAR & LOWER FRONT 'N' STRUT ENDS ATTACHED TO WING SPAR FITTINGS BY ADJUSTABLE BALL-SOCKET THREADED "EYE BOLTS" WHICH PROVIDED MEANS TO ADJUST ANGLE OF INCIDENCE. SEVERAL VARIATIONS OF ENGINE EXHAUST STACKS WERE USED. SHOWN IS THE TYPE MOST CONVENTIONAL WITH 180 H.P. MERCEDES.

DIMENSIONS:

WINGSPAN, UPPER PLANE.	29' 3½"
" LOWER "	23' 3½"
CHORD, UPPER PLANE.	5' 3"
" LOWER "	4' 0"
OVERALL LENGTH.	22' 11½"
GAP BETWEEN PLANES (AT BODY SIDE).	4' 3½"

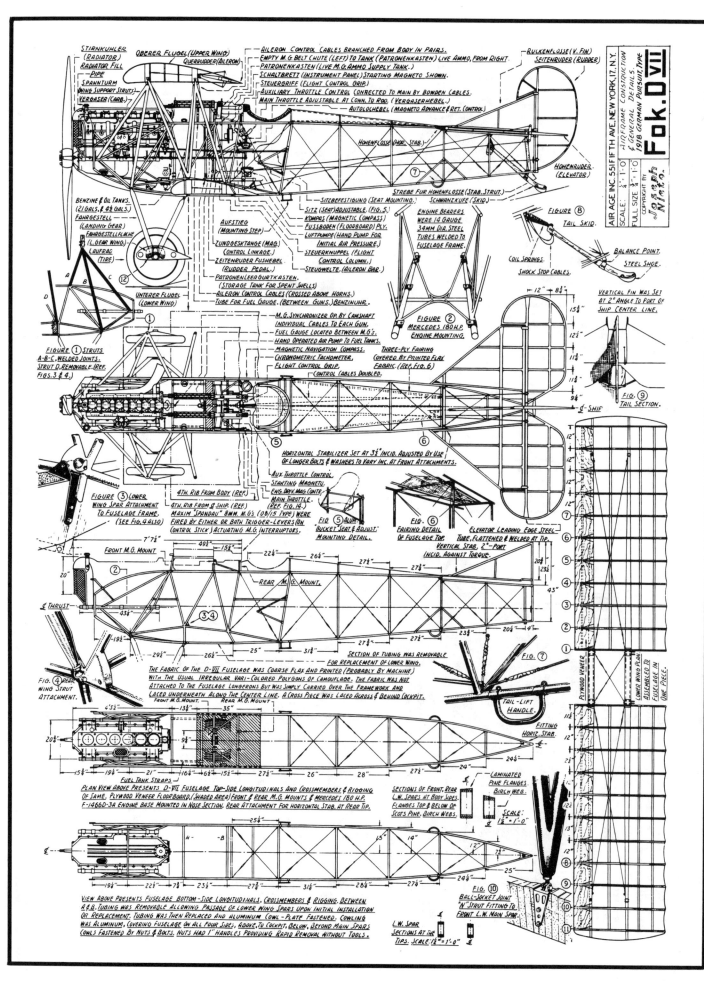

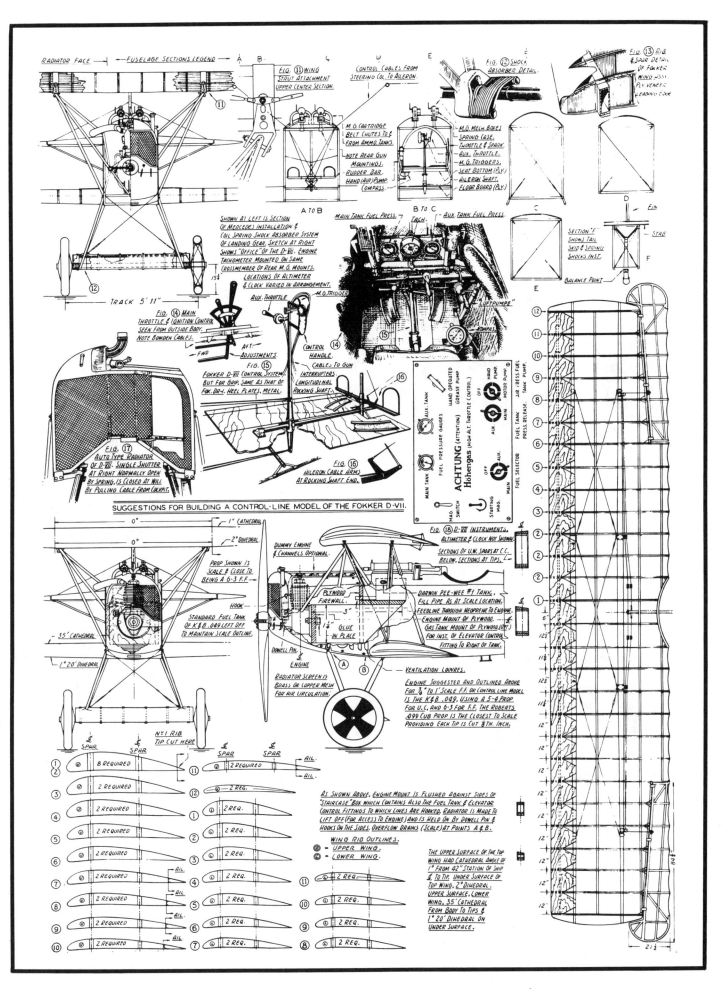

SUGGESTIONS FOR BUILDING A CONTROL-LINE MODEL OF THE FOKKER D-VII.

Fokker E.V/D.VIII

drawings by PHILLIP DREWS

The Fokker D.VIII was unique in several respects. Full cantilever wing, no struts and good performance gave its pilots a tremendous advantage over their foes. Photo courtesy of "Fokker, the Man and the Aircraft."

The 110-hp Oberursel rotary, Siemens-Halske, Goebel, and Le Rhone engines were used on various versions of the D.VIII.

An extremely clean design for WW I, the Fokker D.VIII was a formidable weapon in the hands of German pilots.

DURING the closing weeks of WW I, there appeared over the front lines a nimble little monoplane that is generally credited as being the finest fighter of its day. This was the famous Fokker D.VIII of the German Imperial Air Force.

Powered by a rotary Oberursel engine of 110 hp, the D.VIII had a speed of 127 mph. It climbed at a rate of 1,500 fpm and could ascend over 4 miles high. In its ability to maneuver and dive it was unequaled. The first production E.V's (called D.VIII) were so badly built by the Fokker factory that several crashes resulted, and the type was grounded until the defects could be located and remedied. By the time proper construction procedures were established at the factory, the War was almost over; the D.VIII saw almost no service.

Also known as the Fokker E.V and the "Flying Razor," it gained much of its reputation in the hands of the famous German pilot Ernst Udet. Even after the war Udet toured small German towns giving mock demonstrations of aerial dog fights. Strangely, these illegal performances were not detected by the Allied Occupation authorities.

Of the many designs credited to Anthony Fokker, the D.VIII or E.V was probably one of the best—and most controversial.

Note: recent research has shown that the two spars in each wing were not parallel, as in Drews' drawing, but tapered together toward each tip—and each spar was made in one piece.

One D.VIII survives, now on exhibition in Italy. □

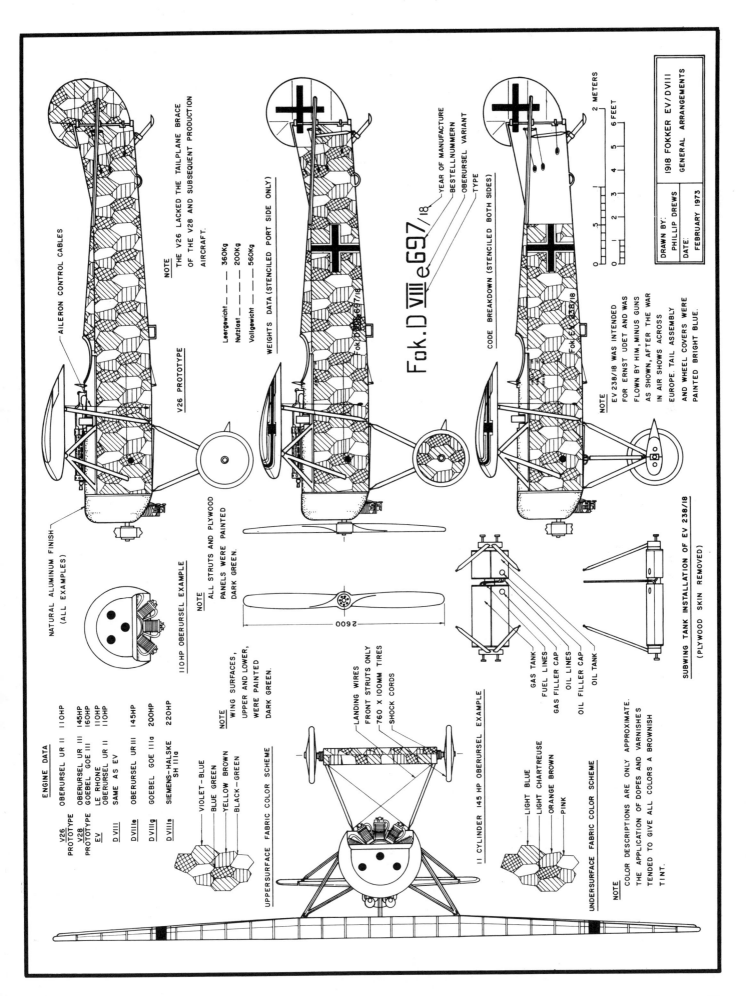

AILERON CONTROL CABLES

NOTE
THE V26 LACKED THE TAILPLANE BRACE OF THE V28 AND SUBSEQUENT PRODUCTION AIRCRAFT.

V26 PROTOTYPE

WEIGHTS DATA (STENCILED PORT SIDE ONLY)

Leergewicht ——— 360Kg
Nutzlast ——— 200Kg
Vollgewicht ——— 560Kg

Fok.D VIII e697/18

CODE BREAKDOWN (STENCILED BOTH SIDES)

YEAR OF MANUFACTURE
BESTELLNUMMERN
OBERURSEL VARIANT
TYPE

NOTE
EV 238/18 WAS INTENDED FOR ERNST UDET AND WAS FLOWN BY HIM, MINUS GUNS AS SHOWN, AFTER THE WAR IN AIR SHOWS ACROSS EUROPE. TAIL ASSEMBLY AND WHEEL COVERS WERE PAINTED BRIGHT BLUE.

NATURAL ALUMINUM FINISH (ALL EXAMPLES)

110HP OBERURSEL EXAMPLE

NOTE
ALL STRUTS AND PLYWOOD PANELS WERE PAINTED DARK GREEN.

NOTE
WING SURFACES, UPPER AND LOWER, WERE PAINTED DARK GREEN.

2600

SUBWING TANK INSTALLATION OF EV 238/18 (PLYWOOD SKIN REMOVED)

GAS TANK
FUEL LINES
GAS FILLER CAP
OIL LINES
OIL FILLER CAP
OIL TANK

ENGINE DATA

V26 PROTOTYPE	OBERURSEL UR II	110HP
V28 PROTOTYPE	OBERURSEL UR III	145HP
	GOEBEL GOE III	160HP
EV	LE RHONE	110HP
	OBERURSEL UR II	110HP
DVIII	SAME AS EV	
DVIIIe	OBERURSEL UR III	145HP
DVIIIg	GOEBEL GOE IIIa	200HP
DVIIIa	SIEMENS-HALSKE SH IIIa	220HP

UPPERSURFACE FABRIC COLOR SCHEME

— VIOLET-BLUE
— BLUE GREEN
— YELLOW BROWN
— BLACK-GREEN

LANDING WIRES
FRONT STRUTS ONLY
760 x 100MM TIRES
SHOCK CORDS

11 CYLINDER 145 HP OBERURSEL EXAMPLE

UNDERSURFACE FABRIC COLOR SCHEME

— LIGHT BLUE
— LIGHT CHARTREUSE
— ORANGE BROWN
— PINK

NOTE
COLOR DESCRIPTIONS ARE ONLY APPROXIMATE. THE APPLICATION OF DOPES AND VARNISHES TENDED TO GIVE ALL COLORS A BROWNISH TINT.

DRAWN BY:
PHILLIP DREWS
DATE:
FEBRUARY 1973

1918 FOKKER EV/DVIII
GENERAL ARRANGEMENTS

2 METERS
6 FEET

57

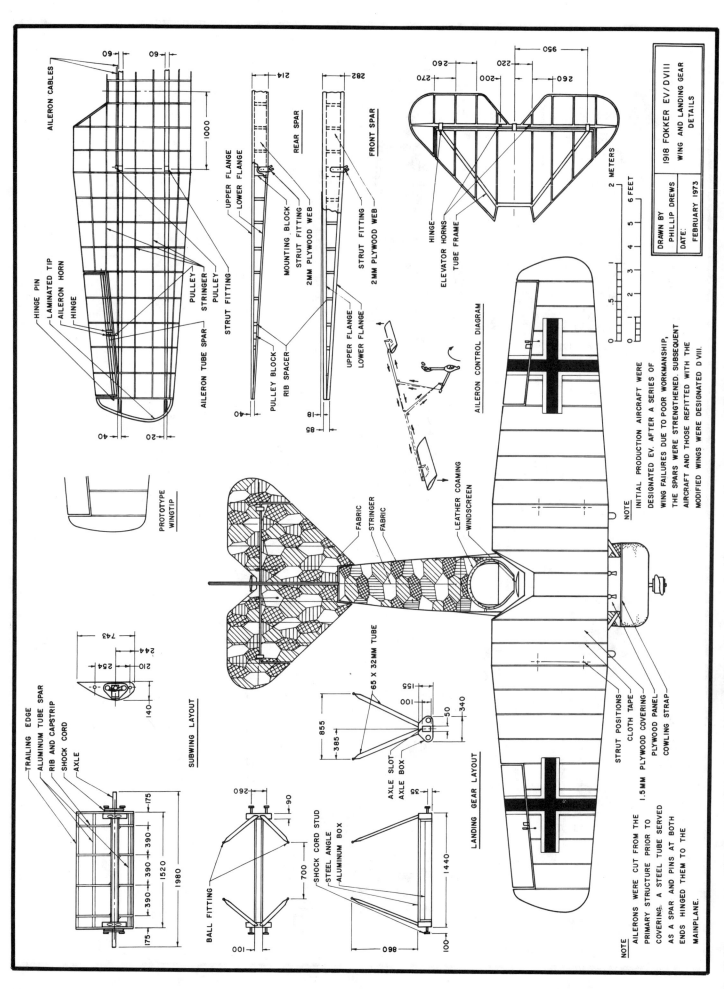

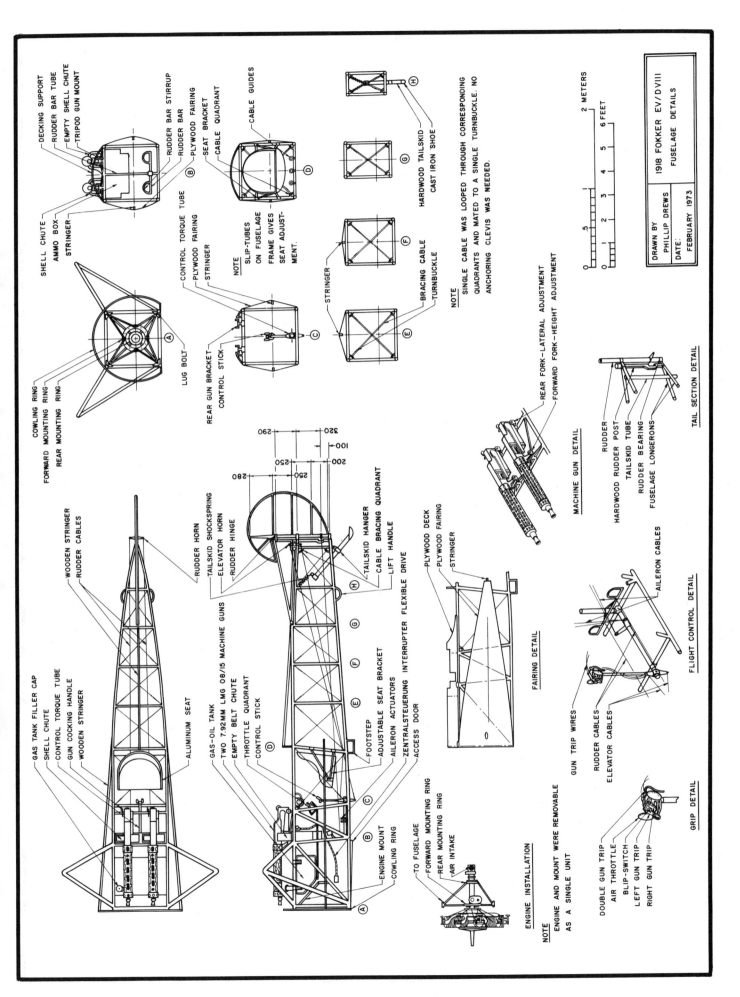

DECKING SUPPORT
RUDDER BAR TUBE
EMPTY SHELL CHUTE
TRIPOD GUN MOUNT
RUDDER BAR STIRRUP
RUDDER BAR
PLYWOOD FAIRING
SEAT BRACKET
CABLE QUADRANT
CABLE GUIDES

SHELL CHUTE
AMMO BOX
STRINGER
CONTROL TORQUE TUBE
PLYWOOD FAIRING
STRINGER

NOTE
SLIP-TUBES ON FUSELAGE FRAME GIVES SEAT ADJUSTMENT.

COWLING RING
FORWARD MOUNTING RING
REAR MOUNTING RING
LUG BOLT
REAR GUN BRACKET
CONTROL STICK
STRINGER
BRACING CABLE
TURNBUCKLE

HARDWOOD TAILSKID
CAST IRON SHOE

NOTE
SINGLE CABLE WAS LOOPED THROUGH CORRESPONDING QUADRANTS AND MATED TO A SINGLE TURNBUCKLE. NO ANCHORING CLEVIS WAS NEEDED.

REAR FORK-LATERAL ADJUSTMENT
FORWARD FORK-HEIGHT ADJUSTMENT

RUDDER
HARDWOOD RUDDER POST
TAILSKID TUBE
RUDDER BEARING
FUSELAGE LONGERONS

MACHINE GUN DETAIL

TAIL SECTION DETAIL

GAS TANK FILLER CAP
SHELL CHUTE
CONTROL TORQUE TUBE
GUN COCKING HANDLE
WOODEN STRINGER
WOODEN STRINGER
RUDDER CABLES
ALUMINUM SEAT

RUDDER HORN
TAILSKID SHOCKSPRING
ELEVATOR HORN
RUDDER HINGE
TAILSKID HANGER
CABLE BRACING QUADRANT
LIFT HANDLE

GAS-OIL TANK
TWO 7.92MM LMG 08/15 MACHINE GUNS
EMPTY BELT CHUTE
THROTTLE QUADRANT
CONTROL STICK
FOOTSTEP
ADJUSTABLE SEAT BRACKET
AILERON ACTUATORS
ZENTRALSTEUERUNG INTERRUPTER FLEXIBLE DRIVE
ACCESS DOOR

PLYWOOD DECK
PLYWOOD FAIRING
STRINGER

FAIRING DETAIL

ENGINE MOUNT
COWLING RING
TO FUSELAGE
FORWARD MOUNTING RING
REAR MOUNTING RING
AIR INTAKE

ENGINE INSTALLATION

NOTE
ENGINE AND MOUNT WERE REMOVABLE AS A SINGLE UNIT

GUN TRIP WIRES
RUDDER CABLES
ELEVATOR CABLES
AILERON CABLES

FLIGHT CONTROL DETAIL

DOUBLE GUN TRIP
AIR THROTTLE
BLIP-SWITCH
LEFT GUN TRIP
RIGHT GUN TRIP

GRIP DETAIL

DRAWN BY PHILLIP DREWS
DATE: FEBRUARY 1973
1918 FOKKER EV/DVIII
FUSELAGE DETAILS

2 METERS
6 FEET

290
320
100
250
200
250
280

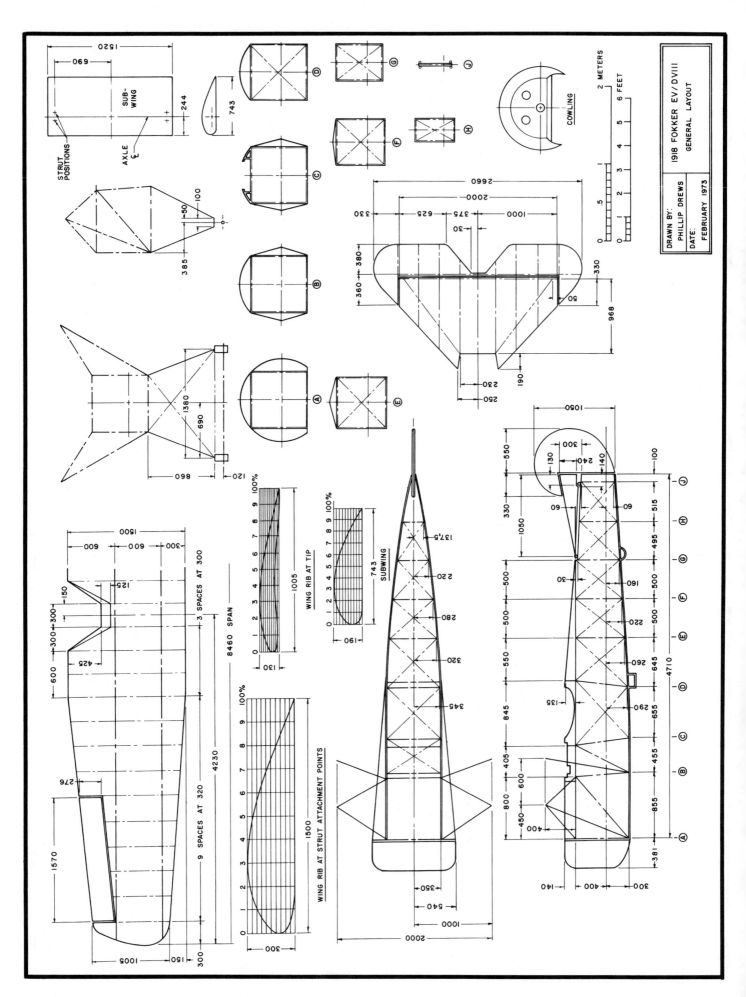

Hansa-Brandenburg
C.I

drawings by WILLIS NYE

Having a top speed of a little over 100 mph, the C.I was still able to carry a heavy load but was vulnerable to Allied fighters. Photo courtesy of Leonard Opdycke, World War I Aeroplanes.

ERNST HEINKEL designed this big two-seater for the German Brandenburg firm, and it was built under license in Austria. Powered by a variety of engines of 160-230 hp, the C.I carried a heavy load with good performance, cruising at over 100 mph.

Willis Nye's drawing is mistitled Brandenburg LDD: this was a smaller Austrian two-seater, sometimes referred to as "The Little Brandenburg," to distinguish it from the C.I, "The Big Brandenburg."

There are none left. □

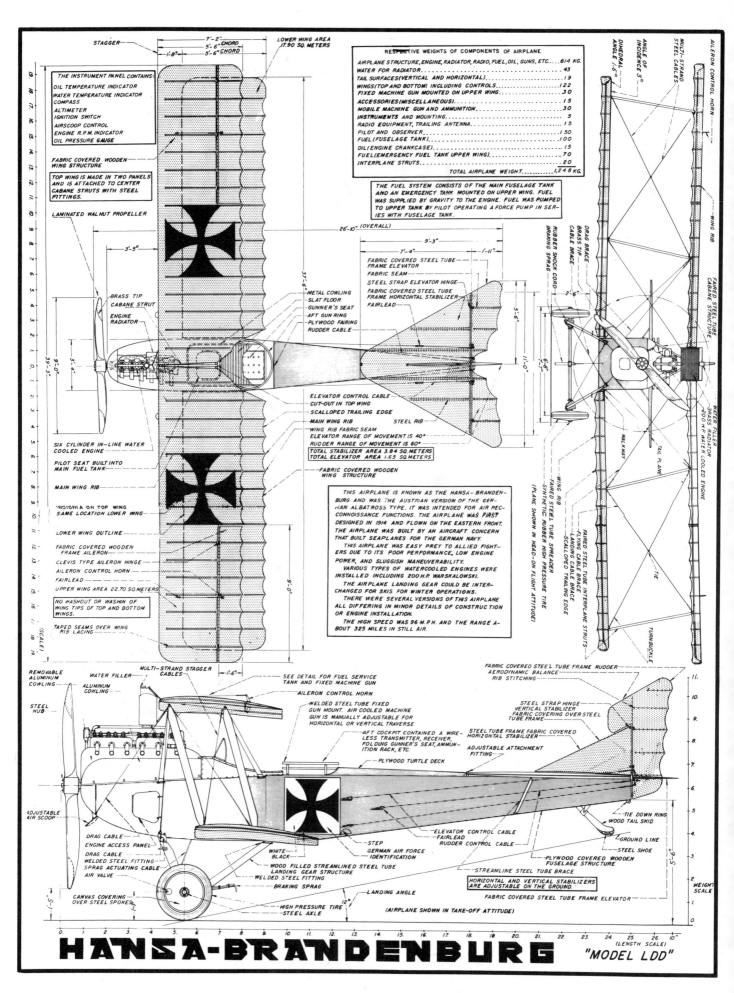

STAGGER

7'-2" CHORD
5'-6" CHORD
5'-6" CHORD

1'-8"

LOWER WING AREA
17.90 SQ. METERS

THE INSTRUMENT PANEL CONTAINS:
OIL TEMPERATURE INDICATOR
WATER TEMPERATURE INDICATOR
COMPASS
ALTIMETER
IGNITION SWITCH
AIRSCOOP CONTROL
ENGINE R.P.M. INDICATOR
OIL PRESSURE GAUGE

FABRIC COVERED WOODEN
WING STRUCTURE

TOP WING IS MADE IN TWO PANELS
AND IS ATTACHED TO CENTER
CABANE STRUTS WITH STEEL
FITTINGS.

LAMINATED WALNUT PROPELLER

3'-5"

BRASS TIP
CABANE STRUT
ENGINE
RADIATOR

9'-0"
3'-4"
39'-3"

37'-6"

SIX CYLINDER IN-LINE WATER
COOLED ENGINE

PILOT SEAT BUILT INTO
MAIN FUEL TANK

MAIN WING RIB

INSIGNIA ON TOP WING
SAME LOCATION LOWER WING

LOWER WING OUTLINE

FABRIC COVERED WOODEN
FRAME AILERON
CLEVIS TYPE AILERON HINGE
AILERON CONTROL HORN
FAIRLEAD
UPPER WING AREA 22.70 SQ.METERS

NO WASHOUT OR WASHIN OF
WING TIPS OF TOP AND BOTTOM
WINGS.

TAPED SEAMS OVER WING
RIB LACING

(SCALE)

METAL COWLING
SLAT FLOOR
GUNNER'S SEAT
AFT GUN RING
PLYWOOD FAIRING
RUDDER CABLE

ELEVATOR CONTROL CABLE
CUT-OUT IN TOP WING
SCALLOPED TRAILING EDGE
MAIN WING RIB
WING RIB FABRIC SEAM
ELEVATOR RANGE OF MOVEMENT IS 40°
RUDDER RANGE OF MOVEMENT IS 60°
TOTAL STABILIZER AREA 3.84 SQ.METERS
TOTAL ELEVATOR AREA 1.65 SQ.METERS

FABRIC COVERED WOODEN
WING STRUCTURE

RESPECTIVE WEIGHTS OF COMPONENTS OF AIRPLANE

AIRPLANE STRUCTURE, ENGINE, RADIATOR, RADIO, FUEL, OIL, GUNS, ETC.	614 KG.
WATER FOR RADIATOR	43
TAIL SURFACES (VERTICAL AND HORIZONTAL)	19
WINGS (TOP AND BOTTOM) INCLUDING CONTROLS	122
FIXED MACHINE GUN MOUNTED ON UPPER WING	30
ACCESSORIES (MISCELLANEOUS)	15
MOBILE MACHINE GUN AND AMMUNITION	30
INSTRUMENTS AND MOUNTING	5
RADIO EQUIPMENT, TRAILING ANTENNA	15
PILOT AND OBSERVER	150
FUEL (FUSELAGE TANK)	100
OIL (ENGINE CRANKCASE)	15
FUEL (EMERGENCY FUEL TANK UPPER WING)	70
INTERPLANE STRUTS	20
TOTAL AIRPLANE WEIGHT	1,248 KG.

THE FUEL SYSTEM CONSISTS OF THE MAIN FUSELAGE TANK
AND AN EMERGENCY TANK MOUNTED ON UPPER WING. FUEL
WAS SUPPLIED BY GRAVITY TO THE ENGINE. FUEL WAS PUMPED
TO UPPER TANK BY PILOT OPERATING A FORCE PUMP IN SE-
RIES WITH FUSELAGE TANK.

26'-10" (OVERALL)

9'-3"
7'-4"
1'-11"

FABRIC COVERED STEEL TUBE
FRAME ELEVATOR
FABRIC SEAM
STEEL STRAP ELEVATOR HINGE
FABRIC COVERED STEEL TUBE
FRAME HORIZONTAL STABILIZER
FAIRLEAD

2'-6"

5'-6"

11'-0"

6'-6"

THIS AIRPLANE IS KNOWN AS THE HANSA-BRANDEN-
BURG AND WAS THE AUSTRIAN VERSION OF THE GER-
MAN ALBATROSS TYPE. IT WAS INTENDED FOR AIR REC-
CONNOISSANCE FUNCTIONS. THE AIRPLANE WAS FIRST
DESIGNED IN 1914 AND FLOWN ON THE EASTERN FRONT.
THE AIRPLANE WAS BUILT BY AN AIRCRAFT CONCERN
THAT BUILT SEAPLANES FOR THE GERMAN NAVY.
THIS AIRPLANE WAS EASY PREY TO ALLIED FIGHT-
ERS DUE TO ITS POOR PERFORMANCE, LOW ENGINE
POWER, AND SLUGGISH MANEUVERABILITY.
VARIOUS TYPES OF WATERCOOLED ENGINES WERE
INSTALLED INCLUDING 200 H.P. WARSKALOWSKI.
THE AIRPLANE LANDING GEAR COULD BE INTER-
CHANGED FOR SKIS FOR WINTER OPERATIONS.
THERE WERE SEVERAL VERSIONS OF THIS AIRPLANE
ALL DIFFERING IN MINOR DETAILS OF CONSTRUCTION
OR ENGINE INSTALLATION.
THE HIGH SPEED WAS 96 M.P.H. AND THE RANGE A-
BOUT 325 MILES IN STILL AIR.

ANGLE OF
INCIDENCE 3°
DIHEDRAL
ANGLE 1-6°

AILERON CONTROL HORN
MULTI-STRAND
STEEL CABLES

WING RIB

FAIRED STEEL TUBE
CABANE STRUCTURE

DRAG BRACE
BRASS TIP
CABLE BRACE

RUBBER SHOCK CORD
BRAKING SPRAG

WING RIB
FAIRED STEEL TUBE
SYNTHETIC RUBBER HIGH PRESSURE TIRE
STEEL TUBE SPREADER
FLYING CABLE BRACE
LANDING CABLE BRACE
SCALLOPED TRAILING EDGE

FAIRED STEEL TUBE INTERPLANE STRUTS
FLYING CABLE BRACE
LANDING CABLE BRACE
SCALLOPED TRAILING EDGE

WATER FILLER
BRASS RADIATOR
200 H.P. WATER COOLED ENGINE

HALKWAY

TAIL PLANE

TIE

TURNBUCKLE

(PLANE SHOWN IN HEAD-ON FLIGHT ATTITUDE)

REMOVABLE
ALUMINUM
COWLING
WATER FILLER
MULTI-STRAND STAGGER
CABLES
1'-6"

ALUMINUM
COWLING

STEEL
HUB

AILERON CONTROL HORN

SEE DETAIL FOR FUEL SERVICE
TANK AND FIXED MACHINE GUN

WELDED STEEL TUBE FIXED
GUN MOUNT. AIR COOLED MACHINE
GUN IS MANUALLY ADJUSTABLE FOR
HORIZONTAL OR VERTICAL TRAVERSE

AFT COCKPIT CONTAINED A WIRE-
LESS TRANSMITTER, RECEIVER,
FOLDING GUNNER'S SEAT, AMMUN-
ITION RACK, ETC.

PLYWOOD TURTLE DECK

FABRIC COVERED STEEL TUBE FRAME RUDDER
AERODYNAMIC BALANCE
RIB STITCHING

STEEL STRAP HINGE
VERTICAL STABILIZER
FABRIC COVERING OVER STEEL
TUBE FRAME

STEEL TUBE FRAME FABRIC COVERED
HORIZONTAL STABILIZER

ADJUSTABLE ATTACHMENT
FITTING

ADJUSTABLE
AIR SCOOP

DRAG CABLE
ENGINE ACCESS PANEL
DRAG CABLE
WELDED STEEL FITTING
SPRAG ACTUATING CABLE
AIR VALVE

CANVAS COVERING
OVER STEEL SPOKES

WHITE
BLACK

WOOD FILLED STREAMLINED STEEL TUBE
LANDING GEAR STRUCTURE
WELDED STEEL FITTING
BRAKING SPRAG

HIGH PRESSURE TIRE
STEEL AXLE

STEP
GERMAN AIR FORCE
IDENTIFICATION

LANDING ANGLE

12°

ELEVATOR CONTROL CABLE
FAIRLEAD
RUDDER CONTROL CABLE

TIE DOWN RING
WOOD TAIL SKID

GROUND LINE
STEEL SHOE

PLYWOOD COVERED WOODEN
FUSELAGE STRUCTURE

STREAMLINE STEEL TUBE BRACE

HORIZONTAL AND VERTICAL STABILIZERS
ARE ADJUSTABLE ON THE GROUND.

FABRIC COVERED STEEL TUBE FRAME ELEVATOR

(AIRPLANE SHOWN IN TAKE-OFF ATTITUDE)

WEIGHT
SCALE

HANSA-BRANDENBURG "MODEL LDD"

0. 1. 2. 3. 4. 5. 6. 7. 8. 9. 10. 11. 12. 13. 14. 15. 16. 17. 18. 19. 20. 21. 22. 23. 24. 25. 26. 10"
(LENGTH SCALE)

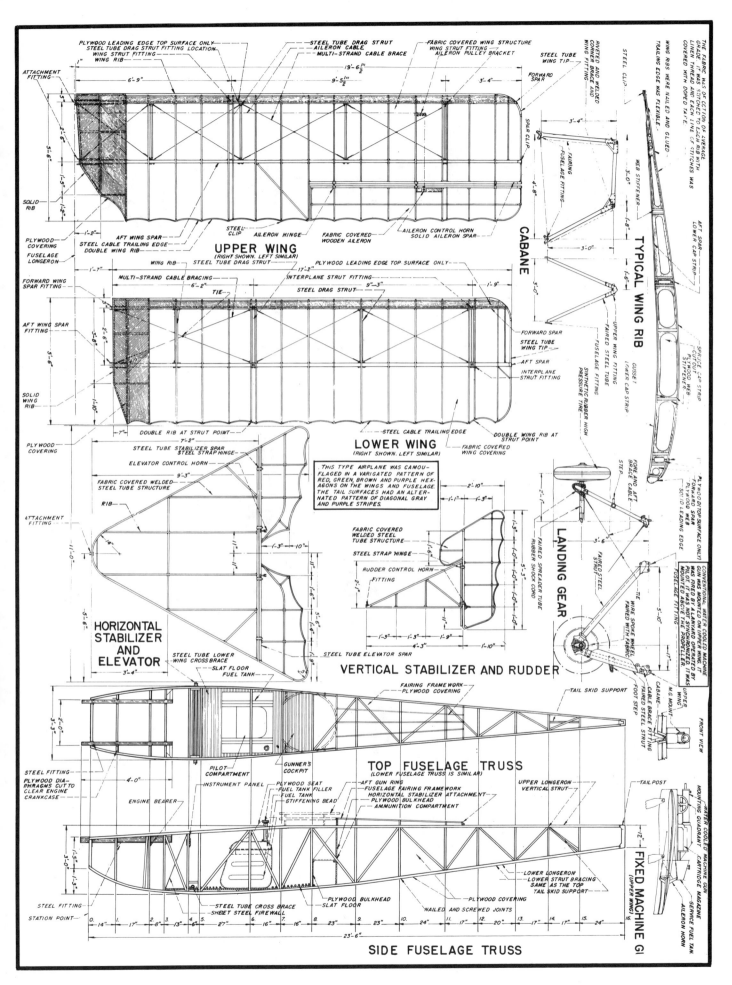

UPPER WING
(RIGHT SHOWN, LEFT SIMILAR)

LOWER WING
(RIGHT SHOWN, LEFT SIMILAR)

CABANE

TYPICAL WING RIB

This type airplane was camouflaged in a varigated pattern of red, green, brown and purple hexagons on the wings and fuselage. The tail surfaces had an alternated pattern of diagonal gray and purple stripes.

HORIZONTAL STABILIZER AND ELEVATOR

VERTICAL STABILIZER AND RUDDER

LANDING GEAR

TOP FUSELAGE TRUSS
(LOWER FUSELAGE TRUSS IS SIMILAR)

FIXED MACHINE G

SIDE FUSELAGE TRUSS

Hansa-Brandenburg
W.29

drawings by TAGE LARSEN

ERNST Heinkel designed the W.29 for the Brandenburg factory in 1918. It was used on the North Sea, its most famous pilot being Oberleutenant Christiensen. It was later built in Denmark and served several countries in modified forms almost until WW II.

One Brandenburg seaplane, the later W.33, is being restored in Finland. □

The Hansa-Brandenburg W.29 had several unique design features for its time. The structure was almost entirely from wood and explored the cantilever concept. "Jane's History of Aviation" photo.

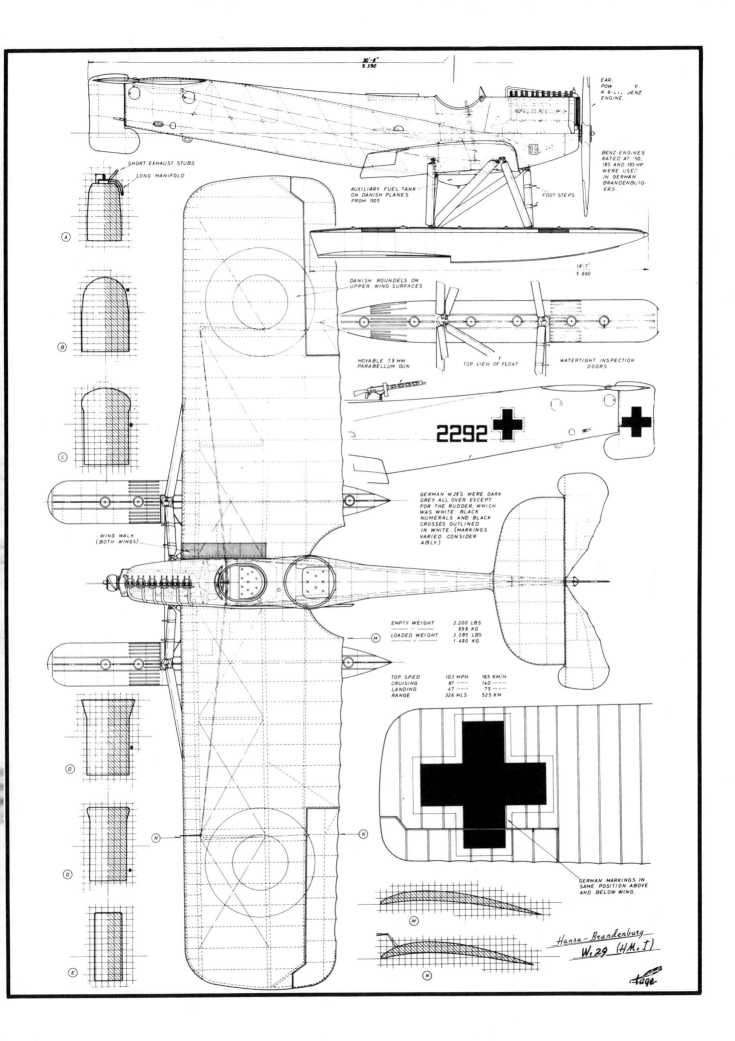

SHORT EXHAUST STUBS

LONG MANIFOLD

EAR.
POW   Y
A 6-CYL BENZ ENGINE.

BENZ ENGINES RATED AT '50, 185 AND 195 HP WERE USED IN GERMAN BRANDENBURGERS.

AUXILIARY FUEL TANK ON DANISH PLANES FROM 1925

FOOT STEPS

DANISH ROUNDELS ON UPPER WING SURFACES

MOVABLE 7.9 MM PARABELLUM GUN

TOP VIEW OF FLOAT

WATERTIGHT INSPECTION DOORS

2292 ✠   ✠

GERMAN W.29'S WERE DARK GREY ALL OVER EXCEPT FOR THE RUDDER, WHICH WAS WHITE. BLACK NUMERALS AND BLACK CROSSES OUTLINED IN WHITE. (MARKINGS VARIED CONSIDER ABLY)

WING WALK (BOTH WINGS)

EMPTY WEIGHT	2.200 LBS
	998 KG
LOADED WEIGHT	3.285 LBS
	1.490 KG

TOP SPED	103 MPH	165 KM/H
CRUISING	87 — " —	140
LANDING	47 — " —	75
RANGE	326 MLS	525 KM

GERMAN MARKINGS IN SAME POSITION ABOVE AND BELOW WING.

Hansa-Brandenburg
W.29 (H.M.I)

Tage

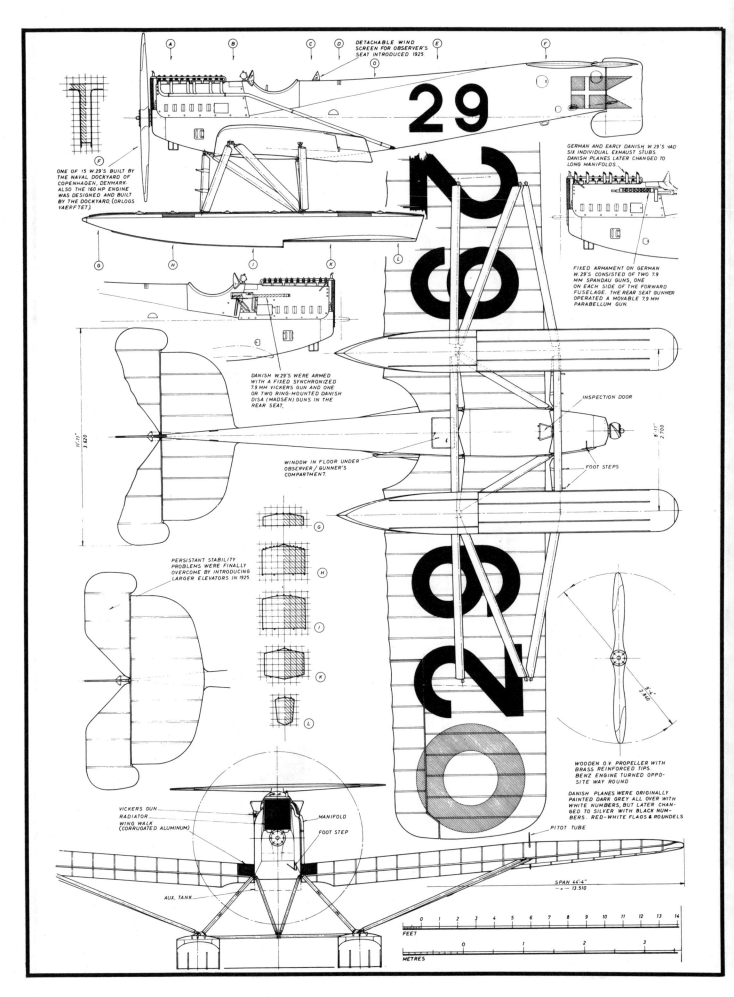

DETACHABLE WIND SCREEN FOR OBSERVER'S SEAT INTRODUCED 1925.

ONE OF 15 W.29'S BUILT BY THE NAVAL DOCKYARD OF COPENHAGEN, DENMARK. ALSO THE 160 HP ENGINE WAS DESIGNED AND BUILT BY THE DOCKYARD (ORLOGS VAERFTET).

GERMAN AND EARLY DANISH W.29'S HAD SIX INDIVIDUAL EXHAUST STUBS. DANISH PLANES LATER CHANGED TO LONG MANIFOLDS.

FIXED ARMAMENT ON GERMAN W.29'S CONSISTED OF TWO 7.9 MM SPANDAU GUNS, ONE ON EACH SIDE OF THE FORWARD FUSELAGE. THE REAR SEAT GUNNER OPERATED A MOVABLE 7.9 MM PARABELLUM GUN.

DANISH W.29'S WERE ARMED WITH A FIXED SYNCHRONIZED 7.9 MM VICKERS GUN AND ONE OR TWO RING-MOUNTED DANISH DISA (MADSEN) GUNS IN THE REAR SEAT.

WINDOW IN FLOOR UNDER OBSERVER / GUNNER'S COMPARTMENT.

INSPECTION DOOR

FOOT STEPS

PERSISTANT STABILITY PROBLEMS WERE FINALLY OVERCOME BY INTRODUCING LARGER ELEVATORS IN 1925.

WOODEN O.V. PROPELLER WITH BRASS REINFORCED TIPS. BENZ ENGINE TURNED OPPOSITE WAY ROUND.

DANISH PLANES WERE ORIGINALLY PAINTED DARK GREY ALL OVER WITH WHITE NUMBERS, BUT LATER CHANGED TO SILVER WITH BLACK NUMBERS. RED-WHITE FLAGS & ROUNDELS

VICKERS GUN
RADIATOR
WING WALK (CORRUGATED ALUMINUM)

MANIFOLD
FOOT STEP

AUX. TANK

PITOT TUBE

SPAN 44'-4"
13.510

11'-11"
3.620

8'-11"
2.700

9'4"
2.840

FEET
0 1 2 3 4 5 6 7 8 9 10 11 12 13 14

METRES
0 1 2 3

66

Junkers D.I

drawing by CHARLES GRAHAM

Junkers first design, the J 1, paved the way to success for the firm.

The Junkers D.1, above and below, was all-metal with full cantilever wings. "Jane's Encyclopedia of the World's Aircraft" photo.

THE FIRST JUNKERS factory design was the J 1 (Army designation E.I); it was known as The Tin Donkey, and only one was built. The 9th Junkers design, the J 9, appeared in October 1917, and with its 160 hp Mercedes was entered in the fighter competitions of 1918. The Army ordered it built as the D.I. Armament consisted of a pair of fixed, forward-firing Spandau guns ahead of the cockpit.

Because of lack of experience with the aircraft's then-unconventional metal construction, only forty-one D.1s were completed and delivered to the Front before the Armistice in November 1918. The aircraft featured a number of unique innovations, one of which was a full cantilever wing.

Four Junkers all-metal monoplanes of the WW I period survive in museums.

□

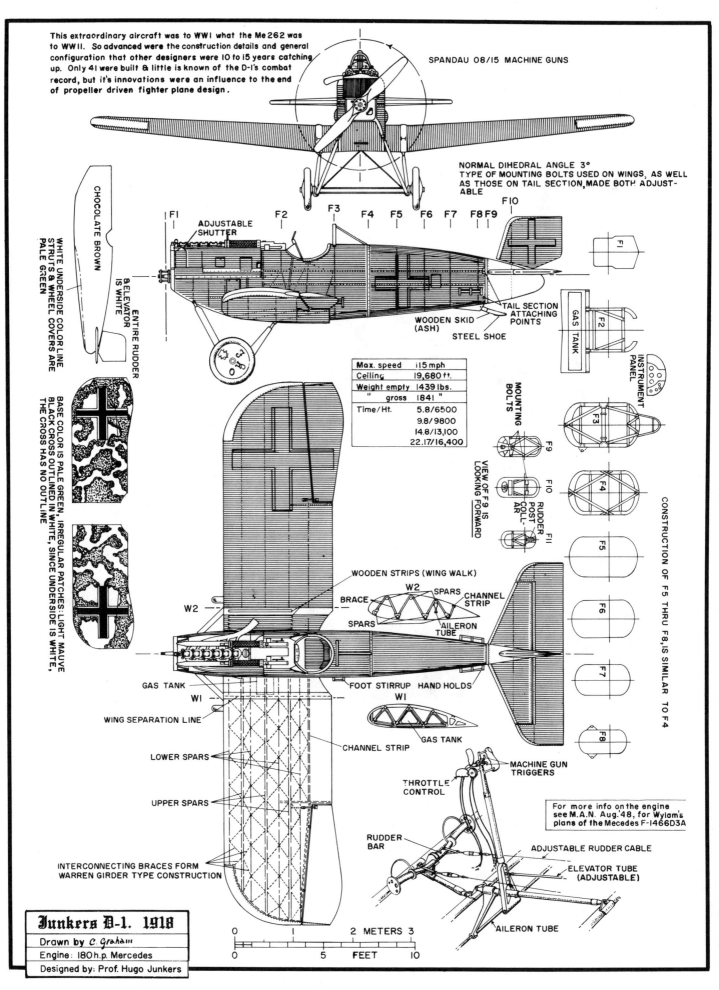

This extraordinary aircraft was to WWI what the Me 262 was to WWII. So advanced were the construction details and general configuration that other designers were 10 to 15 years catching up. Only 41 were built & little is known of the D-I's combat record, but it's innovations were an influence to the end of propeller driven fighter plane design.

SPANDAU 08/15 MACHINE GUNS

NORMAL DIHEDRAL ANGLE 3°
TYPE OF MOUNTING BOLTS USED ON WINGS, AS WELL AS THOSE ON TAIL SECTION, MADE BOTH ADJUST-ABLE

CHOCOLATE BROWN

WHITE UNDERSIDE COLOR LINE
STRUTS & WHEEL COVERS ARE PALE GREEN

ENTIRE RUDDER & ELEVATOR IS WHITE

BASE COLOR IS PALE GREEN, IRREGULAR PATCHES: LIGHT MAUVE
BLACK CROSS OUTLINED IN WHITE, SINCE UNDERSIDE IS WHITE,
THE CROSS HAS NO OUTLINE

ADJUSTABLE SHUTTER

F1 F2 F3 F4 F5 F6 F7 F8 F9 F10

WOODEN SKID (ASH)
STEEL SHOE
TAIL SECTION ATTACHING POINTS

Max. speed	115 mph
Ceiling	19,680 ft.
Weight empty	1439 lbs.
" gross	1841 "
Time/Ht.	5.8/6500
	9.8/9800
	14.8/13,100
	22.17/16,400

GAS TANK
INSTRUMENT PANEL

MOUNTING BOLTS

F9
F10
RUDDER POST COLL-AR
F11

VIEW OF F9 IS LOOKING FORWARD

F1
F2
F3
F4
F5
F6
F7
F8

CONSTRUCTION OF F5 THRU F8, IS SIMILAR TO F4

WOODEN STRIPS (WING WALK)
BRACE
W2
SPARS
CHANNEL STRIP
SPARS
AILERON TUBE

W2

W1

GAS TANK
WING SEPARATION LINE
LOWER SPARS
UPPER SPARS

CHANNEL STRIP

FOOT STIRRUP HAND HOLDS
W1
GAS TANK

INTERCONNECTING BRACES FORM
WARREN GIRDER TYPE CONSTRUCTION

MACHINE GUN TRIGGERS
THROTTLE CONTROL

For more info on the engine see M.A.N. Aug.'48, for Wylam's plans of the Mecedes F-1466D3A

RUDDER BAR
ADJUSTABLE RUDDER CABLE
ELEVATOR TUBE (ADJUSTABLE)
AILERON TUBE

Junkers D-1. 1918
Drawn by *C. Graham*
Engine: 180 h.p. Mercedes
Designed by: Prof. Hugo Junkers

0   1   2 METERS 3
0   5   FEET   10

Loening M-8

drawings by TOM STARK

Although too late to see action in WW I, the Loening M-8 was to establish several world aviation records. "Jane's All the World's Aircraft" photo.

THE LOENING M-8 was described by Grover Loening as "nearer to being inspired than anything I ever did." While its pot-bellied appearance may be anything but inspired by modern standards, when it was designed it represented quite an advancement over the biplanes that dominated that era. It pioneered the strut-braced high-wing configuration and the use of lifting struts that characterized so many commercial airplanes a few years later, including Lindberg's Ryan NYP.

The M-8 was designed near the close of World War I and grew out of America's desire to contribute first line fighting airplanes to the war. The American aircraft industry had not been able to develop and build combat airplanes, and our pilots flew French and British designs in combat. The two-place Bristol Fighter served as the model for the M-8, but was a model in capability and characteristics only, since the M-8 had another requirement—ease of rapid manufacture. In this it succeeded very well, having only one-fifth the number of fittings and requiring only one-fourth the manufacturing time as the Bristol. In addition, it weighed 500 pounds less than

Lifting strut wing braces designed for the M-8 were a breakthrough that has been carried over into lightplane designs of current manufacturing.

the Bristol while carrying the same military load, but at a speed 30 mph faster.

By the time the prototype was flying, the Armistice was signed and plans to build 5,000 M-8s were dropped. Only two were built for the Army and four for the Navy, and they served as engine test-beds, racing planes, and research vehicles. In December 1918, one broke the world's altitude record for carrying one and two passengers.

None survive. □

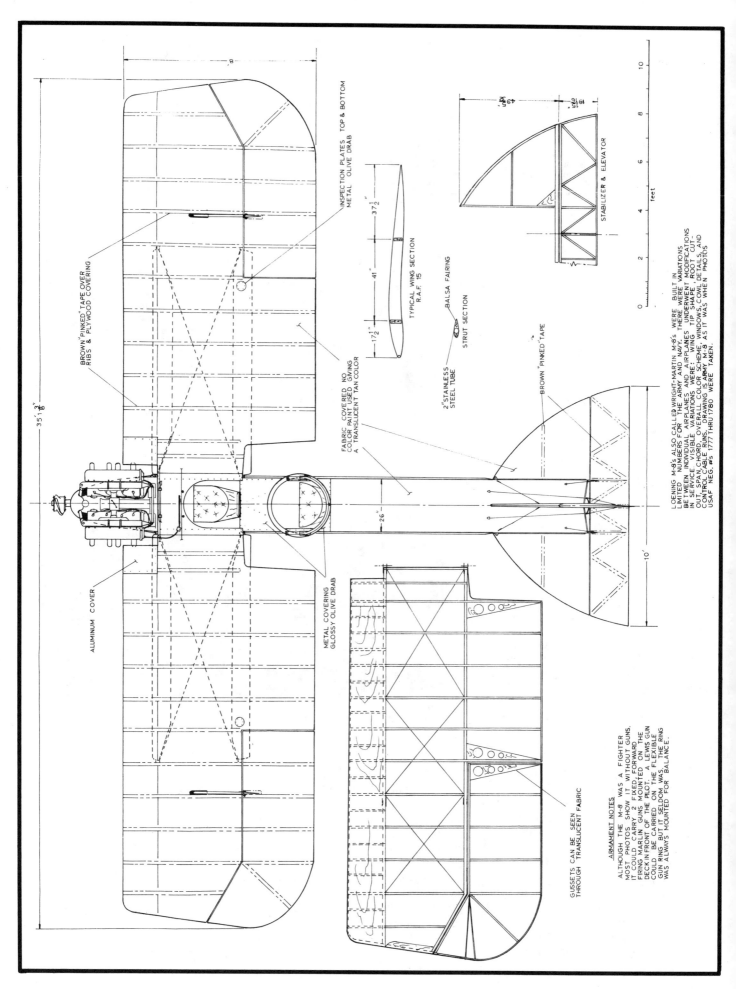

INSPECTION PLATES TOP & BOTTOM
METAL OLIVE DRAB

BROWN "PINKED" TAPE OVER
RIBS & PLYWOOD COVERING

TYPICAL WING SECTION
R.A.F. 15

BALSA FAIRING

STRUT SECTION

2" STAINLESS
STEEL TUBE

FABRIC COVERED NO
COLOR PAINT USED GIVING
A TRANSLUCENT TAN COLOR

STABILIZER & ELEVATOR

feet

BROWN "PINKED" TAPE

ALUMINUM COVER

METAL COVERING
GLOSSY OLIVE DRAB

GUSSETS CAN BE SEEN
THROUGH TRANSLUCENT FABRIC

LOENING M-8's ALSO CALLED WRIGHT-MARTIN M-8's WERE BUILT IN
LIMITED NUMBERS FOR THE ARMY AND NAVY. THERE WERE VARIATIONS
BETWEEN INDIVIDUAL AIRPLANES AND AIRPLANES UNDERWENT MODIFICATIONS
IN SERVICE. VISIBLE VARIATIONS WERE; WING TIP SHAPE, ROOT CUT-
OUT, SPAN, CHORD, OVERALL COLOR SCHEME, WINDOWS, COWL DETAILS, AND
CONTROL CABLE RUNS. DRAWING IS ARMY M-8 AS IT WAS WHEN PHOTO'S
USAF NEG. #'s 17777 THRU 17780 WERE TAKEN.

ARMAMENT NOTES

ALTHOUGH THE M-8 WAS A FIGHTER
MOST PHOTOS SHOW IT WITHOUT GUNS.
IT COULD CARRY 2 FIXED, FORWARD
FIRING MARLIN GUNS MOUNTED ON THE
DECK IN FRONT OF THE PILOT. A LEWIS GUN
COULD BE CARRIED ON THE FLEXIBLE
GUN RING BUT IT SELDOM WAS. THE RING
WAS ALWAYS MOUNTED FOR BALANCE.

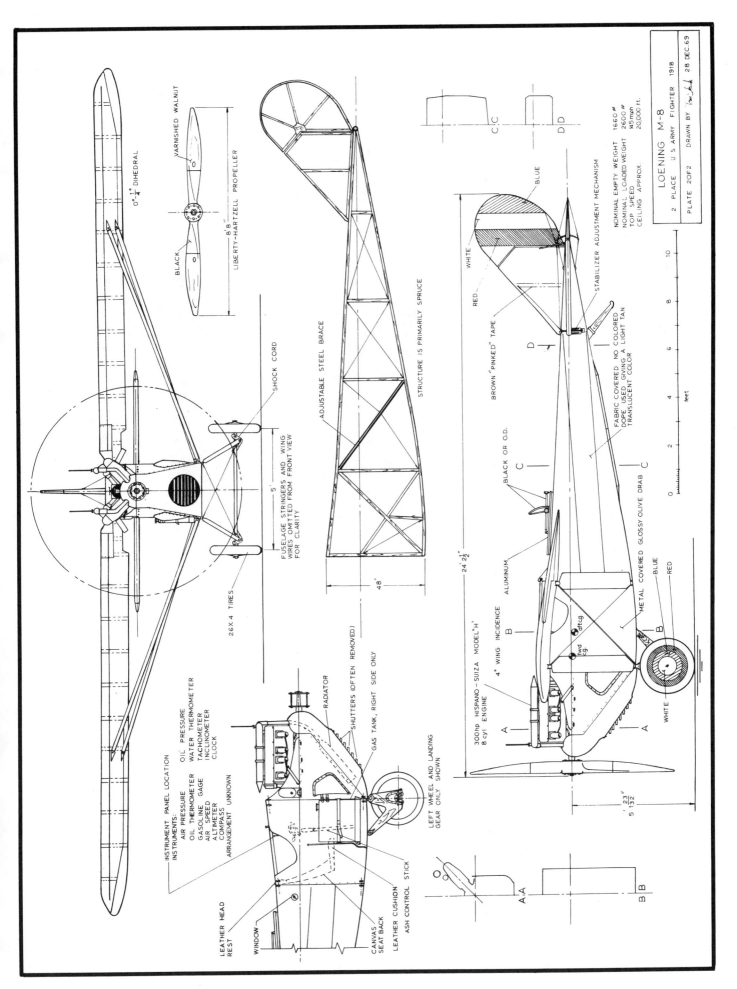

LEATHER HEAD REST

INSTRUMENT PANEL LOCATION
INSTRUMENTS:
AIR PRESSURE   OIL PRESSURE
OIL THERMOMETER WATER THERMOMETER
GASOLINE GAGE   TACHOMETER
AIR SPEED   INCLINOMETER
ALTIMETER   CLOCK
COMPASS
ARRANGEMENT UNKNOWN

0°-1°-¼ DIHEDRAL

VARNISHED WALNUT

BLACK

8'8"

LIBERTY-HARTZELL PROPELLER

SHOCK CORD

5'

FUSELAGE STRINGERS AND WING
WIRES OMITTED FROM FRONT VIEW
FOR CLARITY

26 X 4 TIRES

ADJUSTABLE STEEL BRACE

STRUCTURE IS PRIMARILY SPRUCE

48"

RADIATOR

SHUTTERS (OFTEN REMOVED)

GAS TANK, RIGHT SIDE ONLY

LEFT WHEEL AND LANDING
GEAR ONLY SHOWN

WINDOW

CANVAS SEAT BACK

LEATHER CUSHION

ASH CONTROL STICK

C.C

D.D

BLUE

RED

WHITE

STABILIZER ADJUSTMENT MECHANISM

BROWN "PINKED" TAPE

BLACK OR O.D.

D

C

C

FABRIC COVERED NO COLORED
DOPE USED GIVING A LIGHT TAN
TRANSLUCENT COLOR

METAL COVERED GLOSSY OLIVE DRAB

ALUMINUM

B

A

300hp HISPANO-SUIZA MODEL "H"
8 cyl ENGINE

4° WING INCIDENCE

24' 21½"

aftcg

fwd cg

B

A

BLUE

RED

WHITE

23"
5' 132

feet

0   2   4   6   8   10

A.A

B.B

LOENING M-8
2 PLACE   U S ARMY   FIGHTER   1918
DRAWN BY   28 DEC. 69
PLATE 2 OF 2

NOMINAL EMPTY WEIGHT   1660 #
NOMINAL LOADED WEIGHT   2600 #
TOP SPEED   145mph
CEILING APPROX.   20,000 ft.

Nieuport Nighthawk

drawings by JOSEPH NIETO

THE BRITISH Nieuport Nighthawk was chosen for mass production by the Royal Air Force because of its remarkable performance and because it had been designed to use many S.E.5 parts. It also met the strength requirements as demonstrated by load tests throughout the entire machine. The general arrangements regarding position and accessibility of guns, instruments, etc., provided the facilities most suitable to combat conditions, aided by a minimum "blind" area. Intended for quick mass production of a "knock-out-punch" fighter to finish up the war, it was a bit late for front line service before the armistice. The Nighthawk was fully capable of carrying on for the RAF where the S.E.5 and Snipe had left off. As the RAF's first truly modern radial-powered production airplane, the Nighthawk was powered by a 9-cylinder 320-hp A.B.C. Dragonfly air-cooled engine, giving it a climb rate of 1,500 fpm and a top speed of 151 mph.

Built by Nieuport and the General Aircraft Co. Ltd. of Cricklewood, London, it was designed by H.P. Folland, formerly of the Royal Aircraft Factory.

The nearest thing to a surviving Nighthawk is one of the existing seven S.E.5a's. □

Too late to see service in WW I, the Nieuport Nighthawk carried British fighter pilots for nearly a decade, almost into WW II. "Aircraft of the Royal Air Force, 1918-1957" photo.

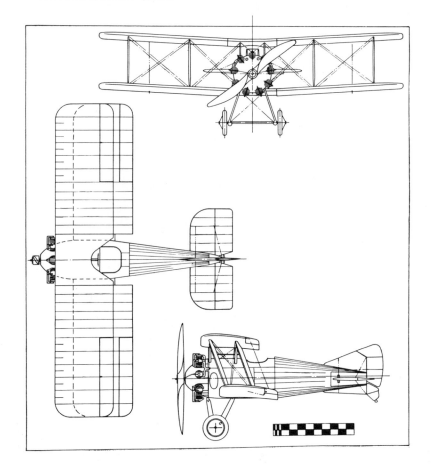

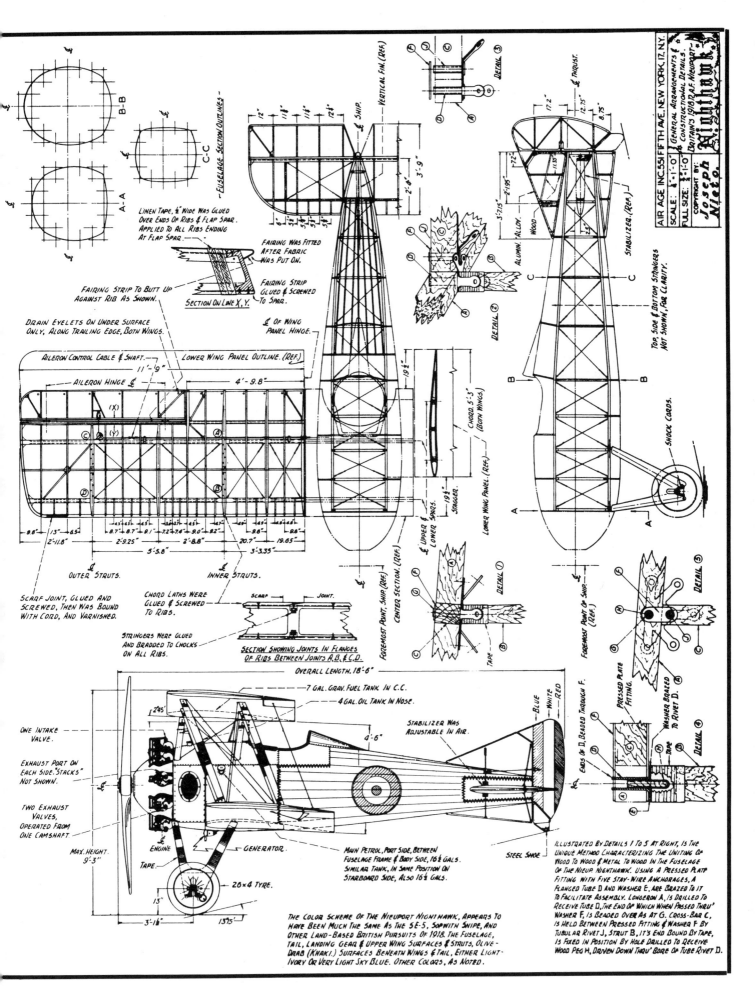

FUSELAGE SECTION OUTLINES.

B-B
A-A
C-C

LINEN TAPE, ½" WIDE WAS GLUED
OVER ENDS OF RIBS & FLAP SPAR.
APPLIED TO ALL RIBS ENDING
AT FLAP SPAR.

FAIRING WAS FITTED
AFTER FABRIC
WAS PUT ON.

FAIRING STRIP TO BUTT UP
AGAINST RIB AS SHOWN.

FAIRING STRIP
GLUED & SCREWED
TO SPAR.

SECTION ON LINE X, Y.

DRAIN EYELETS ON UNDER SURFACE
ONLY, ALONG TRAILING EDGE, BOTH WINGS.

℄ OF WING
PANEL HINGE.

AILERON CONTROL CABLE & SHAFT.   LOWER WING PANEL OUTLINE. (REF.)

AILERON HINGE ℄

11'-9"   4'-9.8"

CHORD 5'-3"
(BOTH WINGS).

STAGGER.

℄ UPPER &
LOWER SPARS.

LOWER WING PANEL. (REF.)

CENTER SECTION. (REF.)

FOREMOST POINT, SHIP. (REF.)

OUTER STRUTS.   INNER STRUTS.

SCARF JOINT, GLUED AND
SCREWED, THEN WAS BOUND
WITH CORD, AND VARNISHED.

CHORD LATHS WERE
GLUED & SCREWED
TO RIBS.

SCARF   JOINT.

STRINGERS WERE GLUED
AND BRADDED TO CHOCKS
ON ALL RIBS.

SECTION SHOWING JOINTS IN FLANGES
OF RIBS BETWEEN JOINTS A, B, & C, D.

VERTICAL FIN. (REF.)

℄ SHIP.

2'-8"   3'-9"

DETAIL ③

℄ THRUST.
17.2"   12.75"
8.75"

ALUMN. ALLOY.
WOOD.

STABILIZER. (REF.)

DETAIL ②

TOP, SIDE & BOTTOM STRINGERS
NOT SHOWN, FOR CLARITY.

SHOCK CORDS.

DETAIL ①

FOREMOST POINT OF SHIP.
(REF.)

DETAIL ⑤

PRESSED PLATE
FITTING.

WASHER BRAZED
TO RIVET D.

DETAIL ④

TAPE.

OVERALL LENGTH, 18'-6"

7 GAL. GRAV. FUEL TANK IN C.C.
4 GAL. OIL TANK IN NOSE.

STABILIZER WAS
ADJUSTABLE IN AIR.

BLUE
WHITE
RED

ONE INTAKE
VALVE.

EXHAUST PORT ON
EACH SIDE. "STACKS"
NOT SHOWN.

TWO EXHAUST
VALVES,
OPERATED FROM
ONE CAMSHAFT.

MAX. HEIGHT.
9'-3"

ENGINE
TAPE.   GENERATOR.

26 × 4 TYRE.

STEEL SHOE.

MAIN PETROL, PORT SIDE, BETWEEN
FUSELAGE FRAME & BODY SIDE, 16¼ GALS.
SIMILAR TANK, IN SAME POSITION ON
STARBOARD SIDE, ALSO 16¼ GALS.

ILLUSTRATED BY DETAILS 1 TO 5 AT RIGHT, IS THE
UNIQUE METHOD CHARACTERIZING THE UNITING OF
WOOD TO WOOD & METAL TO WOOD IN THE FUSELAGE
OF THE NIEUP. NIGHTHAWK, USING A PRESSED PLATE
FITTING WITH FIVE STAY-WIRE ANCHORAGES, A
FLANGED TUBE D AND WASHER E, ARE BRAZED TO IT
TO FACILITATE ASSEMBLY. LONGERON A, IS DRILLED TO
RECEIVE TUBE D, THE END OF WHICH WHEN PASSED THRU'
WASHER F, IS BEADED OVER AS AT G. CROSS-BAR C,
IS HELD BETWEEN PRESSED FITTING & WASHER F BY
TUBULAR RIVET J, STRUT B, IT'S END BOUND BY TAPE,
IS FIXED IN POSITION BY HOLE DRILLED TO RECEIVE
WOOD PEG H, DRIVEN DOWN THRU' BORE OF TUBE RIVET D.

THE COLOR SCHEME OF THE NIEUPORT NIGHTHAWK, APPEARS TO
HAVE BEEN MUCH THE SAME AS THE SE-5, SOPWITH SNIPE, AND
OTHER LAND-BASED BRITISH PURSUITS OF 1918. THE FUSELAGE,
TAIL, LANDING GEAR & UPPER WING SURFACES & STRUTS, OLIVE-
DRAB (KHAKI.) SURFACES BENEATH WINGS & TAIL, EITHER LIGHT-
IVORY OR VERY LIGHT SKY BLUE. OTHER COLORS, AS NOTED.

AIR AGE INC. 551 FIFTH AVE. NEW YORK, 17, N.Y.
SCALE: ¼"=1'-0"   GENERAL ARRANGEMENTS &
FULL SIZE: ¼"=1'-0"   CONSTRUCTIONAL DETAILS.
BRITAIN'S 1918 R.A.F. NIEUPORT
COPYRIGHT BY:
Joseph Nieto.   Nighthawk.

73

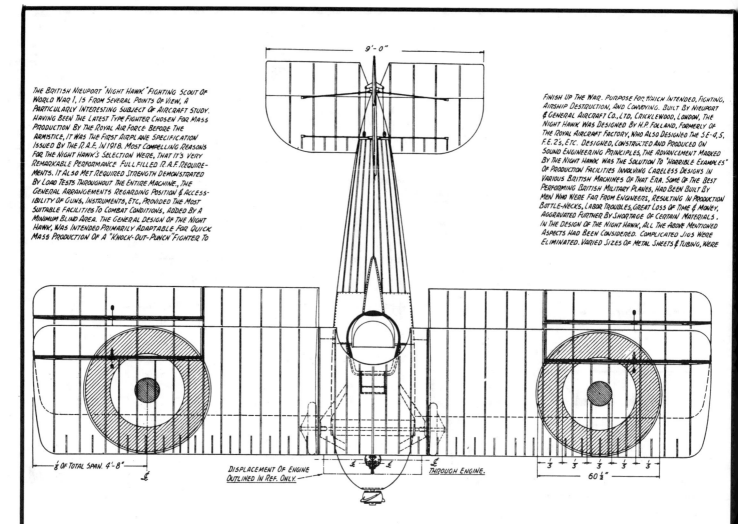

THE BRITISH NIEUPORT "NIGHT HAWK" FIGHTING SCOUT OF WORLD WAR 1, IS FROM SEVERAL POINTS OF VIEW, A PARTICULARLY INTERESTING SUBJECT OF AIRCRAFT STUDY. HAVING BEEN THE LATEST TYPE FIGHTER CHOSEN FOR MASS PRODUCTION BY THE ROYAL AIR FORCE BEFORE THE ARMISTICE, IT WAS THE FIRST AIRPLANE SPECIFICATION ISSUED BY THE R.A.F. IN 1918. MOST COMPELLING REASONS FOR THE NIGHT HAWK'S SELECTION WERE, THAT IT'S VERY REMARKABLE PERFORMANCE FULL FILLED R.A.F. REQUIRE-MENTS. IT ALSO MET REQUIRED STRENGTH DEMONSTRATED BY LOAD TESTS THROUGHOUT THE ENTIRE MACHINE., THE GENERAL ARRANGEMENTS REGARDING POSITION & ACCESS-IBILITY OF GUNS, INSTRUMENTS, ETC, PROVIDED THE MOST SUITABLE FACILITIES TO COMBAT CONDITIONS, ADDED BY A MINIMUM BLIND AREA. THE GENERAL DESIGN OF THE NIGHT HAWK, WAS INTENDED PRIMARILY ADAPTABLE FOR QUICK MASS PRODUCTION OF A "KNOCK-OUT-PUNCH" FIGHTER TO

FINISH UP THE WAR. PURPOSE FOR WHICH INTENDED, FIGHTING, AIRSHIP DESTRUCTION, AND CONVOYING. BUILT BY NIEUPORT & GENERAL AIRCRAFT CO., LTD, CRICKLEWOOD, LONDON, THE NIGHT HAWK WAS DESIGNED BY H.P. FOLLAND, FORMERLY OF THE ROYAL AIRCRAFT FACTORY, WHO ALSO DESIGNED THE S.E-4, S, F.E. 2's, ETC. DESIGNED, CONSTRUCTED AND PRODUCED ON SOUND ENGINEERING PRINCIPLES, THE ADVANCEMENT MARKED BY THE NIGHT HAWK WAS THE SOLUTION TO "HORRIBLE EXAMPLES" OF PRODUCTION FACILITIES INVOLVING CARELESS DESIGNS IN VARIOUS BRITISH MACHINES OF THAT ERA. SOME OF THE BEST PERFORMING BRITISH MILITARY PLANES, HAD BEEN BUILT BY MEN WHO WERE FAR FROM ENGINEERS, RESULTING IN PRODUCTION BOTTLE-NECKS, LABOR TROUBLES, GREAT LOSS OF TIME & MONEY, AGGRAVATED FURTHER BY SHORTAGE OF CERTAIN MATERIALS. IN THE DESIGN OF THE NIGHT HAWK, ALL THE ABOVE MENTIONED ASPECTS HAD BEEN CONSIDERED. COMPLICATED JIGS WERE ELIMINATED. VARIED SIZES OF METAL SHEETS & TUBING, WERE

9'-0"

⅛ OF TOTAL SPAN. 4'-8"

DISPLACEMENT OF ENGINE OUTLINED IN REF. ONLY.

⅌ THROUGH ENGINE.

60½"

NO LONGER A PRODUCTION HINDRANCE. QUANTITIES OF PLENTIFUL, STOCK PARTS & FITTINGS USED IN S.E-5's, WENT INTO THE NEW DESIGN. SCRAP MATERIALS, RESIDUAL FROM WING CONSTRUCTION, WERE USED IN THE FUSELAGE & TAIL FRAMES. BRIEFLY, STANDARDIZATION, SIMPLICITY & FLEXIBILITY OF PRODUCTION FACILITY INCORPORATED IN THE NIGHT HAWK, WAS FURTHER GRATIFIED BY IT'S EXCELLENT AND SPECIFIC PERFORMANCE. A BIT LATE FOR FRONT LINE SERVICE BEFORE THE

ARMISTICE WAS SIGNED, THE NIGHT HAWK WAS FULLY CAPABLE OF CARRYING ON FOR THE R.A.F., WHERE THE S.E-5 AND THE "SNIPE" (WHICH IT RESEMBLED) HAD LEFT OFF, AND WAS AFTER "THE BIG FUSS." PRODUCED IN CONSIDERABLE QUANTITY, FOR THE AIR FORCE'S PEACE PROGRAM. AS THE R.A.F.'s FIRST TRULY MODERN, RADIAL POWERED PRODUCTION AIRPLANE, THE NIGHT HAWK WAS POWERED BY A 9 CYL. 320 H.P. "DRAGON-FLY" AIRCOOLED RADIAL ENGINE, GIVING IT A CLIMB OF APP. 1500 F.P.M.,

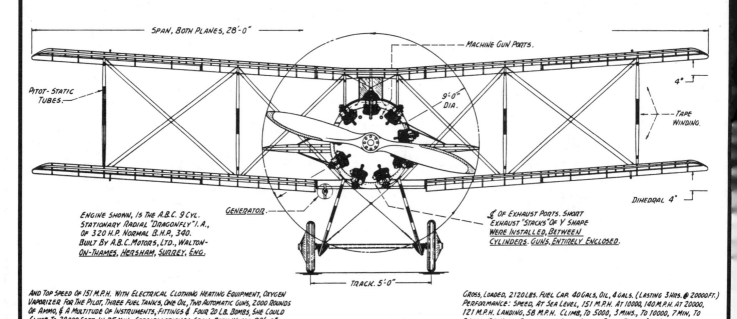

SPAN, BOTH PLANES, 28'-0"

MACHINE GUN PORTS.

PITOT-STATIC TUBES.

9'-0" DIA.

4"

TAPE WINDING.

ENGINE SHOWN, IS THE A.B.C. 9 CYL. STATIONARY RADIAL "DRAGONFLY" I.A., OF 320 H.P. NORMAL B.H.P. 340. BUILT BY A.B.C. MOTORS, LTD., WALTON-ON-THAMES, HERSHAM, SURREY, ENG.

GENERATOR.

DIHEDRAL 4°

⅌ OF EXHAUST PORTS. SHORT EXHAUST "STACKS" OF Y SHAPE WERE INSTALLED, BETWEEN CYLINDERS. GUNS, ENTIRELY ENCLOSED.

TRACK. 5'-0"

AND TOP SPEED OF 151 M.P.H. WITH ELECTRICAL CLOTHING HEATING EQUIPMENT, OXYGEN VAPORIZER FOR THE PILOT, THREE FUEL TANKS, ONE OIL, TWO AUTOMATIC GUNS, 2000 ROUNDS OF AMMO, & A MULTITUDE OF INSTRUMENTS, FITTINGS & FOUR 20 LB. BOMBS, SHE COULD CLIMB TO 28000 FEET IN 25 MIN. SPECIFICATIONS: SPAN, BOTH WINGS, 28'-0". O.A. LENGTH, 18'-6". MAX. HEIGHT, 9'3" (LEV. FL. POS.) CHORD, BOTH, 63", INCIDENCE, 2½'-3". DIHEDRAL, BOTH, 4°. GAP. 4'-6". WEIGHTS: EMPTY, 1500LBS. WT. PER H.P. 6.62 LBS.

GROSS, LOADED, 2120 LBS. FUEL CAP. 40 GALS, OIL, 4 GALS. (LASTING 3 HRS. @ 20000FT.) PERFORMANCE: SPEED, AT SEA LEVEL, 151 M.P.H. AT 10000, 140 M.P.H. AT 20000, 121 M.P.H. LANDING, 58 M.P.H. CLIMB, TO 5000, 3 MINS., TO 10000, 7 MIN, TO 20000, 20 MINS. DISPOSABLE LOAD APART FROM FUEL, 400 LBS. TOTAL AREA OF WINGS, 270 ☐ TOTAL AREA OF TAIL, 28 ☐ (ADDITIONAL REFERENCE AVAILABLE IN "JANES ALL THE WORLD'S AIRCRAFT" FOR 1919.)

Pfalz D.III

drawings by WILLIAM WYLAM

The Pfalz D.III was Germany's attempt to get an edge in the skies over Europe in WW I. Clean in design and very maneuverable, it was still outclassed by Allied aircraft of the era. "Jane's All the World's Aircraft" photos.

The Wylam drawings have been used by countless builders and by the producers of at least one D.III plastic kit. His forward fuselage line under the engine is too full, and the characteristic arrow-shaped profile of the original is lost.

AFTER A SERIES of monoplanes patterned after the French Morane-Saulniers, the D.III was Pfalz's first attempt at producing a modern, high-powered, single-seat fighter. It entered service in 1917 powered by a 160-hp Mercedes engine. Armament was comprised of the usual twin forward-firing Spandaus. Although useful for German units needing replacements, it was considered inferior to other types. None-theless, several hundred were built. For the last months of WW I the D.IIIa became available, which was basically a refined D.III with a more powerful (180-hp) engine. Clean in design, light in weight, and very maneuverable, it was one of the first attempts at streamlining by the Germans in order to develop a scout machine with good performance.

No D.III's still exist. □

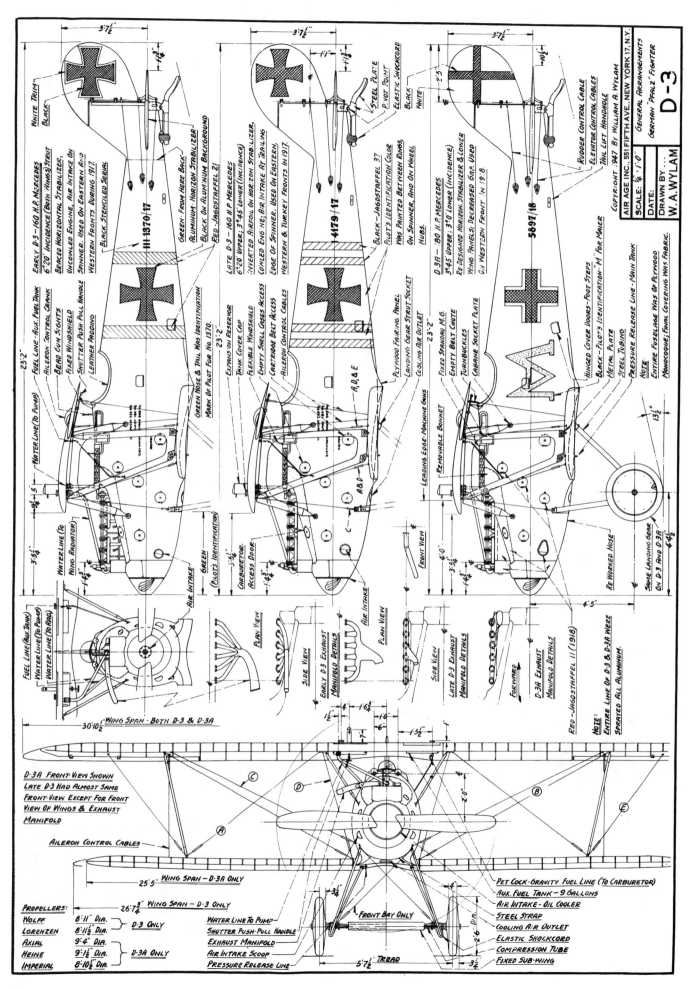

General Arrangements
German "Pfalz" Fighter
D-3

AIR AGE INC. 551 FIFTH AVE. NEW YORK 17, N.Y.
COPYRIGHT 1947 BY WILLIAM R. WYLAM
SCALE: ¼"=1'-0"
DATE:
DRAWN BY
W.A. WYLAM

WHITE TRIM
BLACK
Early D-3-160 H.P. Mercedes
6°20' Incidence (Both Wings) Strut
Braced Horizontal Stabilizer.
Uncowled Engine. Air Intake On
Spinner. Used On Eastern And
Western Fronts During 1917.
Green - From Here Back
Aluminum - Horizon Background
Black On Aluminum Background
Red-Jagdstaffel 21
H 1370/17
Green Nose & Tail Was Identification
Mark Of Pilot For No. 1370.

WHITE
BLACK
STEEL PLATE
PIVOT POINT
ELASTIC SHOCKCORD
TAIL LIFT HANDHOLE
Late D-3-160 H.P. Mercedes
6°20' Upper; 3°45' Lower (Incidence)
Inverted Airfoil On Horizon. Stabilizer.
Cowled Engine; Air Intake At Trailing
Edge Of Spinner. Used On Eastern,
Western And Turkey Fronts In 1917.
Black - Jagdstaffel 37
Pilot's Identification Color
Was Painted Between Rings,
On Spinner, And On Wheel
Hubs.
4179/17

RUDDER CONTROL CABLE
ELEVATOR CONTROL CABLES
BLACK
WHITE
D-3A - 180 H.P. Mercedes
3°45' Upper; 3°0' Lower (Incidence)
Re-Designed Horizon. Stabilizer & Lower
Wing Panels; Decreased Gap. Used
On Western Front In 1918.
5897/18

FUEL LINE - AUX. FUEL TANK
FUEL LINE
AILERON CONTROL CRANK
BEAD GUN SIGHTS
FIXED WINDSHIELD
SHUTTER PUSH-PULL HANDLE
LEATHER PADDING
23'-2"
WATER LINE (TO PUMP)
WATERLINE (TO WING RADIATOR)
FUEL LINE (AUX. TANK)
WATER LINE (TO PUMP)
WATER LINE (TO RAD.)
AIR INTAKE
WING SPAN - BOTH D-3 & D-3A
30'-10½"
PLAN VIEW
SIDE VIEW
Early D-3 Exhaust
Manifold Details
GREEN
(PILOT'S IDENTIFICATION)

EXPANSION RESERVOIR
TANK COVER CAP
FLEXIBLE WINDSHIELD
EMPTY SHELL GASES ACCESS
CARTRIDGE BELT ACCESS
AILERON CONTROL CABLES
A, D, & E
A & D
CARBURETOR
ACCESS DOOR
23'-2"
PLYWOOD FAIRING PANEL
LANDING GEAR STRUT SOCKET
COOLING AIR OUTLET
LEADING EDGE - MACHINE GUNS
AIR INTAKE
AIR VIEW
PLAN VIEW
Late D-3 Exhaust
Manifold Details
SIDE VIEW
Front View

REMOVABLE BONNET
FIXED SPANDAU M.G.
EMPTY BELT CHUTE
TURNBUCKLES
CABANE SOCKET PLATE
HINGED COVER DOORS - FOOT-STEPS
BLACK - PILOT'S IDENTIFICATION - "M" FOR MAIER
METAL PLATE
STEEL TUBING
PRESSURE RELEASE LINE - MAIN TANK
NOTE
Entire Fuselage Was Of Plywood
Monocoque; Final Covering Was Fabric.
4'-0"
3'-5¼"
FORWARD
D-3A Exhaust
Manifold Details
13½"
4'-4½"
RE-WORKED NOSE
Same Landing Gear
On D-3 And D-3A
4'-5"
NOTE:
Entire Line Of D-3 & D-3A Were
Sprayed All Aluminum.
Red - Jagdstaffel II (1918)

D-3A Front-View Shown
Late D-3 Had Almost Same
Front-View Except For Front
View Of Wings & Exhaust
Manifold

AILERON CONTROL CABLES

WING SPAN - D-3A ONLY
25'-5"
WING SPAN - D-3 ONLY
26'-7¾"

PROPELLERS:
WOLFF   8'-11" DIA.   D-3 ONLY
LORENZEN   8'-11½" DIA.
AXIAL   9'-4" DIA.   D-3A ONLY
HEINE   9'-1½" DIA.
IMPERIAL   8'-10½" DIA.

WATER LINE TO PUMP
SHUTTER PUSH-PULL HANDLE
EXHAUST MANIFOLD
AIR INTAKE SCOOP
PRESSURE RELEASE LINE

FRONT BAY ONLY
2'-0"
5'-7½" TREAD

PET COCK - GRAVITY FUEL LINE (TO CARBURETOR)
AUX. FUEL TANK - 9 GALLONS
AIR INTAKE - OIL COOLER
STEEL STRAP
COOLING AIR OUTLET
ELASTIC SHOCKCORD
COMPRESSION TUBE
FIXED SUB-WING

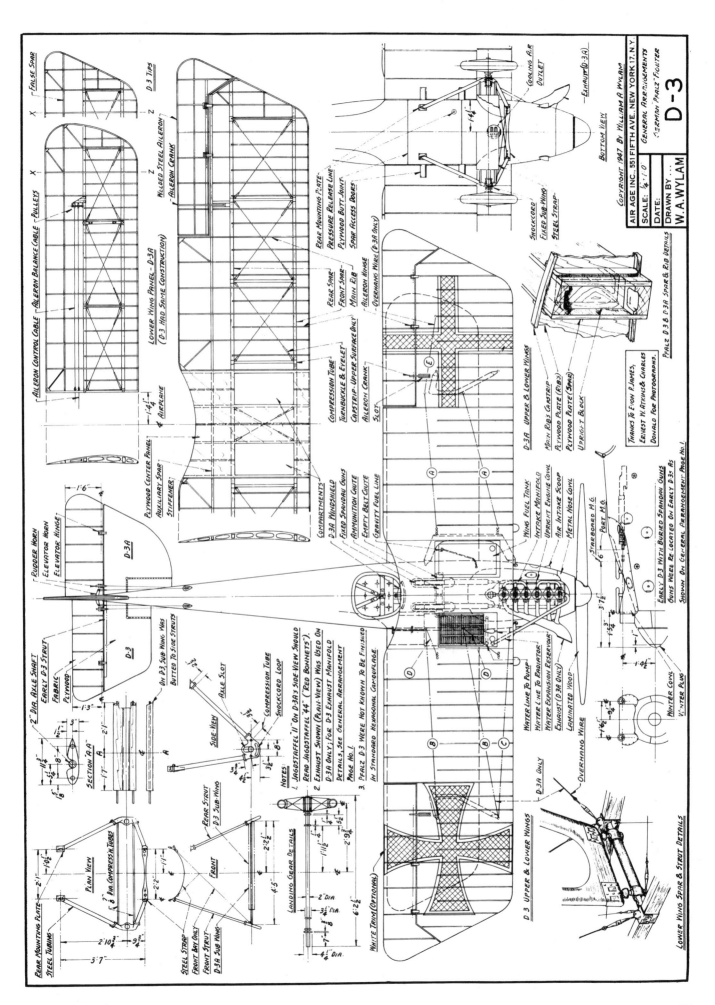

General Arrangements
"GERMAN" PFALZ FIGHTER
D-3

SCALE: ¼" : 0
DATE:
DRAWN BY
W. A. WYLAM

AIR AGE INC. 551 FIFTH AVE. NEW YORK 17, N.Y.
COPYRIGHT 1947 BY WILLIAM A. WYLAM

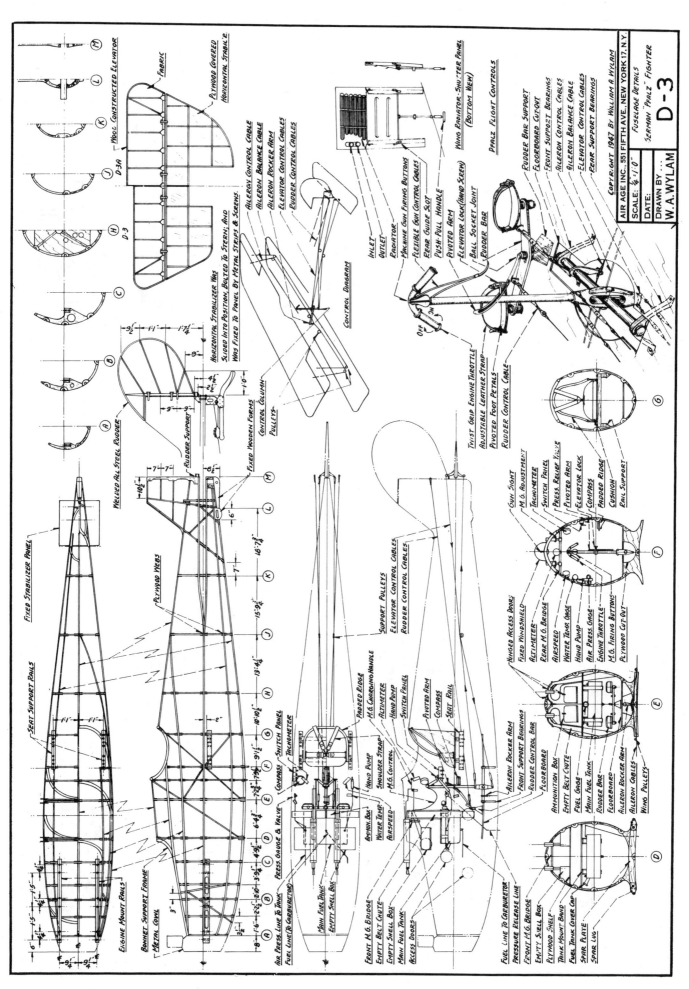

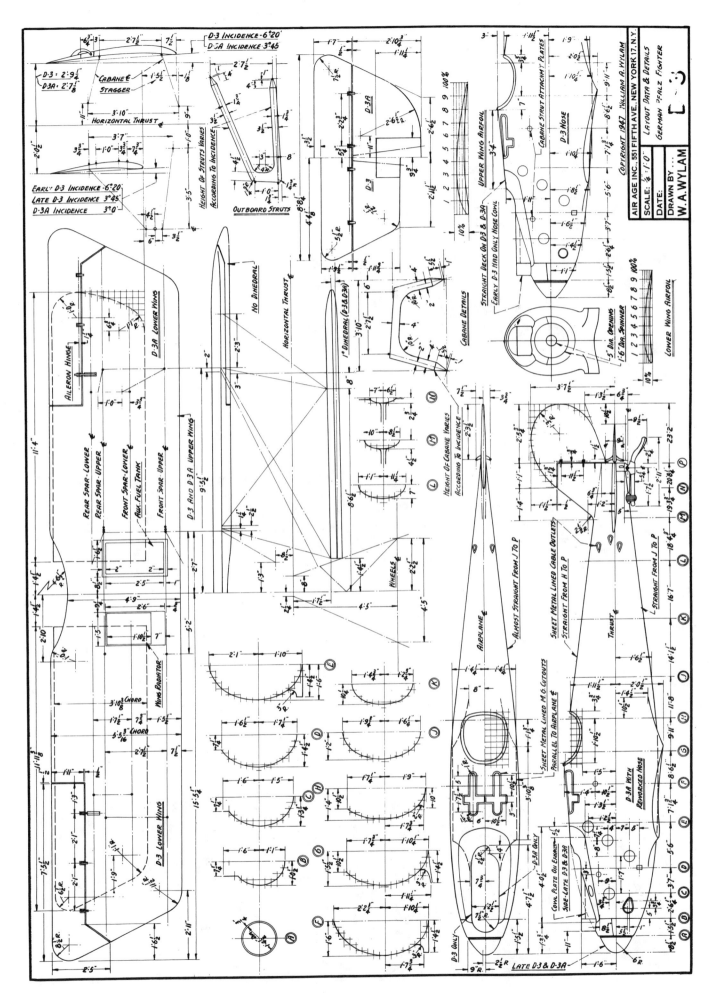

Pfalz D.XII

drawings by WILLIAM WYLAM

THE PFALZ D.XII was designed late in 1917 as a high-performance single-seat pursuit plane. Economy of construction was a prime prerequisite in view of Germany's increasing shortage of strategic materials, and the airplane was built largely of wood at a time when metal fabrication was coming into the picture. The fuselage utilized plywood skin.

Pilots found the D.XII to be a stable airplane and easy to fly. It required little attention when cruising, although it was somewhat difficult to keep straight on the ground due to a sluggish rudder effect. But mechanics found its two-bay rigging difficult to keep in trim, especially when compared to the wire-less Fokker D.VII.

Beautiful in form, the D.XII was advanced for its time. Equipped with either a Mercedes 160- or 180-hp power-plant, depending on date of manufacture, the engine was cooled by a nose radiator located entirely above the propeller shaft. It had two fuel tanks located in the fuselage and worked under air pressure.

The D.XII reached the front too late in the war to make an imposing record for itself.

There are four left, all in museums. □

This Pfalz D.XII was a rugged design as seen in photo of wreckage below. "Jane's All the World's Aircraft" photos.

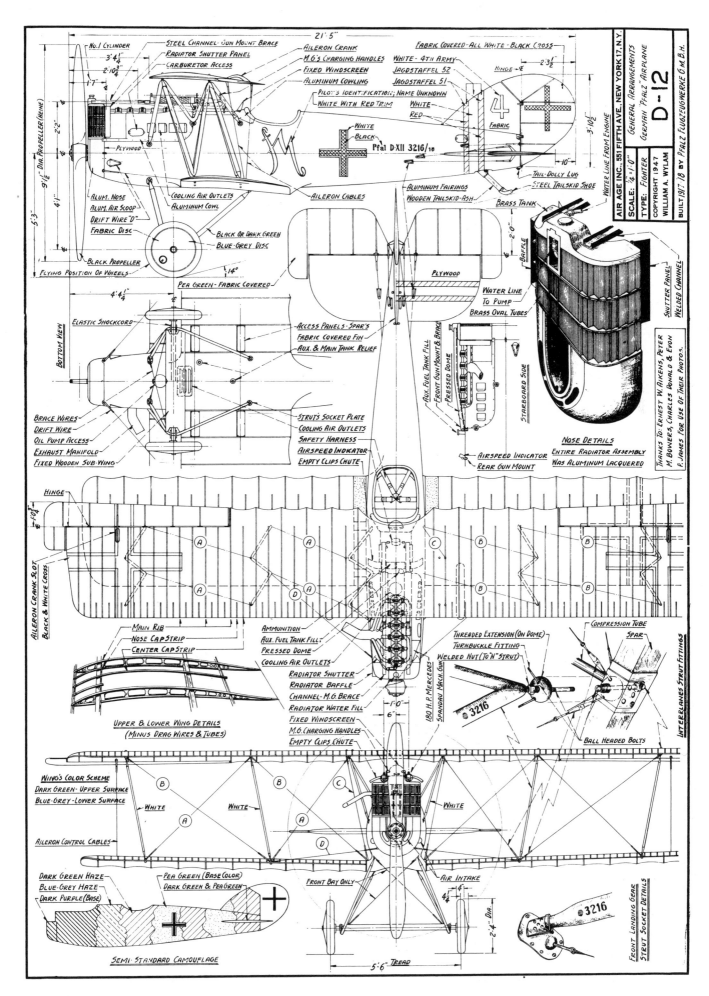

Upper & Lower Wing Details
(Minus Drag Wires & Tubes)

Semi-Standard Camouflage

Nose Details
Entire Radiator Assembly
Was Aluminum Lacquered

Front Landing Gear
Strut Socket Details

AIR AGE INC., 551 FIFTH AVE., NEW YORK 17, N.Y.
General Arrangements
German "Pfalz" Airplane
D-12
SCALE: ¼"-1'-0"
TYPE: Fighter
COPYRIGHT 1947
WILLIAM A. WYLAM
BUILT 1917-'18 BY PFALZ FLUGZEUGWERKE G.M.B.H.

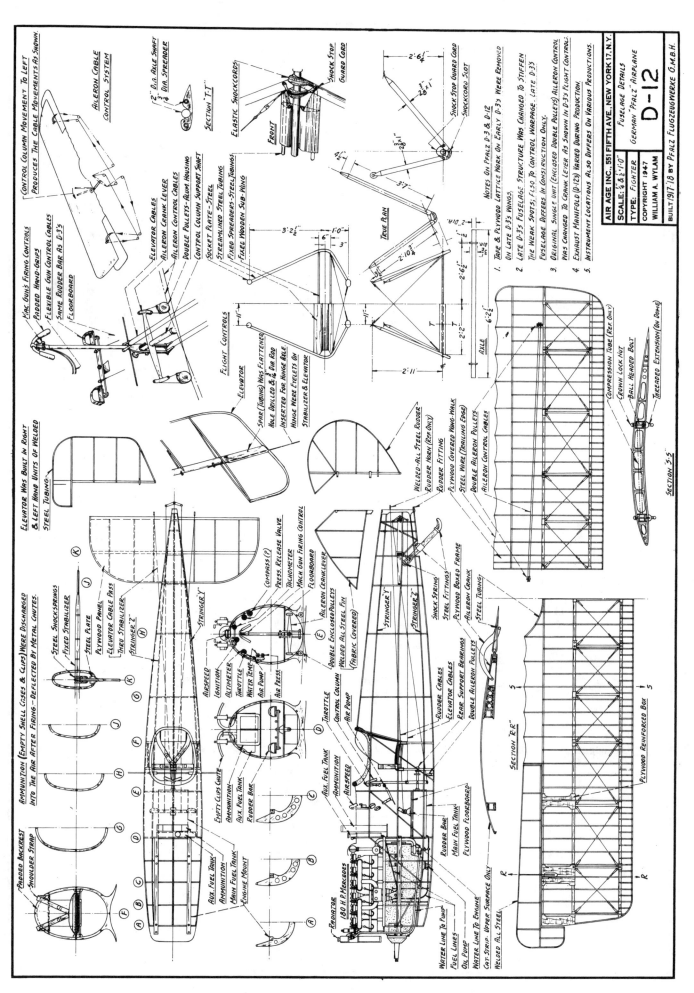

Title block (right side):

AIR AGE INC., 551 FIFTH AVE., NEW YORK 17, N.Y.

SCALE: ¼ & ⅛"=1'-0"

TYPE: FIGHTER

COPYRIGHT 1947
WILLIAM A. WYLAM

BUILT 1917 ⅛ BY PFALZ FLUGZEUGWERKE G.M.B.H.

FUSELAGE DETAILS
GERMAN "PFALZ" AIRPLANE

D-12

Notes on Pfalz D-3 & D-12

1. TAPE & PLYWOOD LATTICE WORK ON EARLY D-33 WERE REMOVED ON LATE D-33'S WINGS.
2. LATE D-33'S FUSELAGE STRUCTURE WAS CHANGED TO STIFFEN THE WEAK SPOTS; FLS.O TO CONTROL WARPAGE. LATE D-33 FUSELAGE DIFFERS IN CONSTRUCTION ONLY.
3. ORIGINAL SINGLE UNIT (ENCLOSED DOUBLE PULLEYS) AILERON CONTROL WAS CHANGED TO CRANK LEVER AS SHOWN IN D-33'S FLIGHT CONTROLS.
4. EXHAUST MANIFOLD (D-12) VARIED DURING PRODUCTION.
5. INSTRUMENT LOCATIONS ALSO DIFFERS ON VARIOUS PRODUCTIONS.

Various labels throughout the drawing:

AILERON CABLE CONTROL SYSTEM

CONTROL COLUMN MOVEMENT TO LEFT PRODUCES THE CABLE MOVEMENTS AS SHOWN.

¾" DIA. AXLE SHAFT
¾" DIA. SPREADER

SECTION "T-T"

ELASTIC SHOCKCORDS

SHOCK STOP GUARD CORD
SHOCKCORD SLOT

FRONT

SHOCK STOP GUARD CORD

ELEVATOR CABLES
AILERON CRANK LEVER
AILERON CONTROL CABLES
DOUBLE PULLEYS-ALUM. HOUSING
CONTROL COLUMN SUPPORT SHAFT
SOCKET PLATE-STEEL
STREAMLINED STEEL TUBING
FIXED SPREADERS-STEEL TUBINGS
FIXED WOODEN SUB-WING

TRUE PLAN

MAC. GUNS FIRING CONTROLS
PADDED HAND-GRIPS
FLEXIBLE GUN CONTROL CABLES
SAME RUDDER BAR AS D-33
FLOORBOARD

FLIGHT CONTROLS

ELEVATOR

SPAR (TUBING) WAS FLATTENED
HOLE DRILLED & ¼ DIA. ROD INSERTED FOR HINGE AXLE
HINGE WERE EYELETS ON STABILIZER & ELEVATOR

ELEVATOR WAS BUILT IN RIGHT & LEFT HAND UNITS OF WELDED STEEL TUBING.

WELDED-ALL STEEL RUDDER
RUDDER HORN (REF. ONLY)
RUDDER FITTING
PLYWOOD COVERED HAND-WALK
STEEL WIRE (TRAILING EDGE)
DOUBLE AILERON PULLEYS
AILERON CONTROL CABLES

COMPRESSION TUBE (REF. ONLY)
CROWN LOCK NUT
BALL HEADED BOLT
THREADED EXTENSION (ON DOME)

SECTION 5-5

AMMUNITION (EMPTY SHELL CASES & CLIPS) WERE DISCHARGED INTO THE AIR AFTER FIRING—DEFLECTED BY METAL CHUTES.

PADDED BACKREST
SHOULDER STRAP
STEEL SHOCKSPRINGS
FIXED STABILIZER
STEEL PLATE
PLYWOOD PANEL
ELEVATOR CABLE PASS THRU STABILIZER
STRINGER "Z"
STRINGER "Y"

COMPASS (2)
PRESS. RELEASE VALVE
TACHOMETER
FLOORBOARD
MACH GUN FIRING CONTROL
AILERON CRANKLEVER
DOUBLE ENCLOSE PULLEYS
WELDED ALL STEEL FIN
(FABRIC COVERED)
THROTTLE
CONTROL COLUMN
AIR PUMP

STRINGER "Y"
STRINGER "Z"
SHOCK SPRING
STEEL FITTINGS
PLYWOOD BOXED FRAME
AILERON CRANK
STEEL TUBING

RUDDER CABLES
ELEVATOR CABLES
REAR SUPPORT BEARINGS
DOUBLE AILERON PULLEYS

SECTION "R-R"

AIRSPEED
IGNITION
ALTIMETER
THROTTLE
WATER TEMP.
AIR PUMP
AIR PRESS

EMPTY CLIPS CHUTE
AMMUNITION
AUX. FUEL TANK
RUDDER BAR

AUX. FUEL TANK
AMMUNITION
AUX. FUEL TANK
AIRSPEED
MAIN FUEL TANK

AUX. FUEL TANK
AMMUNITION
MAIN FUEL TANK
ENGINE MOUNT

RADIATOR
(180 H.P. MERCEDES)

RUDDER BAR
MAIN FUEL TANK
PLYWOOD FLOORBOARD

WATER LINE TO PUMP
FUEL LINES
OIL PUMP
WATER LINE TO ENGINE
CAT STRIP, UPPER SURFACE ONLY
WELDED ALL STEEL

PLYWOOD REINFORCED BOX

AXLE

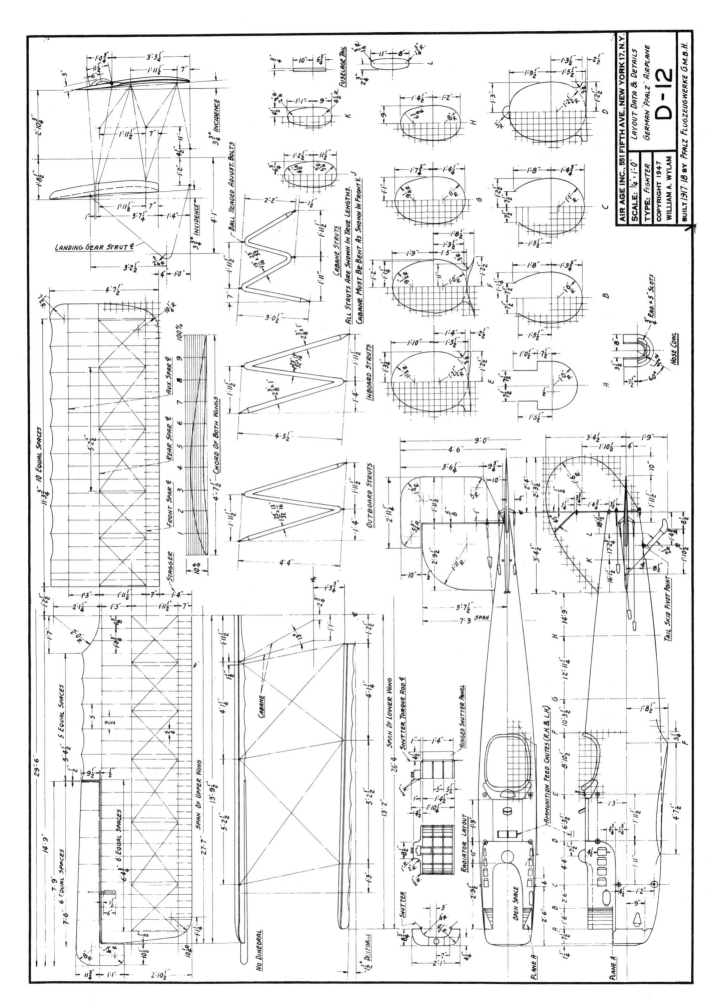

AIR AGE INC., 551 FIFTH AVE., NEW YORK 17, N.Y.

Layout Data & Details
German "Pfalz" Airplane

D-12

SCALE: ¼" = 1'-0"
TYPE: Fighter
COPYRIGHT 1947
WILLIAM A. WYLAM
BUILT 1917-18 BY Pfalz Flugzeugwerke G.M.B.H.

ALL STRUTS ARE SHOWN IN TRUE LENGTHS.
CABANE MUST BE BENT AS SHOWN IN FRONT V.

CABANE STRUTS

INBOARD STRUTS

OUTBOARD STRUTS

BALL HEADED ADJUST. BOLTS

LANDING GEAR STRUT ℄

NOSE COWL

CHORD OF BOTH WINGS

FRONT SPAR ℄
REAR SPAR ℄
AUX. SPAR ℄

STAGGER

NO DIHEDRAL

DIHEDRAL

CABANE

SPAN OF LOWER WING

SPAN OF UPPER WING

SHUTTER

SHUTTER TORQUE ROD ℄

HINGED SHUTTER PANEL

RADIATOR LAYOUT

OPEN SPACE

AMMUNITION FEED CHUTES (R.H. & L.H.)

TAIL SKID PIVOT POINT

PLANE A

FUSELAGE TAIL

drawing by BARNETT FEINBERG

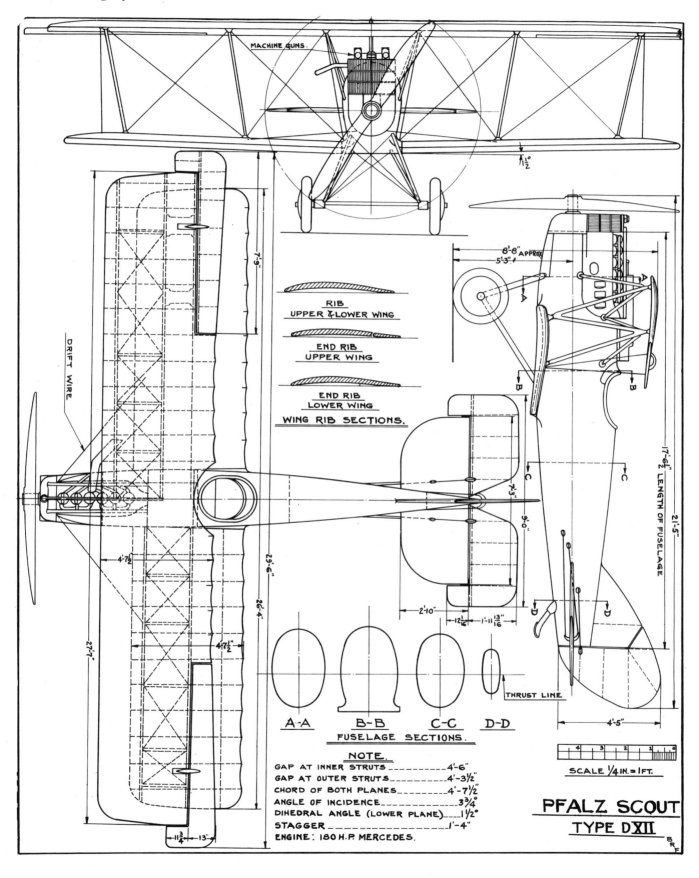

MACHINE GUNS.

RIB
UPPER & LOWER WING

END RIB
UPPER WING

END RIB
LOWER WING

WING RIB SECTIONS.

DRIFT WIRE

7'-9"

4'-7½"

29'-6"

26'-4"

27'-7"

4'-7½"

11¾" 13"

8'-8" APPROX
5'-3"

17'-6½" LENGTH OF FUSELAGE

21'-5"

7'-3"

9'-0"

2'-10"

12 1/16" 1'-11 13/16"

THRUST LINE

4'-5"

A-A   B-B   C-C   D-D
FUSELAGE SECTIONS.

1½°

NOTE.
GAP AT INNER STRUTS _____ 4'-6"
GAP AT OUTER STRUTS _____ 4'-3½"
CHORD OF BOTH PLANES _____ 4'-7½"
ANGLE OF INCIDENCE _____ 3¾°
DIHEDRAL ANGLE (LOWER PLANE) __ 1½°
STAGGER _____ 1'-4"
ENGINE: 180 H.P. MERCEDES.

SCALE ¼ IN.= 1 FT.

PFALZ SCOUT
TYPE D XII

B R F

RAF S.E.5a

drawings by WILLIAM WYLAM

One of the most famous aircraft of WW I was the S.E.5a and it is credited with turning the tide in air supremacy over the Allied forces. "Jane's All the World's Aircraft" photos.

THE SCOUTING Experimental Number 5 was produced by the British Royal Aircraft Factory and appeared at the front during "bloody April" of 1917, the blackest month of the war in terms of casualties for the British RFC. Armed with either two Vickers guns or a Vickers and a Lewis gun, the Scout soon proved a match for the German Albatros, which up until that time had ruled the skies.

The S.E.5, and the later S.E.5a with a geared engine, was renowned for its ruggedness and proof of this fact came during a battle when a pilot actually flew an S.E.5 through the side of a house and emerged unhurt. It was also a favorite for fighter pilots of the Royal Flying Corps. Britain's leading Ace, Major Edward Mannock, scored 50 of his 73 victories while flying the S.E.5 Scout. William Bishop and Ray Collishaw also downed a majority of their credits in this aircraft.

A major contribution to the war effort, the 25th Aero Squadron was formed at

Kelly Field in June 1917. The unit was made up of American pilots and ground personnel and their participation in the Great War has gone down in history as one of the turning points in favor of the Allies. The S.E.5 was a great aid to that end. In October 1918, no less than 16 units of the RFC were equipped with the

S.E.5 and 5a. The speed of the airplane was reported to be 132 mph at 6,500 feet, with a climb of 765 fpm and a service ceiling of 20,000 feet. □

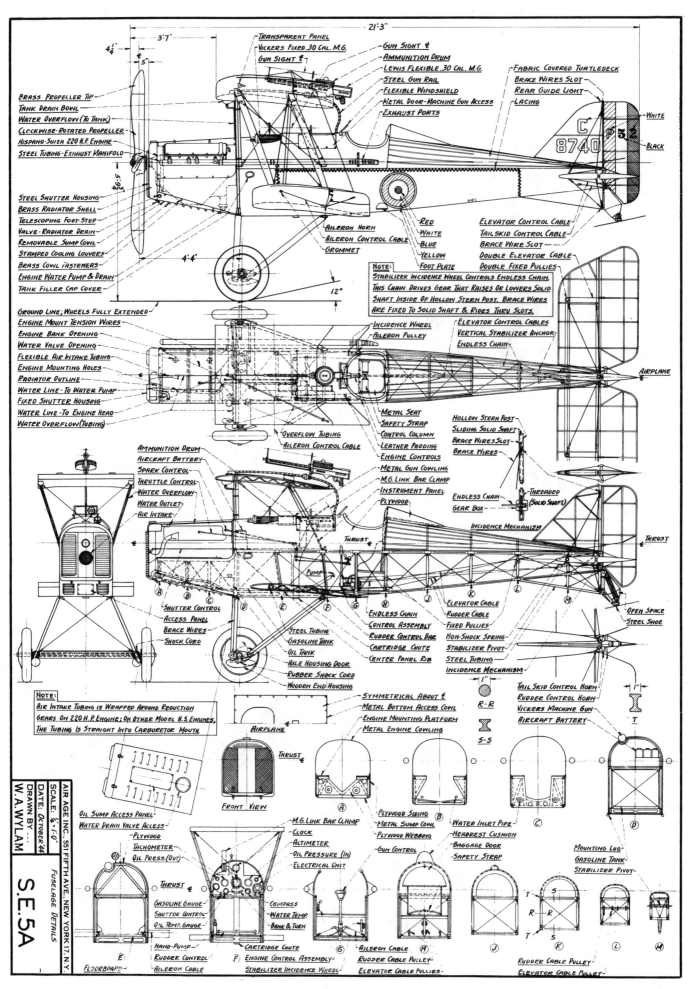

21'-3"

3'-7"

4 1/4"
5

Brass Propeller Tip
Tank Drain Bowl
Water Overflow (To Tank)
Clockwise-Rotated Propeller
Hispano-Suiza 220 H.P. Engine
Steel Tubing-Exhaust Manifold

Transparent Panel
Vickers Fixed .30 Cal. M.G.
Gun Sight ℄

Gun Sight ℄
Ammunition Drum
Lewis Flexible .30 Cal. M.G.
Steel Gun Rail
Flexible Windshield
Metal Door-Machine Gun Access
Exhaust Ports

Fabric Covered Turtledeck
Brace Wires
Rear Guide Light
Lacing

C 5
8740

WHITE
BLACK

Steel Shutter Housing
Brass Radiator Shell
Telescoping Foot-Step
Valve-Radiator Drain
Removable Sump Cowl
Stamped Cooling Louvers
Brass Cowl Fasteners
Engine Water Pump & Drain
Tank Filler Cap Cover

4'-4"

12°

Aileron Horn
Aileron Control Cable
Grommet

Red
White
Blue
Yellow
Foot Plate

Elevator Control Cable
Tail Skid Control Cable
Brace Wire Slot
Double Elevator Cable
Double Fixed Pullies

Note:
Stabilizer Incidence Wheel Controls Endless Chain.
This Chain Drives Gear That Raises Or Lowers Solid
Shaft Inside Of Hollow Stern Post. Brace Wires
Are Fixed To Solid Shaft & Rides Thru Slots.

Ground Line; Wheels Fully Extended
Engine Mount Tension Wires
Engine Bank Opening
Water Valve Opening
Flexible Air Intake Tubing
Engine Mounting Holes
Radiator Outline
Water Line - To Water Pump
Fixed Shutter Housing
Water Line - To Engine Head
Water Overflow (Tubing)

Incidence Wheel
Aileron Pulley

Elevator Control Cables
Vertical Stabilizer Anchor
Endless Chain

AIRPLANE

Metal Seat
Safety Strap
Control Column
Leather Padding
Engine Controls
Metal Gun Cowling
M.G. Link Bar Clamp
Instrument Panel
Plywood

Hollow Stern Post
Sliding Solid Shaft
Brace Wires Slot
Brace Wires

Endless Chain
Gear Box

Threaded
(Solid Shaft)

Incidence Mechanism

Overflow Tubing
Aileron Control Cable

Ammunition Drum
Aircraft Battery
Spark Control
Throttle Control
Water Overflow
Water Outlet
Air Intake

Thrust

Pump

Thrust

Endless Chain
Control Assembly
Rudder Control Bar
Cartridge Chute
Center Panel Rib

Elevator Cable
Rudder Cable
Fixed Pullies
Non-Shock Spring
Stabilizer Pivot
Steel Tubing
Incidence Mechanism

Open Space
Steel Shoe

Shuttor Control
Access Panel
Brace Wires
Shock Cord

Steel Tubing
Gasoline Tank
Oil Tank
Axle Housing Door
Rubber Shock Cord
Wooden End Housing

A B C D E F G H J K L M

1"
R-R

1"
I
T

Tail Skid Control Horn
Rudder Control Horn
Vickers Machine Gun
Aircraft Battery

Note:
Air Intake Tubing Is Wrapped Around Reduction
Gears On 220 H.P. Engine; On Other Model H.S. Engines,
The Tubing Is Straight Into Carburetor Mouth.

Airplane

Symmetrical About ℄
Metal Bottom Access Cowl
Engine Mounting Platform
Metal Engine Cowling

S-S

Thrust

Front View

A

Plywood Siding
Metal Sump Cowl
Plywood Webbing
Gun Control

B

C

Water Inlet Pipe
Headrest Cushion
Baggage Door
Safety Strap

D

Oil Sump Access Panel
Water Drain Valve Access
Plywood
Tachometer
Oil Press. (Out)

M.G. Link Bar Clamp
Clock
Altimeter
Oil Pressure (In)
Electrical Unit

Mounting Lug
Gasoline Tank
Stabilizer Pivot

AIR AGE INC., 551 FIFTH AVE., NEW YORK 17, N.Y.

SCALE: 1/4" = 1'-0"
DATE: October '44
DRAWN BY... W. A. WYLAM

S.E.5A

FUSELAGE DETAILS

Thrust ℄

Gasoline Gauge
Shuttor Control
Oil Temp. Gauge

Compass
Water Temp.
Bank & Turn

Hand-Pump
Rudder Control
Aileron Cable

Cartridge Chute
Engine Control Assembly
Stabilizer Incidence Wheel

Aileron Cable
Rudder Cable Pulley
Elevator Cable Pullies

Rudder Cable Pulley
Elevator Cable Pulley

E

F

G

H

J

K

L

M

Floorboard

T S
R R
T S

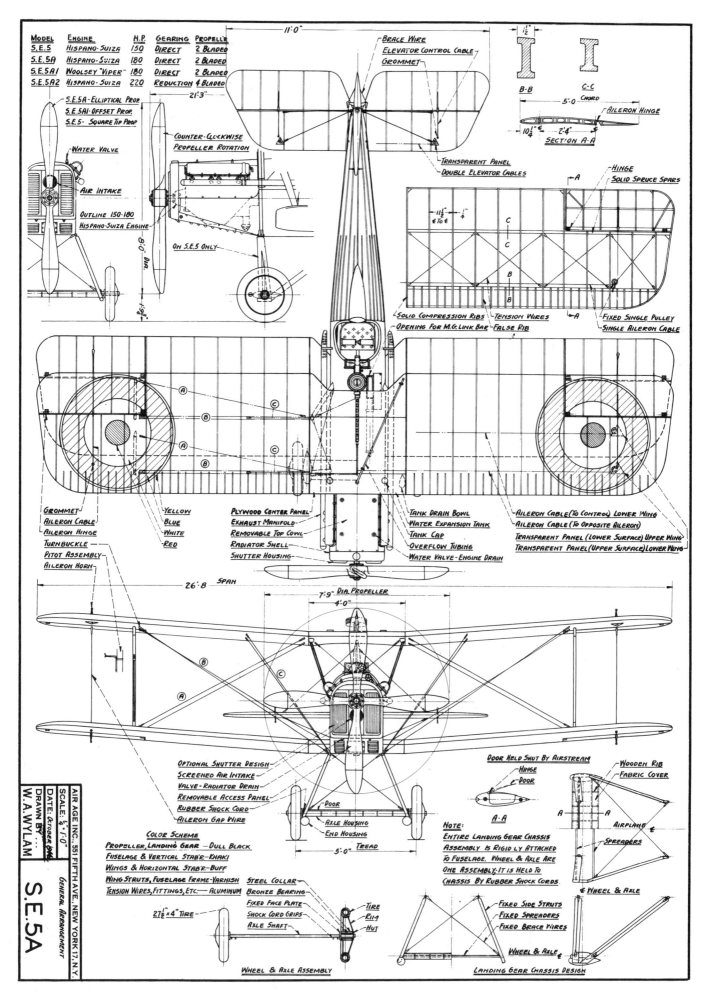

Model	Engine	H.P.	Gearing	Propell'r
S.E.5	Hispano-Suiza	150	Direct	2 Bladed
S.E.5A	Hispano-Suiza	180	Direct	2 Bladed
S.E.5A1	Woolsey "Viper"	180	Direct	2 Bladed
S.E.5A2	Hispano-Suiza	220	Reduction	4 Bladed

S.E.5A—Elliptical Prop.
S.E.5A1—Offset Prop.
S.E.5—Square Tip Prop.

Water Valve
Air Intake
Outline 150-180 Hispano-Suiza Engine

Counter-Clockwise Propeller Rotation
On S.E.5 Only

Brace Wire
Elevator Control Cable
Grommet

Transparent Panel
Double Elevator Cables

B-B   C-C Chord
Aileron Hinge
Section A-A

Solid Compression Ribs — Tension Wires
Opening for M.G. Link Bar — False Rib

Hinge — Solid Spruce Spars
Fixed Single Pulley
Single Aileron Cable

Grommet
Aileron Cable
Aileron Hinge
Turnbuckle
Pitot Assembly
Aileron Horn

Yellow
Blue
White
Red

Plywood Center Panel
Exhaust Manifold
Removable Top Cowl
Radiator Shell
Shutter Housing

Tank Drain Bowl
Water Expansion Tank
Tank Cap
Overflow Tubing
Water Valve-Engine Drain

Aileron Cable (To Control) Lower Wing
Aileron Cable (To Opposite Aileron)
Transparent Panel (Lower Surface) Upper Wing
Transparent Panel (Upper Surface) Lower Wing

26'-8" SPAN
7'-9" Dia. Propeller
4'-0"

Optional Shutter Design
Screened Air Intake
Valve-Radiator Drain
Removable Access Panel
Rubber Shock Cord
Aileron Gap Wire

Color Scheme
Propeller, Landing Gear — Dull Black
Fuselage & Vertical Stab'r — Khaki
Wings & Horizontal Stab'r — Buff
Wing Struts, Fuselage Frame — Varnish
Tension Wires, Fittings, Etc. — Aluminum

Door
Axle Housing
End Housing
5'-0" Tread

Door Held Shut By Airstream
Hinge
Door
A-A

Note: Entire Landing Gear Chassis Assembly Is Rigidly Attached To Fuselage. Wheel & Axle Are One Assembly; It Is Held To Chassis By Rubber Shock Cords.

Wooden Rib
Fabric Cover
Airplane
Spreaders
Wheel & Axle

Steel Collar
Bronze Bearing
Fixed Face Plate
Shock Cord Grips
Axle Shaft
Tire
Rim
Nut

27½"x4" Tire

Wheel & Axle Assembly

Fixed Side Struts
Fixed Spreaders
Fixed Brace Wires
Wheel & Axle
Landing Gear Chassis Design

AIR AGE INC, 551 FIFTH AVE, NEW YORK 17, N.Y.
SCALE: ¼"=1'-0"
DATE: October 1946
DRAWN BY: W. A. WYLAM
GENERAL ARRANGEMENT
S.E.5A

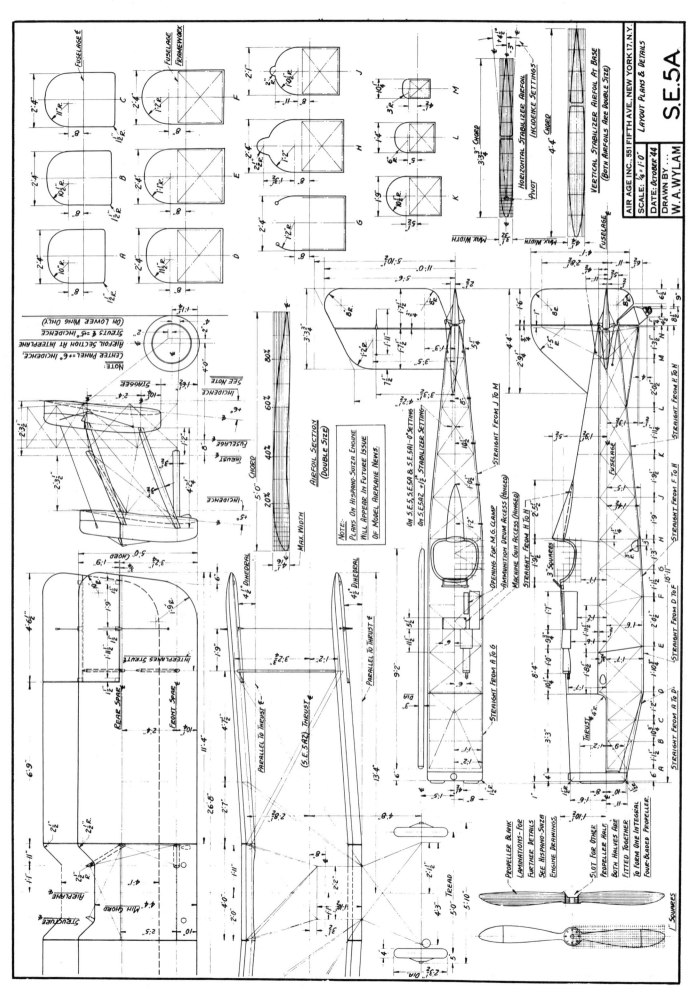

S.E.5A

AIR AGE INC. 551 FIFTH AVE., NEW YORK 17, N.Y.

Layout Plans & Details

SCALE: ¼"=1'·0"

DATE: October '44

DRAWN BY.... W. A. WYLAM

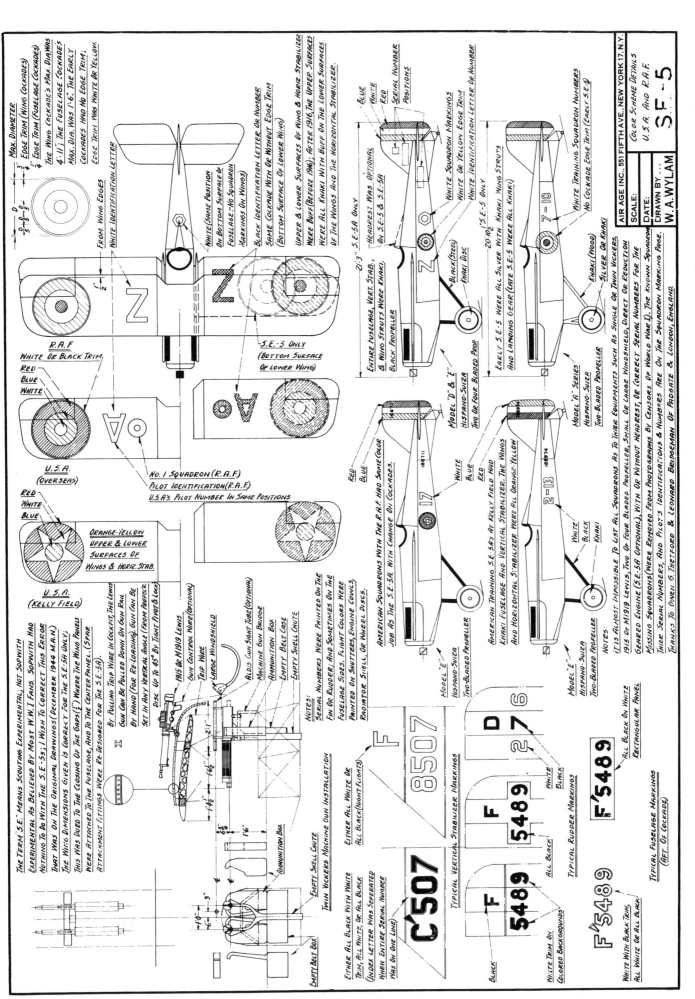

RAF S.E.5a Squadron Markings

drawings by WILLIAM WYLAM

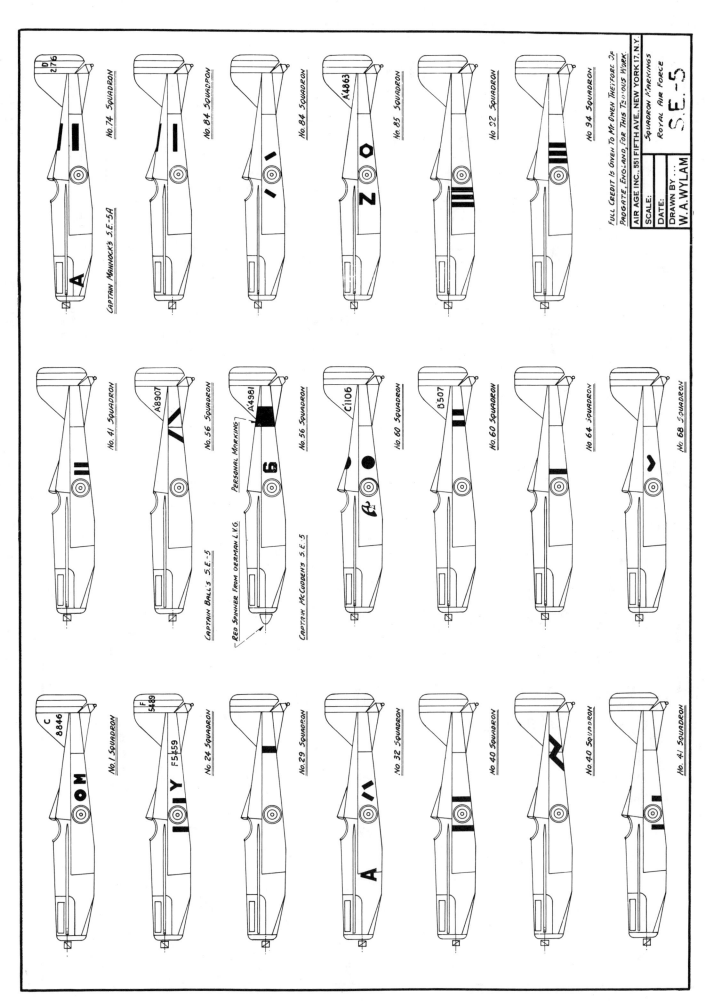

Captain Mannock's S.E.-5A   No. 74 Squadron

No. 84 Squadron

No. 84 Squadron

No. 85 Squadron

No. 22 Squadron

No. 94 Squadron

No. 41 Squadron

No. 56 Squadron

Personal Marking   No. 56 Squadron   Captain Ball's S.E.-5   Red Spinner from German L.V.G.

Captain McCudden's S.E.-5

No. 60 Squadron

No. 60 Squadron

No. 64 Squadron

No. 68 Squadron

No. 1 Squadron

No. 24 Squadron

No. 29 Squadron

No. 32 Squadron

No. 40 Squadron

No. 40 Squadron

No. 41 Squadron

FULL CREDIT IS GIVEN TO MR OWEN THETFORD OF
PADGATE, ENGLAND, FOR THIS TEDIOUS WORK.

AIR AGE INC., 551 FIFTH AVE., NEW YORK 17, N.Y.

SCALE:	ROYAL AIR FORCE
DATE:	SQUADRON MARKINGS
DRAWN BY .... W. A. WYLAM	S.E.-5

Salmson Bomber 2 A.2

drawings by RICHARD ANDERSON

A brute in appearance, yet very maneuverable, the 2.A2 was known for its ability to fly and fly well. "A.A.H.S. Journal" photo.

BUILT by the French firm Societe des Moteurs Salmson, the 2 A.2 was considered by many to be one of the best two-seat fighters developed by any nation during the last half of WW I.

The aircraft featured dive-brakes between the landing gear legs under the fuselage, but the most unusual feature was the 9-cylinder water-cooled radial, the Salmson 9Z. When confronted by this new mechanical apparition, the French Air Ministry was somewhat taken aback, but still supported it, particularly because financing was accomplished entirely through private channels.

The 2 A.2 was intended for use as an Army cooperation type, to carry out any one of several jobs as required. In this respect it was intended to take up where the Sopwith 1½ Strutter left off and to carry on to meet advanced specifications.

The vast majority of pilots who flew it during WW I agree that it was a first-class airplane with few faults and lots of "flyability." Takeoff was relatively short, and the ship landed at about 45 mph tail high and at 40 mph, three-point. What

endeared it most to pilots was its long, flat glide, which saved many a crew who lost an engine far out over the lines.

Two survive; one in Belgium, the other in Japan. □

The Salmson 2A.2 was a large airplane that proved a favorite due to its good handling qualities. "A.A.H.S. Journal" photograph.

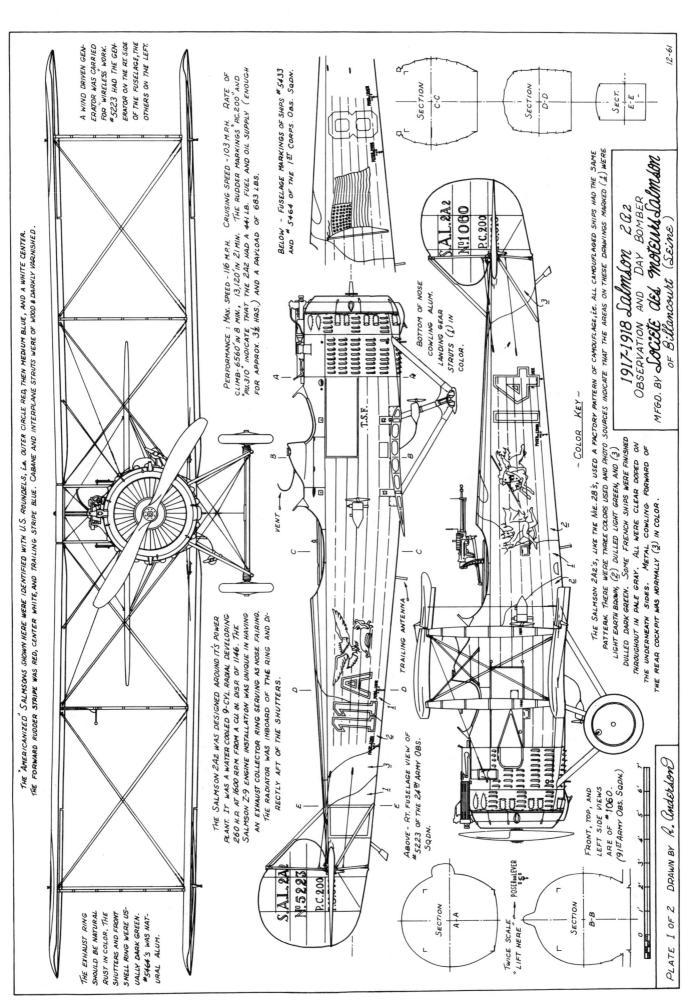

THE "AMERICANIZED" SALMSONS SHOWN HERE WERE IDENTIFIED WITH U.S. ROUNDELS, i.e. OUTER CIRCLE RED, THEN MEDIUM BLUE, AND A WHITE CENTER. THE FORWARD RUDDER STRIPE WAS RED, CENTER WHITE, AND TRAILING STRIPE BLUE. CABANE AND INTERPLANE STRUTS WERE OF WOOD & DARKLY VARNISHED.

A WIND DRIVEN GENERATOR WAS CARRIED FOR "WIRELESS" WORK. #5223 HAD THE GENERATOR ON THE RT. SIDE OF THE FUSELAGE, THE OTHERS ON THE LEFT.

THE EXHAUST RING SHOULD BE NATURAL RUST IN COLOR. THE SHUTTERS AND FRONT SHELL RING WERE USUALLY DARK GREEN. #5464'S WAS NATURAL ALUM.

PERFORMANCE: MAX. SPEED - 116 M.P.H. CRUISING SPEED - 103 M.P.H. RATE OF CLIMB - 6560' IN 8 MIN. 13,120' IN 21 MIN. THE RUDDER MARKINGS "P.C.200" AND "PU.310" INDICATE THAT THE 2A2 HAD A 441 LBS. FUEL AND OIL SUPPLY (ENOUGH FOR APPROX. 3½ HRS.) AND A PAYLOAD OF 683 LBS.

THE SALMSON 2A2 WAS DESIGNED AROUND IT'S POWER PLANT. IT WAS A WATER COOLED 9-CYL. RADIAL DEVELOPING 260 H.P. AT 1600 R.P.M. FROM A CU. IN. DISP. OF 1146. THE SALMSON Z-9 ENGINE INSTALLATION WAS UNIQUE IN HAVING AN EXHAUST COLLECTOR RING SERVING AS NOSE FAIRING. THE RADIATOR WAS INBOARD OF THE RING AND DIRECTLY AFT OF THE SHUTTERS.

BELOW - FUSELAGE MARKINGS OF SHIPS #5433 AND #5464 OF THE 1ST CORPS. OBS. SQDN.

ABOVE - RT. FUSELAGE VIEW OF #5223 OF THE 24TH ARMY OBS. SQDN.

BOTTOM OF NOSE COWLING ALUM. LANDING GEAR STRUTS (1) IN COLOR.

SECTION C-C

SECTION D-D

SECT. E-E

SECTION A-A

SECTION B-B

FRONT, TOP, AND LEFT SIDE VIEWS ARE OF #1060. (91ST ARMY OBS. SQDN.)

~ COLOR KEY ~

THE SALMSON 2A2'S, LIKE THE Me. 28'S, USED A FACTORY PATTERN OF CAMOUFLAGE, i.e. ALL CAMOUFLAGED SHIPS HAD THE SAME PATTERN. THERE WERE THREE COLORS USED AND PHOTO SOURCES INDICATE THAT THE AREAS ON THESE DRAWINGS MARKED (1) WERE LIGHT EARTH BROWN, (2) DULLED LIGHT GREEN, AND (3) DULLED DARK GREEN. SOME FRENCH SHIPS WERE FINISHED THROUGHOUT IN PALE GRAY. ALL WERE CLEAR DOPED ON THE UNDERNEATH SIDES. METAL COWLING FORWARD OF THE REAR COCKPIT WAS NORMALLY (3) IN COLOR.

1917-1918 *Salmson 2A2* OBSERVATION AND DAY BOMBER MFGD. BY *Societe des Moteurs Salmson* of *Billancourt (Seine)*

TWICE SCALE "LIFT HERE"

POSER ou LEVER "ici"

S.A.L.2A2 No 5223 P.C.200

S.A.L.2A2 No 1060 P.C.200

PLATE 1 OF 2   DRAWN BY R. Anderson

12-61

92

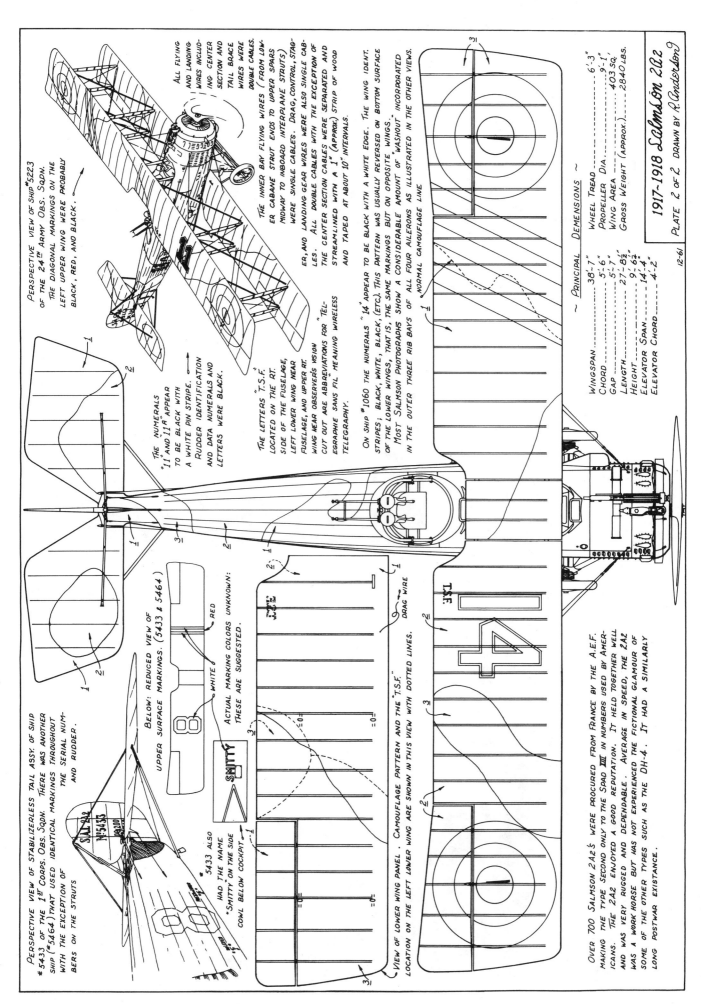

PERSPECTIVE VIEW OF SHIP #5223 OF THE 24TH ARMY OBS. SQDN. THE DIAGONAL MARKINGS ON THE LEFT UPPER WING WERE PROBABLY BLACK, RED, AND BLACK.

ALL FLYING AND LANDING WIRES INCLUDING CENTER SECTION AND TAIL BRACE WIRES WERE DOUBLE CABLES.

THE INNER BAY FLYING WIRES (FROM LOWER CABANE STRUT ENDS TO UPPER SPARS MIDWAY TO INBOARD INTERPLANE STRUTS) WERE SINGLE CABLES. DRAG, CONTROL, STAGGER, AND LANDING GEAR WIRES WERE ALSO SINGLE CABLES. ALL DOUBLE CABLES WITH THE EXCEPTION OF THE CENTER SECTION CABLES WERE SEPARATED AND STREAMLINED WITH A 1" (APPROX.) STRIP OF WOOD AND TAPED AT ABOUT 10" INTERVALS.

PERSPECTIVE VIEW OF STABILIZERLESS TAIL ASSY. OF SHIP #5433 OF THE 1ST CORPS. OBS. SQDN. THERE WAS ANOTHER SHIP (#5464) THAT USED IDENTICAL MARKINGS THROUGHOUT WITH THE EXCEPTION OF THE SERIAL NUMBERS AND RUDDER.

THE NUMERALS "11" AND "11A" APPEAR TO BE BLACK WITH A WHITE PIN STRIPE. RUDDER IDENTIFICATION AND DATA NUMERALS AND LETTERS WERE BLACK.

THE LETTERS T.S.F. LOCATED ON THE RT. SIDE OF THE FUSELAGE, LEFT LOWER WING NEAR FUSELAGE, AND UPPER RT. WING NEAR OBSERVERS VISION CUT OUT ARE ABBREVIATIONS FOR "TÉLÉGRAPHIE SANS FIL MEANING WIRELESS TELEGRAPHY.

ON SHIP #1060 THE NUMERALS "14" APPEAR TO BE BLACK WITH A WHITE EDGE. THE WING IDENT. STRIPES; BLACK, WHITE, BLACK, (ETC.) THIS PATTERN WAS USUALLY REVERSED ON BOTTOM SURFACE OF THE LOWER WINGS, THAT IS, THE SAME MARKINGS BUT ON OPPOSITE WINGS. MOST SALMSON PHOTOGRAPHS SHOW A CONSIDERABLE AMOUNT OF "WASHOUT" INCORPORATED IN THE OUTER THREE RIB BAYS OF ALL FOUR AILERONS AS ILLUSTRATED IN THE OTHER VIEWS.

NORMAL CAMOUFLAGE LINE

BELOW: REDUCED VIEW OF UPPER SURFACE MARKINGS. (5433 & 5464)

ACTUAL MARKING COLORS UNKNOWN: THESE ARE SUGGESTED.

RED
WHITE
SMITTY

*5433 ALSO HAD THE NAME "SMITTY ON THE SIDE COWL BELOW COCKPIT.

VIEW OF LOWER WING PANEL. CAMOUFLAGE PATTERN AND THE "T.S.F. LOCATION ON THE LEFT LOWER WING ARE SHOWN IN THIS VIEW WITH DOTTED LINES.

T.S.F.

DRAG WIRE

14

~ PRINCIPAL DIMENSIONS ~

WINGSPAN ————— 38'-7"
CHORD ————— 5'-6"
GAP ————— 5'-7"
LENGTH ————— 27-8½
HEIGHT ————— 9'-6½
ELEVATOR SPAN ————— 14'-4"
ELEVATOR CHORD ————— 4'-2"

WHEEL TREAD ————— 6'-3"
PROPELLER DIA. ————— 9'-1"
WING AREA ————— 403 SQ.
GROSS WEIGHT (APPROX.)——— 2840 LBS.

1917~1918 Salmson 2A2
PLATE 2 of 2   DRAWN BY R. Anderson

12-61

OVER 700 SALMSON 2A2's WERE PROCURED FROM FRANCE BY THE A.E.F. MAKING THE TYPE SECOND ONLY TO THE SPAD XIII IN NUMBERS USED BY AMERICANS. THE 2A2 ENJOYED A GOOD REPUTATION. IT HELD TOGETHER WELL AND WAS VERY RUGGED AND DEPENDABLE. AVERAGE IN SPEED, THE 2A2 WAS A WORK HORSE BUT HAS NOT EXPERIENCED THE FICTIONAL GLAMOUR OF SOME OF THE OTHER TYPES SUCH AS THE DH-4. IT HAD A SIMILARLY LONG POSTWAR EXISTANCE.

Siemens-Schuckert

D.IV

drawings by WILLIAM WYLAM

As a FIGHTING machine, the SS D.IV was as potent as anything developed by the warring nations of WW I. By skillful and sometimes ingenious methods, Siemens engineers produced an airplane weighing no more than its predecessor, the D.III, but with a reduced wing area and a much higher combat performance, mostly due to a new engine, the 200-hp Siemens Halske SH.IIIa. Many experts believe that without this engine the D.IV would have been just another airplane. The engine was unique among rotaries in that the crankshaft revolved in one direction and the cylinders and crankcase revolved in the opposite direction, thus giving an equivalent engine speed of 1,800 rpm with a propeller speed of 900 rpm, a direct 2-1 reduction. This feature allowed the use of a huge four-bladed propeller that was streamlined with a spun aluminum spinner.

From the pilot's standpoint, the Siemens-Schuckert D.IV was an excellent airplane in which to go to war. Its ability to climb rapidly at high altitudes where other aircraft were sluggish was one of its best attributes. It was easily controlled

Utilizing a rotary engine and a huge reverse rotating propeller, the D.IV could out-climb its adversaries.

and very responsive, although according to pilot reports it had a nasty stall.

Because it was produced in the last stages of WW I, it was too late arriving to have much influence over the fate of the Germans.

An Albatros-built experimental model with long wings for high-altitude flight is stored in Poland. □

Profile view of the D.IV shows the stubbiness of the design, almost bulldog-like. "Jane's All the World's Aircraft" photos.

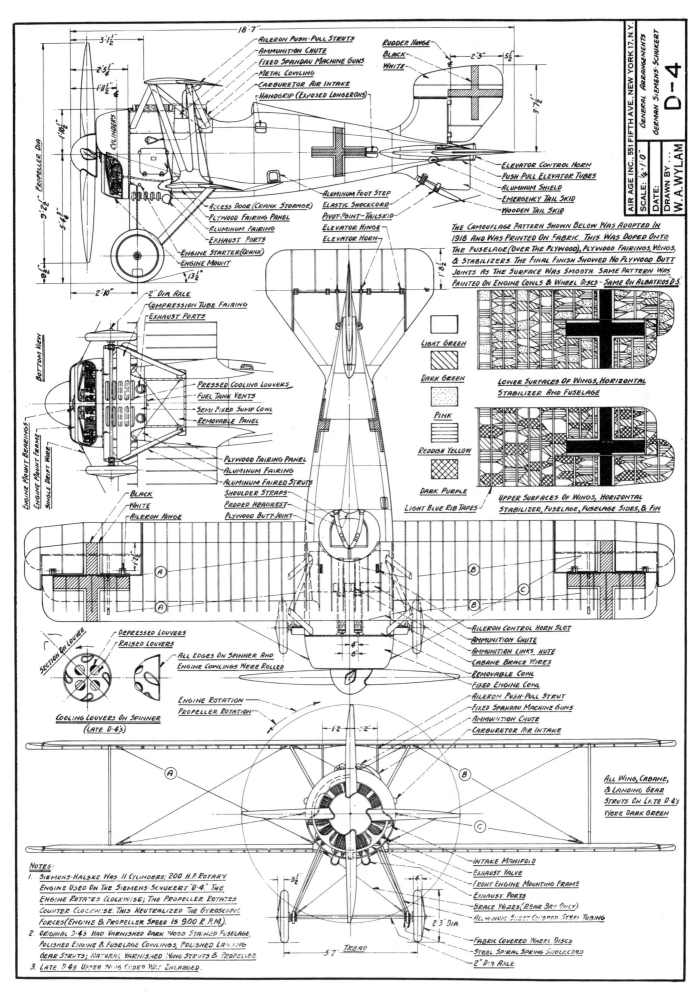

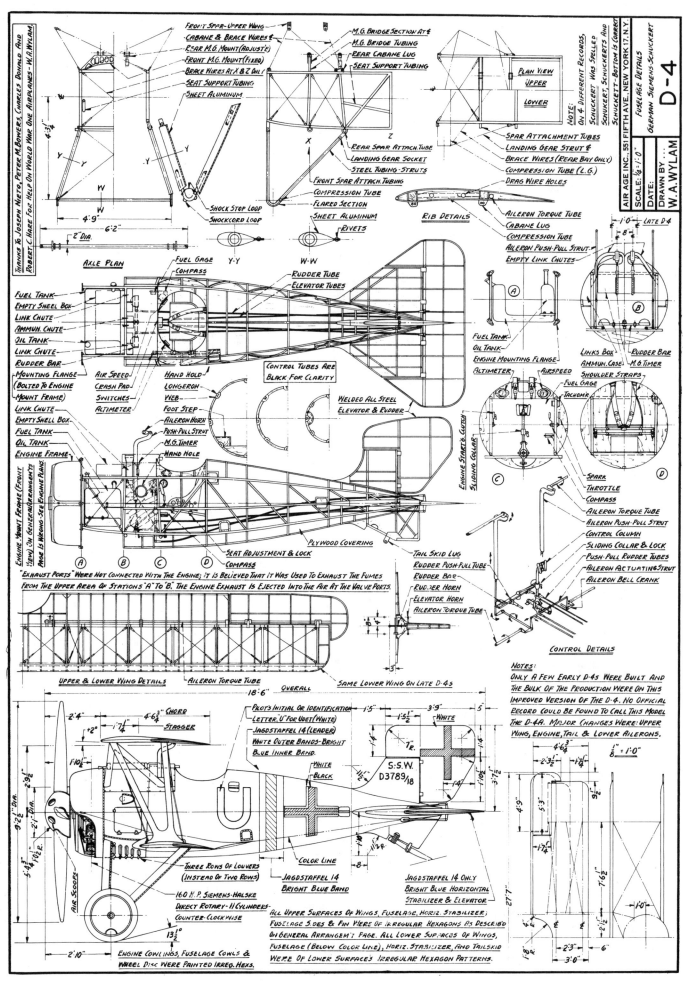

THANKS TO JOSEPH NIETO, PETER M. BOWERS, CHARLES DONALD AND
ROBERT C. HARE FOR HELP ON WORLD WAR ONE AIRPLANES.—W. R. WYLAM

FRONT SPAR-UPPER WING
CABANE & BRACE WIRES
REAR M.G. MOUNT (ADJUST)
FRONT M.G. MOUNT (FIXED)
BRAKE WIRES AT X & Z ONLY
SEAT SUPPORT TUBING
SHEET ALUMINUM

M.G. BRIDGE SECTION AT ℄
M.G. BRIDGE TUBING
REAR CABANE LUG
SEAT SUPPORT TUBING

NOTE:
ON 4 DIFFERENT RECORDS, SCHUCKERT WAS SPELLED SCHUCKERT, SCHUCKERTS AND SCHUCKETT—BOTTOM IS CORRECT

PLAN VIEW
UPPER
LOWER

AIR AGE INC., 551 FIFTH AVE., NEW YORK 17, N.Y.
SCALE: ¼=1'-0"
DATE:
DRAWN BY ...
W. A. WYLAM

FUSELAGE DETAILS
GERMAN SIEMENS-SCHUCKERT

D-4

REAR SPAR ATTACH. TUBE
LANDING GEAR SOCKET
STEEL TUBING-STRUTS
FRONT SPAR ATTACH. TUBING
COMPRESSION TUBE
FLARED SECTION
SHEET ALUMINUM
RIVETS

SPAR ATTACHMENT TUBES
LANDING GEAR STRUT ℄
BRACE WIRES (REAR BAY ONLY)
COMPRESSION TUBE (L.G.)
DRAG WIRE HOLES

SHOCK STOP LOOP
SHOCKCORD LOOP

RIB DETAILS

AILERON TORQUE TUBE
CABANE LUG
COMPRESSION TUBE
AILERON PUSH-PULL STRUT
EMPTY LINK CHUTES

LATE D-4

AXLE PLAN
2" DIA.
2'2"
6'2"
4'9"
4'3½"
Y-Y
W·W

FUEL GAGE
COMPASS

RUDDER TUBE
ELEVATOR TUBES

FUEL TANK
EMPTY SHELL BOX
LINK CHUTE
AMMUN. CHUTE
OIL TANK
LINK CHUTE
RUDDER BAR
MOUNTING FLANGE
(BOLTED TO ENGINE
MOUNT FRAME)
LINK CHUTE
EMPTY SHELL BOX
FUEL TANK
OIL TANK
ENGINE FRAME

AIR SPEED
CRASH PAD
SWITCHES
ALTIMETER

HAND HOLD
LONGERON
WEB
FOOT STEP
AILERON HORN
PUSH-PULL STRUT
M.G. TIMER
HAND HOLE

CONTROL TUBES ARE
BLACK FOR CLARITY

WELDED ALL STEEL
ELEVATOR & RUDDER

FUEL TANK
OIL TANK
ENGINE MOUNTING FLANGE
ALTIMETER

ALTIMETER
AIRSPEED

LINKS BOX
AMMUN. CASE

RUDDER BAR
M.G. TIMER
SHOULDER STRAPS
FUEL GAGE
TACHOMTR.

ENGINE STRUT & CLUTCH
SLIDING COLLAR

Ⓐ
Ⓑ
Ⓒ
Ⓓ

SPARK
THROTTLE
COMPASS
AILERON TORQUE TUBE
AILERON PUSH-PULL STRUT
CONTROL COLUMN
SLIDING COLLAR & LOCK
PUSH-PULL RUDDER TUBES
AILERON ACTUATING STRUT
AILERON BELL CRANK

ENGINE MOUNT FRAME (FRONT VIEW) ON GENERAL ARRANGEM'TS
PAGE IS WRONG—SEE ENGINE PLANS

PLYWOOD COVERING
SEAT ADJUSTMENT & LOCK
COMPASS

TAIL SKID LUG
RUDDER PUSH-PULL TUBE
RUDDER BAR
RUDDER HORN
ELEVATOR HORN
AILERON TORQUE TUBE

CONTROL DETAILS

"EXHAUST PORTS" WERE NOT CONNECTED WITH THE ENGINE; IT IS BELIEVED THAT IT WAS USED TO EXHAUST THE FUMES
FROM THE UPPER AREA OF STATIONS "A" TO "B". THE ENGINE EXHAUST IS EJECTED INTO THE AIR AT THE VALVE PORTS.

NOTES:
ONLY A FEW EARLY D-4s WERE BUILT AND
THE BULK OF THE PRODUCTION WERE ON THIS
IMPROVED VERSION OF THE D-4. NO OFFICIAL
RECORD COULD BE FOUND TO CALL THIS MODEL
THE D-4A. MAJOR CHANGES WERE: UPPER
WING, ENGINE, TAIL & LOWER AILERONS.

UPPER & LOWER WING DETAILS
AILERON TORQUE TUBE
SAME LOWER WING ON LATE D-4s

18'6" OVERALL

2'4"
4'6¾" CHORD
STAGGER
+2°
1'4½"
1'10½"
9'2½" DIA.
2'1" DIA.
5'4¾"
1'0½" R.

PILOT'S INITIAL OR IDENTIFICATION
LETTER, "U" FOR UDET (WHITE)
JAGDSTAFFEL 14 (LEADER)
WHITE OUTER BANDS-BRIGHT
BLUE INNER BAND.

WHITE
BLACK

1'5"
1'5½"
3'9"
5
WHITE
7 R.

S.S.W.
D3789/18

1'4

3'1½"
1'10½"

COLOR LINE
8

THREE ROWS OF LOUVERS
(INSTEAD OF TWO ROWS)
AIR SCOOPS

JAGDSTAFFEL 14
BRIGHT BLUE BAND

JAGDSTAFFEL 14 ONLY
BRIGHT BLUE HORIZONTAL
STABILIZER & ELEVATOR

160 H.P. SIEMENS-HALSKE
DIRECT ROTARY-11 CYLINDERS-
COUNTER-CLOCKWISE

13½°
2'10"

4'6¾"
2'3½"
1'7½"
⅛"=1'-0"
4'9"
5'3"
1'7¼"
9½"
7'6½"
27'7"
1'0"
2'3"
3'6"
1'8"

ENGINE COWLINGS, FUSELAGE COWLS &
WHEEL DISC WERE PAINTED IRREG. HEXS.

ALL UPPER SURFACES OF WINGS, FUSELAGE, HORIZ. STABILIZER,
FUSELAGE SIDES & FIN WERE OF IRREGULAR HEXAGONS AS DESCRIB'D
ON GENERAL ARRANGEM'T PAGE. ALL LOWER SURFACES OF WINGS,
FUSELAGE (BELOW COLOR LINE), HORIZ. STABILIZER, AND TAILSKID
WERE OF LOWER SURFACE'S IRREGULAR HEXAGON PATTERNS.

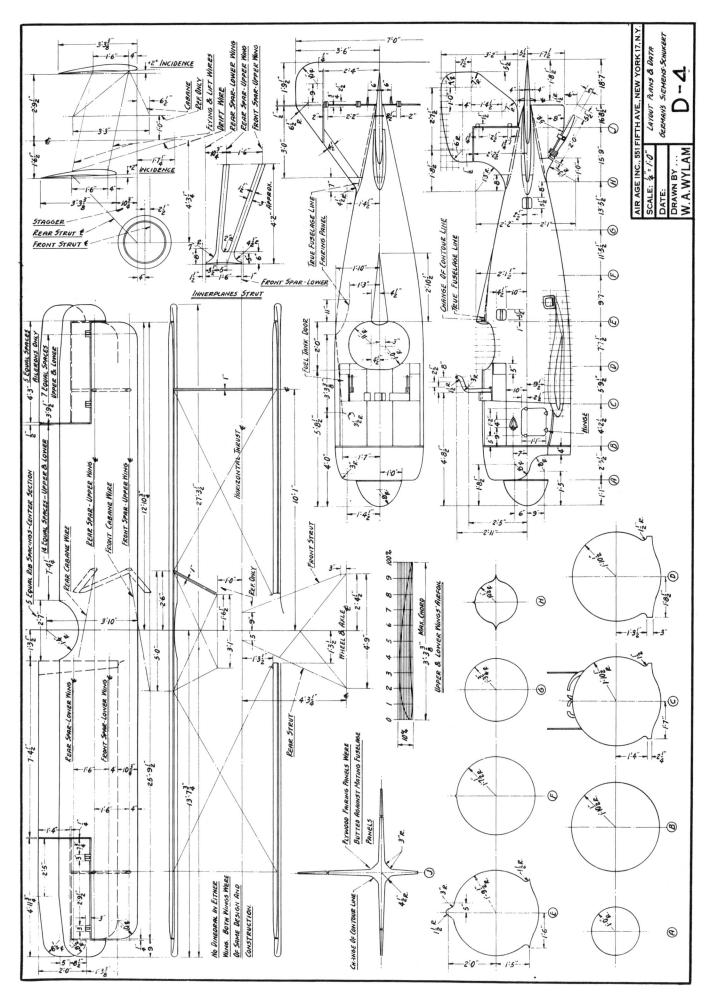

AIR AGE INC., 551 FIFTH AVE., NEW YORK 17, N.Y.

LAYOUT PLANS & DATA

GERMAN'S SIEMENS-SCHUKERT

D-4

SCALE: ½"=1'-0"

DATE:

DRAWN BY .... W. A. WYLAM

Sopwith Camel

drawings by WILLIAM WYLAM

THE SOPWITH Camel was the most widely and most numerously produced aircraft of WW I. A total of 5,490 Camels were constructed by at least nine manufacturers and the design was considered to be one of the best dog fighters of the 1914-1918 conflict. The Camel was responsible for the destruction of more German aircraft than any other design and was the first British aircraft designed for two forward-firing machine guns. Two versions, the F.1 and the 2F.1, were produced, the latter for the Royal Navy with shorter wings, smaller tail surfaces, and a larger engine. It changed the course of Naval aviation. Needing a weapon to counter the activities of German dirigibles that had previously exercised surveillance of British Naval activities without jeopardy, the Camel was to become the first successful attempt to counter the high-flying Germans. On August 11, 1918, Sub-Lieutenant Stuart D. Culley, an American-born member of the British Royal Air Force, took off from a platform in tow by a British destroyer and climbed to 18,000 feet in pursuit of the German dirigible L.53.

Finding the dirigible in his sights at 19,000 feet, Culley's Camel staggered and strained to maintain flight as he emptied his guns upward and directly at the dirigible. The L.53 seemed unaffected until suddenly it burst into flames and dropped into the sea. This was the first aerial victory by a shipboard aircraft.

Culley's Camel is now exhibited at London's Imperial War Museum: there are five other Camels in other museums. □

The Sopwith Camel was produced in large quantities during WW I. Air Age file photo.

Responsible for the destruction of more German aircraft than any other Allied design, the Sopwith Camel was also adapted for use by the Royal Navy. Photo courtesy of Leonard Opdycke, WW I Aeroplanes.

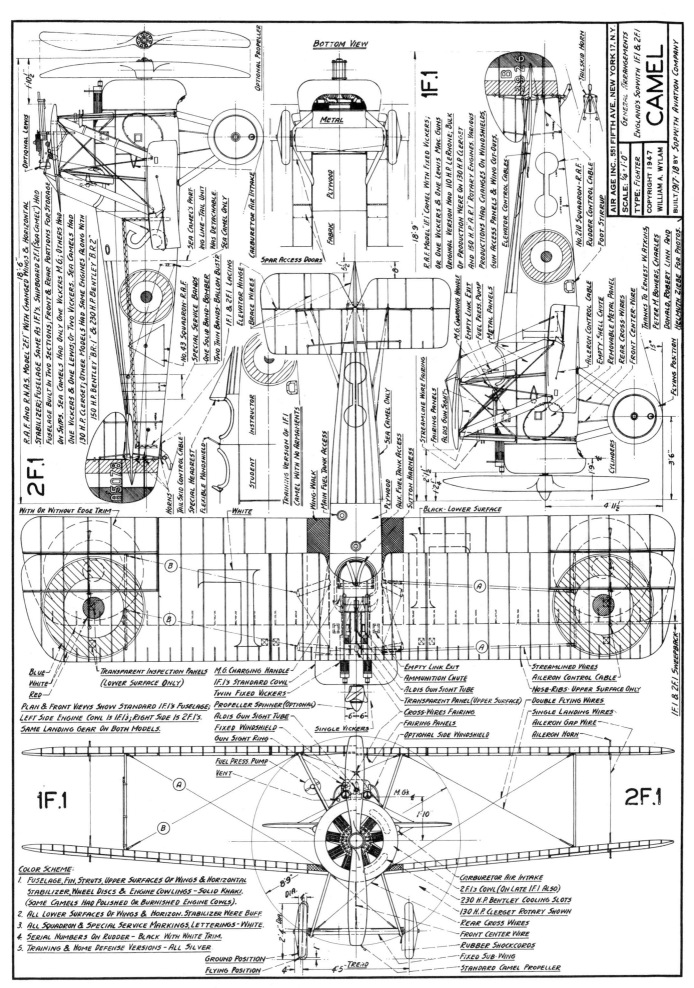

CAMEL

General Arrangements

England's Sopwith 1F.1 & 2F.1

Air Age Inc., 551 Fifth Ave., New York 17, N.Y.

Scale: 1/8" = 1'-0"

Type: Fighter

Copyright 1947

William A. Wylam

Built 1917-18 by Sopwith Aviation Company

Bottom View

1F.1

Metal
Plywood
Fabric

Spar Access Doors

2F.1

Color Scheme:
1. Fuselage, Fin, Struts, Upper Surfaces Of Wings & Horizontal Stabilizer, Wheel Discs & Engine Cowlings - Solid Khaki. (Some Camels Had Polished Or Burnished Engine Cowls).
2. All Lower Surfaces Of Wings & Horizon. Stabilizer Were Buff.
3. All Squadron & Special Service Markings, Letterings - White.
4. Serial Numbers On Rudder - Black With White Trim.
5. Training & Home Defense Versions - All Silver.

1F.1

2F.1

Thanks To Ernest W. Atkins, Peter M. Bowers, Charles Donald, Robert Linn And Helmuth Ziebe For Photos.

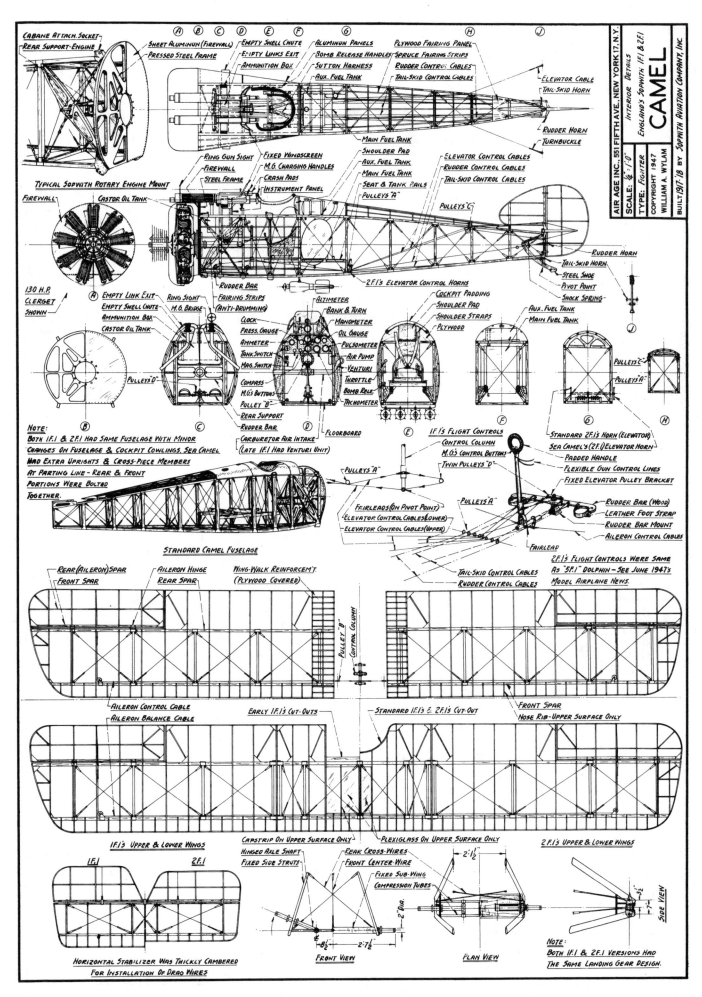

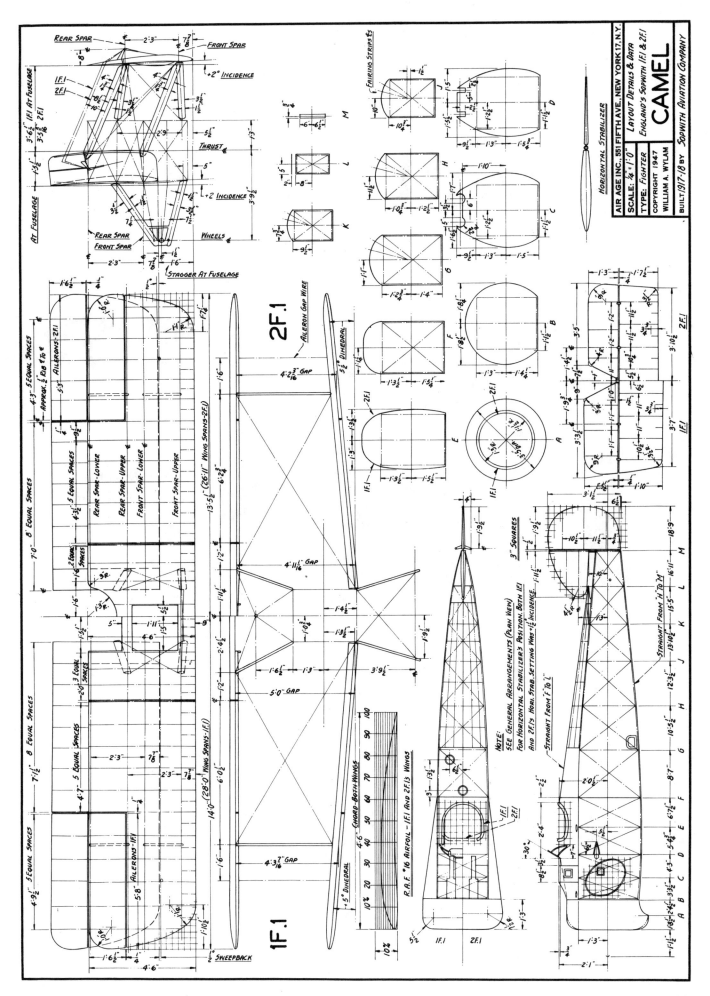

HORIZONTAL STABILIZER

AIR AGE INC., 551 FIFTH AVE. NEW YORK 17, N.Y.

ENGLAND'S SOPWITH IF.1 & 2F.1
LAYOUT DETAILS & DATA

SCALE: ¼ = 1'-0"
TYPE: FIGHTER
COPYRIGHT 1947
WILLIAM A. WYLAM
BUILT 1917-18 BY

CAMEL

SOPWITH AVIATION COMPANY

NOTE:
SEE GENERAL STABILIZER ARRANGEMENTS (PLAN VIEW)
FOR HORIZONTAL STABILIZER'S POSITION. BOTH IF.1
AND 2F.1'S HORZ. STAB. SETTING WAS 1½° INCIDENCE.

R.A.F. "16 AIRFOIL – IF.1 AND 2F.1'S WINGS
CHORD–BOTH WINGS

3" SQUARES

STRAIGHT FROM "H" TO "M"
STRAIGHT FROM "F" TO "L"

IF.1   2F.1

Sopwith Dolphin 5F.1

drawings by WILLIAM WYLAM

THE DESIGN of the Dolphin began as a scratch-pad doodle in the engineering rooms of Sopwith Aviation during the summer of 1916. The doodling engineers pointed with pride at their thumbnail sketches of what might be, if only a 190-hp water-cooled engine were available.

Then, like a bolt from the blue, word came that Wolseley Motors had obtained a license from Hispano-Suiza to manufacture their new 200-hp geared engine. With the promise of an appropriate powerplant, the doodle soon became an engineering project and the forces of Sopwith immediately went to work on Model 5F.1. It was nicknamed "Dolphin" in accordance with Sopwith's custom of naming their products after animals, fish, or fowl.

In performance, the production Dolphins left little to be desired for a 1918 service type. The first operational models officially weighed in at 1,406 pounds empty and grossed 1,881 pounds. Fuel, weighing 194 pounds and sufficient for a 230-mile range, was included in this gross figure. The top speed was 136 mph at sea level and it had a landing speed of 40 mph.

As an all-around single-seater, the Dolphin exceeded anything the British manufacturers were able to put out in squadron quantities before WW I ended. Other types perhaps bettered it in specific items of performance, but as a package the 5F.1 was hard to beat. It possessed enough good characteristics that a 300-hp version was built and tested for production in 1919 and which the U.S. and French air services were contracting at the time of the Armistice.

One Dolphin lives in the RAF Museum in London.   □

Conceived in 1916 as an answer to Allied air squadrons' requirements for air superiority, the Sopwith Dolphin 5F.1 was slow in coming and hardly fulfilled its combat credentials. Air Age file photo.

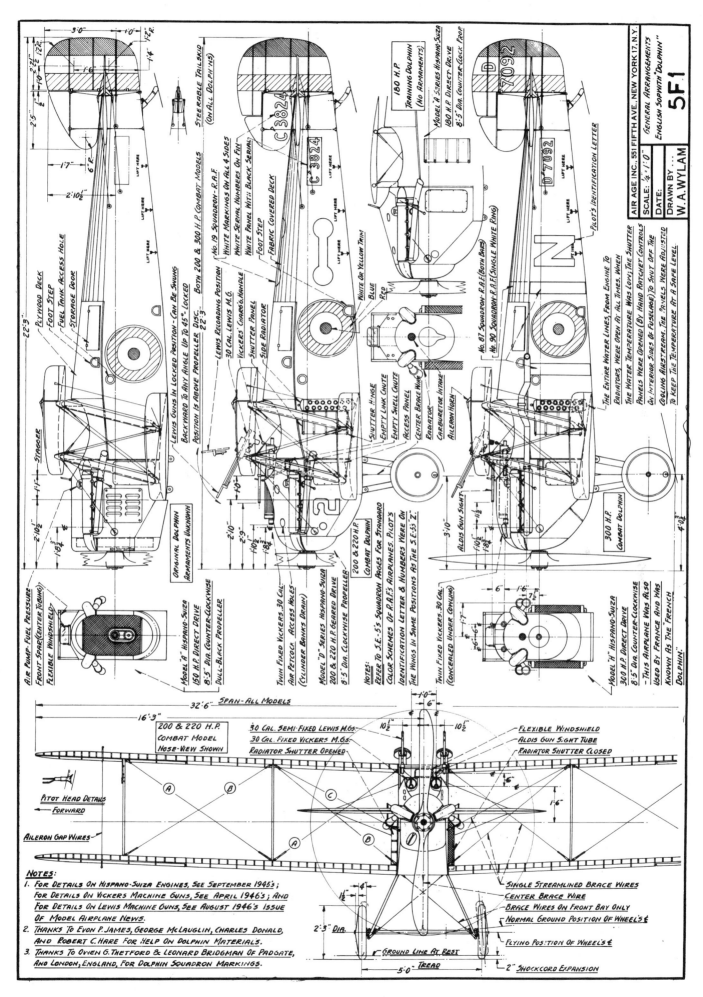

General Arrangements
English Sopwith "Dolphin"
5F1

AIR AGE INC., 551 FIFTH AVE., NEW YORK 17, N.Y.

SCALE: ¼" = 1'-0"

DATE:

DRAWN BY ...
W. A. WYLAM

180 H.P.
TRAINING DOLPHIN
(NO ARMAMENTS)

MODEL "A" SERIES HISPANO-SUIZA
180 H.P. DIRECT-DRIVE
8'-5" DIA. COUNTER-CLOCK. PROP.

PLYWOOD DECK
FOOT STEP
FUEL TANK ACCESS HOLE
STORAGE DOOR

LEWIS GUNS IN LOCKED POSITION - CAN BE SWUNG
BACKWARD TO ANY ANGLE UP TO 45° LOCKED
POSITION IS ABOVE PROPELLER DISC. 22'-3"

STEERABLE TAILSKID
(ON ALL DOLPH.'N'S)

BOTH 200 & 300 H.P. COMBAT MODELS

No. 19 SQUADRON - R.A.F.
WHITE MARKINGS ON ALL 4 SIDES
WHITE SERIAL NUMBERS ON FIN
WHITE PANEL WITH BLACK SERIAL
FOOT STEP
FABRIC COVERED DECK

LEWIS RELOADING POSITION
30 CAL. LEWIS M.G.
VICKERS' CHARG'G. HANDLE
SHUTTER PANEL
SIDE RADIATOR

SHUTTER HINGE
EMPTY LINK CHUTE
EMPTY SHELL CHUTE
ACCESS PANEL
CENTER BRACE WIRE
RADIATOR
CARBURETOR INTAKE
AILERON HORN

WHITE OR YELLOW TRIM
BLUE
RED

No. 87 SQUADRON - R.A.F. (BOTH BARS)
No. 90 SQUADRON - R.A.F. SINGLE WHITE RING

PILOT'S IDENTIFICATION LETTER

MODEL "A" SERIES HISPANO-SUIZA
300 H.P. DIRECT-DRIVE
8'-5" DIA. COUNTER-CLOCK. PROP.

ALDIS GUN SIGHT

300 H.P.
COMBAT DOLPHIN

22'-3"

STAGGER

ORIGINAL DOLPHIN
ARMAMENTS UNKNOWN

AIR PUMP- FUEL PRESSURE
FRONT SPAR (CENTER TUBING)
FLEXIBLE WINDSHIELD

MODEL "A" HISPANO-SUIZA
180 H.P. DIRECT-DRIVE
8'-5" DIA. COUNTER-CLOCKWISE
DULL-BLACK PROPELLER

TWIN FIXED VICKERS 30 CAL.
AIR PETCOCK ACCESS HOLES
(CYLINDER BANKS DRAIN)

MODEL "D" SERIES HISPANO-SUIZA
200 & 220 H.P. GEARED DRIVE
8'-5" DIA. CLOCKWISE PROPELLER

200 & 220 H.P.
COMBAT DOLPHIN

NOTES:
REFER TO S.E.-5's SQUADRON
COLOR SCHEMES OF R.A.F.'S AIRPLANES. PILOT'S
IDENTIFICATION LETTER & NUMBERS WERE ON
THE WINGS IN SAME POSITIONS AS THE S.E.-55 'Z'.

TWIN FIXED VICKERS 30 CAL.
(CONCEALED UNDER COWLING)

MODEL "H" HISPANO-SUIZA
300 H.P. DIRECT-DRIVE
8'-5" DIA. COUNTER-CLOCKWISE
- THIS AIRPLANE WAS ALSO
USED BY FRANCE AND HAS
KNOWN AS THE FRENCH
DOLPHIN.

THE ENTIRE WATER LINES, FROM ENGINE TO
RADIATORS, WERE OPEN AT ALL TIMES. WHEN
THE WATER TEMPERATURE WAS LOW, THE SHUTTER
PANELS WERE OPENED (BY HAND RATCHET CONTROLS
ON INTERIOR SIDES OF FUSELAGE) TO SHUT OFF THE
COOLING AIRSTREAM. THE PANELS WERE ADJUSTED
TO KEEP THE TEMPERATURE AT A SAFE LEVEL.

32'-6"   SPAN - ALL MODELS
16'-3"

200 & 220 H.P.
COMBAT MODEL
NOSE-VIEW SHOWN

30 CAL. SEMI-FIXED LEWIS M.G's.
30 CAL. FIXED VICKERS M.G's.
RADIATOR SHUTTER OPENED

FLEXIBLE WINDSHIELD
ALDIS GUN SIGHT TUBE
RADIATOR SHUTTER CLOSED

PITOT HEAD DETAILS
FORWARD

AILERON GAP WIRES

SINGLE STREAMLINED BRACE WIRES
CENTER BRACE WIRE
BRACE WIRES ON FRONT BAY ONLY
NORMAL GROUND POSITION OF WHEEL'S ₵

FLYING POSITION OF WHEEL'S ₵

2'-3" DIA.

GROUND LINE AT REST
5'-0"   TREAD
2" SHOCKCORD EXPANSION

NOTES:
1. FOR DETAILS ON HISPANO-SUIZA ENGINES, SEE SEPTEMBER 1945's;
   FOR DETAILS ON VICKERS MACHINE GUNS, SEE APRIL 1946's; AND
   FOR DETAILS ON LEWIS MACHINE GUNS, SEE AUGUST 1946'S ISSUE
   OF MODEL AIRPLANE NEWS.
2. THANKS TO EVON P. JAMES, GEORGE McLAUGLIN, CHARLES DONALD,
   AND ROBERT C. HARE FOR HELP ON DOLPHIN MATERIALS.
3. THANKS TO OWEN G. THETFORD & LEONARD BRIDGMAN OF PADGATE,
   AND LONDON, ENGLAND, FOR DOLPHIN SQUADRON MARKINGS.

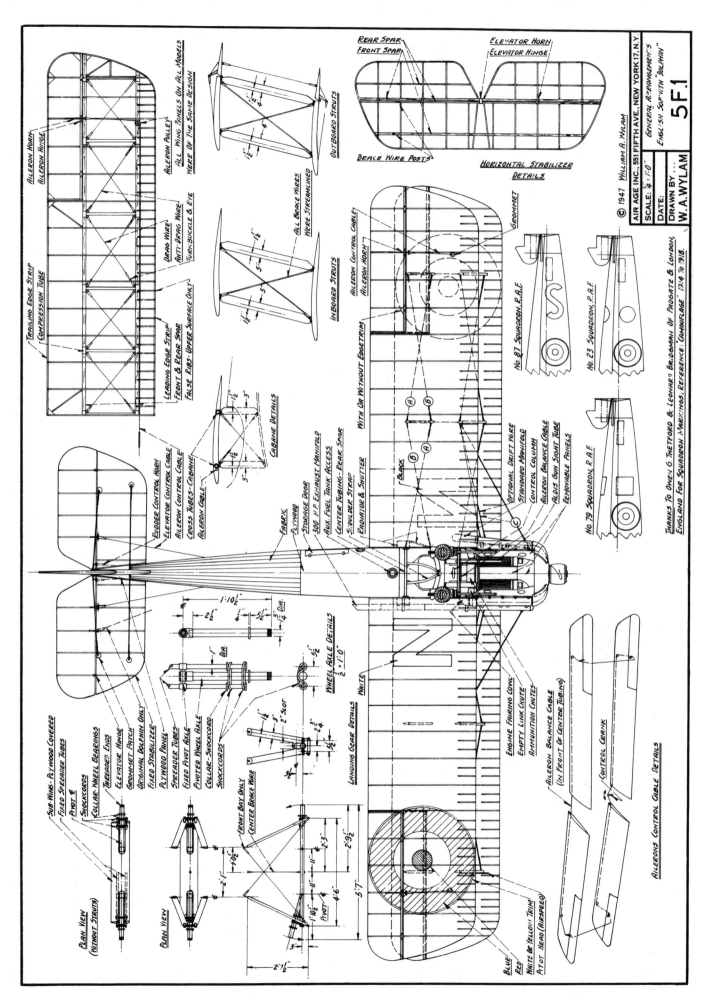

REAR SPAR
FRONT SPAR
ELEVATOR HORN
ELEVATOR HINGE

HORIZONTAL STABILIZER DETAILS

BRACE WIRE POSTS

ALL WING PANELS ON ALL MODELS WERE OF THE SAME DESIGN

ALERON PULLEY

OUTBOARD STRUTS

DRAG WIRE
ANTI-DRAG WIRE
TURN-BUCKLE & EYE

ALL BRACE WIRES WERE STREAMLINED

INBOARD STRUTS

CABANE DETAILS

GENERAL ARRANGEMENTS
ENGLISH SOPWITH "DOLPHIN"

5F.1

© 1947 AIR AGE INC., 551 FIFTH AVE., NEW YORK 17, N.Y.
SCALE: ¼" = 1'-0"
DATE:
DRAWN BY ...
W. A. WYLAM

No. 87 SQUADRON, R.A.F.
No. 23 SQUADRON, R.A.F.
No. 79 SQUADRON, R.A.F.

THANKS TO OWEN G. THETFORD & LEONARD BRIDGMAN OF PROGATE & LONDON, ENGLAND FOR SQUADRON MARKINGS. REFERENCE: CAMOUFLAGE: 1914 TO 1918.

TRAILING EDGE STRIP
COMPRESSION TUBE

ALERON HORN
ALERON HINGE

LEADING EDGE STRIP
FRONT & REAR SPAR
FALSE RIBS- UPPER SURFACE ONLY

RUDDER CONTROL HORN
ELEVATOR CONTROL CABLE
ALERON CONTROL CABLE
CROSS TUBES- CABANE
ALERON CABLE

GROMMET

ALERON CONTROL CABLE
ALERON HORN

WITH OR WITHOUT EDGE TRIM

FABRIC
PLYWOOD
STORAGE DOOR
300 H.P. EXHAUST MANIFOLD
AUX. FUEL TANK ACCESS
CENTER TUBING- REAR SPAR
SHOULDER STRAP
RADIATOR & SHUTTER

OPTIONAL DRIFT WIRE
STANDARD MANIFOLD
CONTROL COLUMN
ALERON BALANCE CABLE
ALDIS GUN SIGHT TUBE
REMOVABLE PANELS

BLACK

ENGINE FAIRING COWL
EMPTY LINK CHUTE
AMMUNITION CHUTES

WHITE

ALERON BALANCE CABLE
(IN FRONT OF CENTER TUBING)

CONTROL CRANK

SUB-WING- PLYWOOD COVERED
FIXED SPREADER TUBES
PIVOT ₵
SHOCKCORDS
COLLAR- WHEEL BEARINGS
THREADED ENDS
ELEVATOR HINGE
GROMMET PATCH
ORIGINAL DOLPHIN ONLY
FIXED STABILIZER
PLYWOOD PANEL
SPREADER TUBES
FIXED PIVOT AXLE
PIVOTED WHEEL AXLE
COLLAR- SHOCKCORD
SHOCKCORDS

1'-10½"
2½"
¼"
5½"
¾" DIA.

WHEEL AXLE DETAILS
½" = 1'-0"

½" DIA.

1"
3"
2" SLOT
2¾"

LANDING GEAR DETAILS

PLAN VIEW
(WITHOUT STRUTS)

PLAN VIEW

FRONT BAY ONLY
CENTER BRAKE WIRE

1'-10½"
2'-3"
2'-9½"
11"
11"
2'-1"
PIVOT ₵
4'-6"
5'-7"
3"
PIVOT ₵
2'-7½"

BLUE
RED
WHITE OR YELLOW TRIM
PITOT HEAD (AIRSPEED)

AILERONS CONTROL CABLE DETAILS

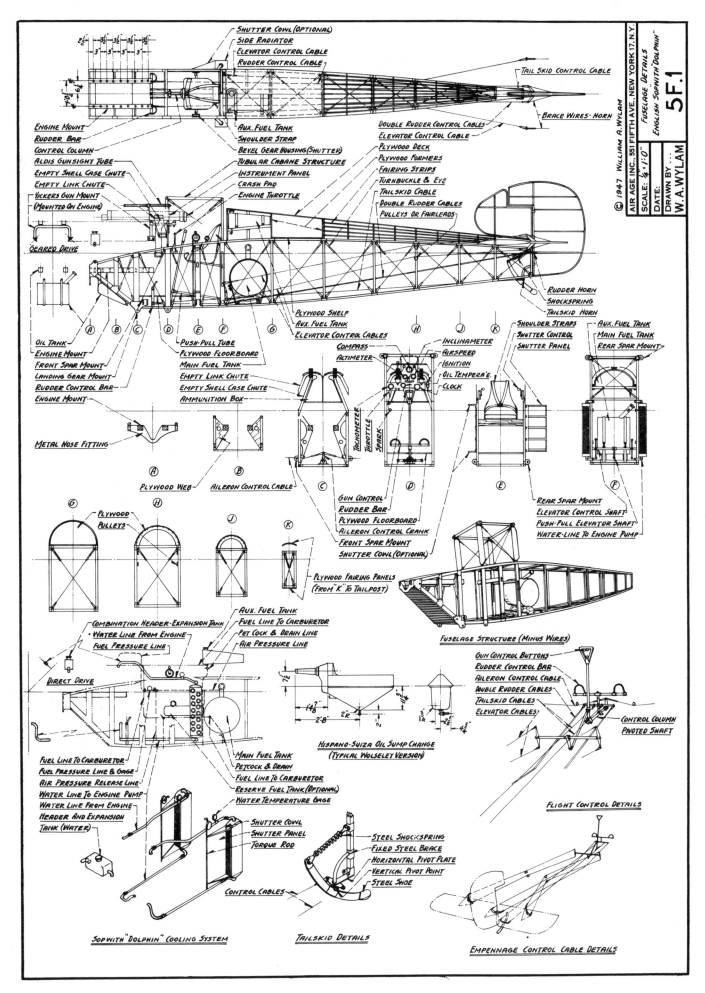

© 1947 — AIR AGE INC., 551 FIFTH AVE., NEW YORK 17, N.Y.

FUSELAGE DETAILS
ENGLISH SOPWITH "DOLPHIN"

SCALE: ¾"=1'-0"

DATE:

DRAWN BY ....
W. A. WYLAM

5F.1

Shutter Cowl (Optional)
Side Radiator
Elevator Control Cable
Rudder Control Cable
Tail Skid Control Cable
Brace Wires - Horn

Engine Mount
Rudder Bar
Control Column
Aldis Gunsight Tube
Empty Shell Case Chute
Empty Link Chute
Vickers Gun Mount
(Mounted On Engine)
Geared Drive

Aux. Fuel Tank
Shoulder Strap
Bevel Gear Housing (Shutter)
Tubular Cabane Structure
Instrument Panel
Crash Pad
Engine Throttle

Double Rudder Control Cables
Elevator Control Cable
Plywood Deck
Plywood Formers
Fairing Strips
Turnbuckle & Eye
Tailskid Cable
Double Rudder Cables
Pulleys Or Fairleads

Rudder Horn
Shockspring
Tailskid Horn

Oil Tank
Engine Mount
Front Spar Mount
Landing Gear Mount
Rudder Control Bar
Engine Mount

Metal Nose Fitting

Push-Pull Tube
Plywood Floorboard
Main Fuel Tank
Empty Link Chute
Empty Shell Case Chute
Ammunition Box

Plywood Shelf
Aux. Fuel Tank
Elevator Control Cables

Compass
Altimeter

Inclinameter
Airspeed
Ignition
Oil Tempera'e.
Clock

Shoulder Straps
Shutter Control
Shutter Panel

Aux. Fuel Tank
Main Fuel Tank
Rear Spar Mount

(A) (B) (C) (D) (E) (F) (G) (H) (J) (K)

Tachometer
Throttle
Spark

Gun Control
Rudder Bar
Plywood Floorboard
Aileron Control Crank
Front Spar Mount
Shutter Cowl (Optional)

Rear Spar Mount
Elevator Control Shaft
Push-Pull Elevator Shaft
Water-Line To Engine Pump

Plywood Web   Aileron Control Cable

(A)   (B)   (C)   (D)   (E)   (F)

(G)   (H)
Plywood
Pulleys

(J)   (K)

Plywood Fairing Panels
(From "K" To Tailpost)

Fuselage Structure (Minus Wires)

Combination Header-Expansion Tank
Water Line From Engine
Fuel Pressure Line

Aux. Fuel Tank
Fuel Line To Carburetor
Pet Cock & Drain Line
Air Pressure Line

Gun Control Buttons
Rudder Control Bar
Aileron Control Cable
Double Rudder Cables
Tailskid Cables
Elevator Cables

Direct Drive

Control Column
Pivoted Shaft

Fuel Line To Carburetor
Fuel Pressure Line & Gage
Air Pressure Release Line
Water Line To Engine Pump
Water Line From Engine
Header And Expansion
Tank (Water)

Main Fuel Tank
Petcock & Drain
Fuel Line To Carburetor
Reserve Fuel Tank (Optional)
Water Temperature Gage

Hispano-Suiza Oil Sump Change
(Typical Wolseley Version)

Flight Control Details

Shutter Cowl
Shutter Panel
Torque Rod

Control Cables

Steel Shockspring
Fixed Steel Brace
Horizontal Pivot Plate
Vertical Pivot Point
Steel Shoe

Sopwith "Dolphin" Cooling System

Tailskid Details

Empennage Control Cable Details

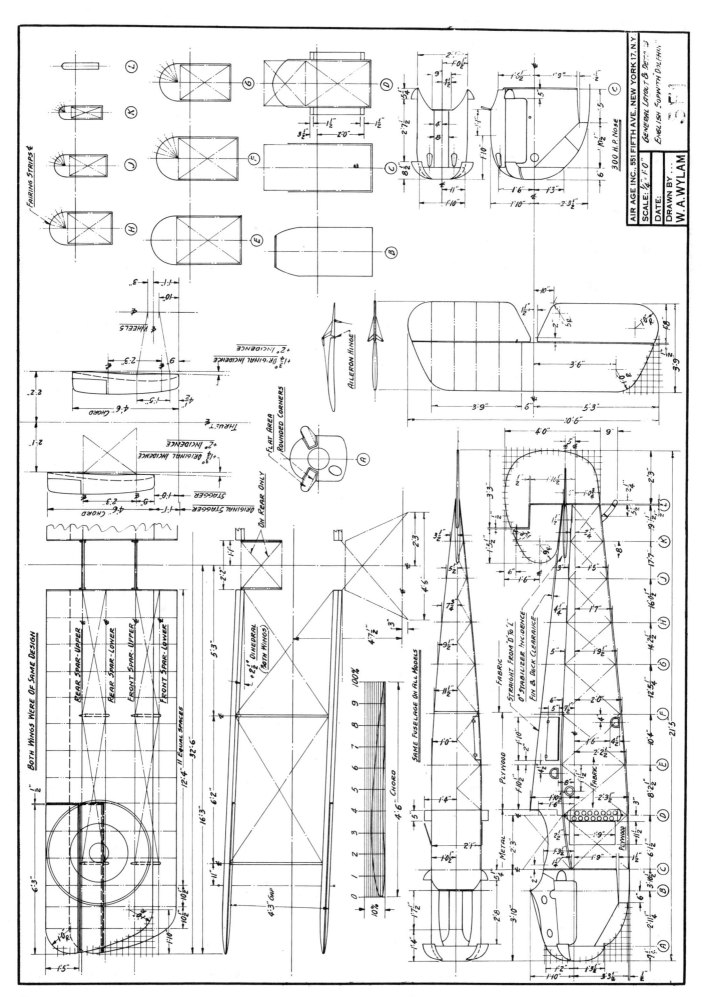

Sopwith Snipe 7F.1

drawings by JOSEPH NIETO

The Sopwith Snipe 7F.1 followed the successful Sopwith Camel and was used by the British until 1926. Air Age file photo.

INTRODUCED as a successor to the famous Sopwith Camel, the Snipe first reached the Western Front in September 1918. In the three months before the war's end it proved the best of the Allied fighters, though less than a hundred were in action. It was while flying a Snipe that Major W.G. Barker of No. 201 Squadron fought his celebrated single-handed engagement with 15 Fokker D.VIIs on October 27, 1918, for which he was awarded the Victorian Cross. The fuselage of Barker's aircraft is to be seen at the Canadian War Museum in Ottawa.

The prototype Snipe had single-bay wings. Photo courtesy of Leonard Opdycke, WW I Aeroplanes.

Of a wooden structure and fabric covering, the makers' designation of the aircraft was the Sopwith 7F.1. Powered by a Bentley B.R.2 engine that developed 230 hp, the Snipe was able to achieve a maximum speed of 121 mph at 10,000 feet and had a rate of climb of 970 fpm.

Due to financial stringencies applied to the British air services, the Snipe remained active with fighter squadrons until as late as 1926.

Four other Snipes can be seen in other museums. □

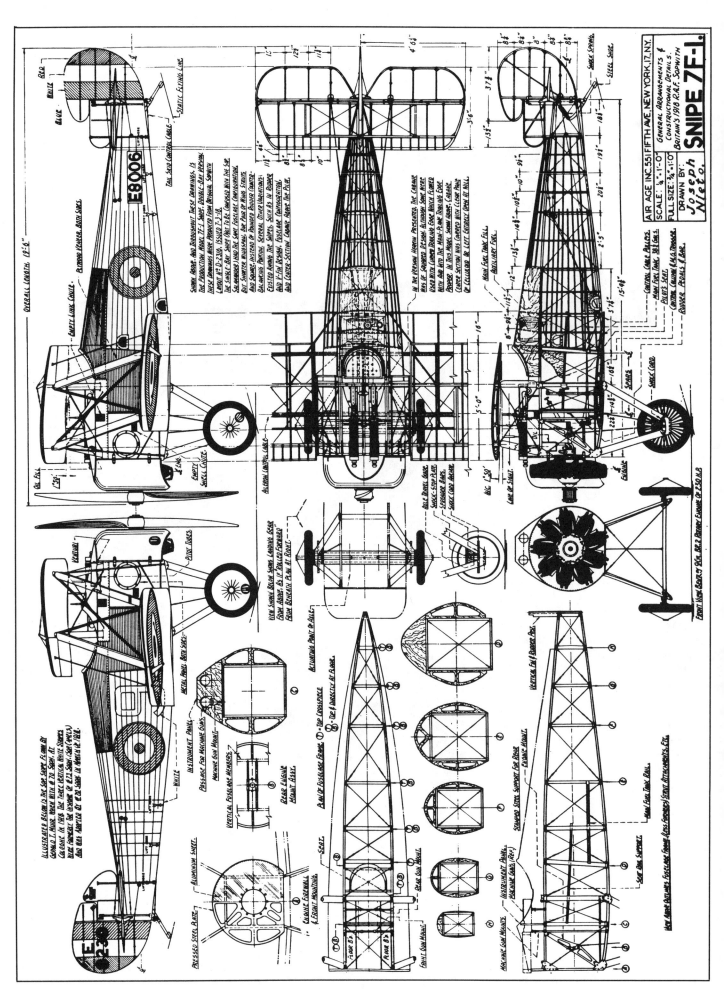

SNIPE 7F-1.
GENERAL ARRANGEMENTS &
CONSTRUCTIONAL DETAILS.
BRITAIN'S 1918 R.A.F. SOPWITH

AIR AGE INC. 551 FIFTH AVE. NEW YORK, 17, N.Y.
SCALE: ¼":1'-0"
FULL SIZE: ¾":1'-0"
DRAWN BY: Joseph Nieto.

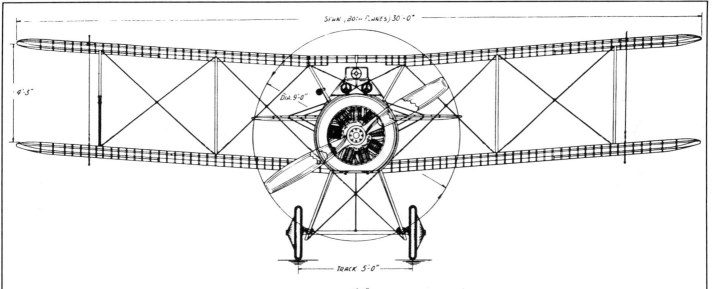

SPAN (BOTH PLANES) 30'-0"

DIA. 9'-0"

4'-3"

TRACK 5'-0"

9'2"

3'-6"

24"

CHORD 5'0" 16"

THE BRITISH SOPWITH "SNIPE" SINGLE SEATER FIGHTER TYPE 7F-1 OF 1918, WAS BUILT BY SOPWITH AVIATION CO. LTD., KINGSTON ON THAMES, ENGLAND, AND IS REPUTED TO HAVE BEEN THE BEST ALL-ROUND FIGHTING SCOUT PRODUCED BY ANY NATION DURING THE FIRST WORLD WAR. IN DEFINING IT'S APPROPRIATE NICKNAME, "TO SHOOT FROM A CONCEALED PLACE AT THOSE WHO BECOME DETACHED FROM A MAIN BODY OR FORCE". THE SNIPE WAS FIRST ATTACHED TO THE BRITISH R.F.C. FEB. 4, 1918, SERVING CONTINUOUSLY THROUGH NOV. 11, AND SUBSEQUENTLY CARRIED ON WITH R.A.F. FIGHTER SQUADRONS UNTIL THE MIDDLE TWENTIES. MASS PRODUCTION ON THE SNIPE WAS STARTED IN THE LATTER HALF OF 1918, AND BY DECEMBER OF THAT YEAR, 500 HAD BEEN BUILT. OF THAT NUMBER, 79 OF THEM WENT TO No. 43 SQDN. AT BOUINCOURT, IN SEPT. 1918, REPLACING CAMELS, No. 71 SQDN. (No. 4 AUSTRALIAN, A.F.C.) AT ENNETIERES, IN NOVEMBER, IN PLACE OF CAMELS, No. 81 SQDN. (ARRIVING AT THE WESTERN FRONT IN SEPT. 1918 WITH SNIPES) No. 201 & 208 (8 NAVAL) BOTH REPLACING BENTLEY CAMELS. PERHAPS THE MOST FAMED SNIPE WAS THAT FLOWN BY MAJOR W.G. BARKER, WHILE C.O. OF No. 201, WHICH REPLACED CAMELS WITH SNIPES IN SEPT. 1918. BARKER RECEIVED THE COVETED VICTORIA CROSS AFTER BEING ATTACKED BY 60 GERMAN PLANES, HE FOUGHT BACK, DOWNING 4 FOKKERS IN FLAMES AND PUT 10 OTHERS OUT OF CONTROL. HIS OFFICIAL RECORD FOR THE DAY WAS 4 VICTORIES, WHICH BROUGHT UP THE TOTAL TO 52. BARKER'S SNIPE WAS IDENTIFIED BY A SINGLE WHITE, VERTICAL BAR JUST AFT OF THE FUSELAGE COCKADE.) A SINGLE SNIPE SQUADRON ACCOUNTED FOR 36 ENEMY PLANES IN 4 DAYS, DOWNING 13 OF THESE IN ONE DAY. IN THE SHORT TIME OF ACTION WHICH THE SOPWITH SNIPE HAD AT IT'S DISPOSAL IN 1918, IT MADE AN ENVIABLE REPUTATION FOR ITSELF WHICH BODE NO JOY FOR THE EXHAUSTED PILOTS OF THE GERMAN AIR SERVICE.

UNDOUBTEDLY, THE SNIPE SAW SERVICE IN OTHER SQUADRONS NOT RECORDED HEREWITH. AMONG THESE PERHAPS, WERE No. 70 SQDN, FIRST TO GET CAMELS IN JULY, 1917, IN WHICH SERVED GERALD I. MUIR OF AUSTRALIA, A WAR 1 AVIATION PILOT, ILLUSTRATOR, PHOTOGRAPHER-COLLECTOR AND FRIEND OF THE AUTHOR, WHOSE SNIPE IS SHOWN IN THESE DRAWINGS WHILE No. 70 WAS CAMPED AT COLOGNE IN 1918. (NOTE: A SOP. SNIPE, FITTED WITH AN A.B.C. ENGINE, ATTAINED A SPEED OF 156 M.P.H. AND CLIMBED TO 10,000 FT. IN 4½ MIN.)

SPECIFICATIONS. (DOUBLE BAY VERSION.)

SPAN. (BOTH WINGS) VARIATIONS EXISTED.	30'-0"
OVERALL LENGTH.	19'-6"
HEIGHT AT CENTER SECTION.	8'-9"
" " WING TIPS.	9'-7"
WING SURFACE INCLUDING AILERONS.	256 ☐
DIHEDRAL ANGLE, BOTH WINGS.	4°
INCIDENCE " "	1° 50'
CHORD " "	5'-0"
GAP " "	4'-3"
STAGGER (POSITIVE)	1'-4"
HORIZONTAL TAIL PLANE AREA, TOTAL.	26 ☐
VERTICAL	11.75 ☐
WING LOADING. (IN POUNDS)	7.5 ☐
POWER LOADING. (IN POUNDS PER H.P.)	8.86
WEIGHT EMPTY.	1312 LBS.
" OF FUEL & OIL. (38½ PETROL & 7 GALS. OIL.)	343 "
MILITARY LOAD & CREW.	365 "
GROSS WEIGHT OF SHIP.	2020 "

ENGINE: 9 CYL. BENTLEY BR.2 ROTARY OF 200-230 H.P.

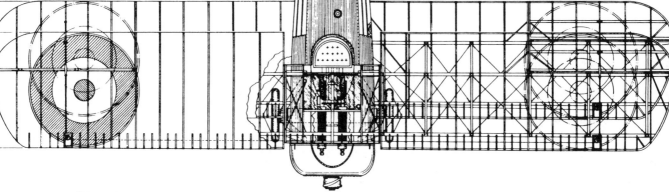

- PERFORMANCE -

NORMAL BRAKE H.P. & R.P.M. @ GROUND LEVEL.   228 AT 1300 R's.

SPEED	TAKE OFF.	60 M.P.H.
	116 "	AT 6500 FT.
	121 "	.10000 "
	113 "	.15000 "
	108.5 "	.16500 "
	40 "	.LANDING.
CLIMB.	6500 FT. IN 5.2 MIN	AT 970 FT. PER. MIN.
	10000 " 9.4 "	710 "
	15000 " 18.8 "	390 "
	16500 " 23.2 "	290 "
SERVICE CEILING.		20,500 FT.
AIR ENDURANCE.		3 HRS.
RANGE.		370 MILES.

ARMAMENT. TWIN MACHINE GUNS, SYNCH. VICKERS.
SIGHT. (OPTIONAL) ALDIS TUBE OR RING TYPE. NO DRAWN.

MANY, MOST SINCERE THANKS TO KENNY ERNST, INDIANAPOLIS, IND., PHUL R. MATT, CINCINNATI, OHIO, DAVE WILLIAMS, IOWA CITY, IOWA, & TO BOB ZUOK, BILL KEE, BERGEN HARDESTY, & PETER L. GREY, (LUTON, BEDS. ENG) AND ALL OTHER SUCH AVID ENTHUSIASTS WHO HAVE SO GENEROUSLY COLLABORATED WITH ME IN THIS AND WORKS THAT FOLLOW. ...

- CONSTRUCTION -

ENTIRE PLANE WAS FABRIC COVERED WOOD CONSTRUCTION. METAL NOSE COWL & SIDE ENGINE PANELS. PLY. VENEER SIDES & REAR OF COCKPIT. EXTERNAL WING BRACING & TAIL, STREAMLINED STEEL CABLES. (TIERODS.)

- COLOR SCHEME -

ENTIRE PLANE COLOURED OLIVE-DRAB (BRITISH KHAKI-GREEN.) METAL PARTS WERE EITHER POLISHED OR PAINTED LIGHT GRAY. LOWER SURFACE OF WINGS EITHER LEFT OLIVE-DRAB, OR PAINTED LIGHT IVORY, CREAM, OR SKY BLUE. INSIGNIA COLOURING NOTED. NUMERALS BLACK & WHITE OUTLINE WHERE SO REQUIRED AS SHOWN.

COST OF SOPWITH SNIPE TO R.A.F. £ 945. 17 s.

ADDITIONAL DATA: COCKADE INSIGNIA SAME DIMENSIONS AS ON SE-5, (CHORD BEING 60, OVERALL DIA. OF COCKADE, 59" WITH ½" CLEARANCE AT LEADING & TR. EDGES. NARROW ENCIRCLING WHITE RING, ⅜ WIDE, BLUE, WHITE & RED SECTIONS, EQUAL WIDTH OR 11⅗. COCKADES ON FUSELAGE SIDES WERE ROUGHLY HALVED.

Spad S.VII C.1

drawings by WILLIAM WYLAM

A very famous airplane, the French-built Spad VII had an excellent performance capability for WW I pilots. Air Age file photo.

IT WAS A nervous group of men that stood on Bleriot Field one morning in July 1916, when the first S.VII was about to demonstrate the theories of its engineers.

After successfully producing the Spad A.I to the order of the Russian government in early 1915, the designers rushed to their boards to reconfigure the platform for the then-radical engine designed by Marc Birkigt, the brilliant designer of engines for Hispano-Suiza motor car company. In addition, the youthful M. Bechereau, designer of Deperdussin's record-breaking racing monoplanes of 1912 and 1913 fame, and Louis Bleriot, famed Channel flier and aerodynamic progressive, were among the firm's design staff.

Bechereau was made chief engineer with a free hand as far as designs were concerned. The result was the Spad (Societe Pour Aviation et ses Derives) S.VII.

At the conclusion of the first test flight the fears of the designers were dismissed. Sea-level speed proved to be 123.5 mph, about 5 mph more than anticipated. The rate of climb was quite good, as it attained an altitude of 10,000 feet in 9 minutes 50 seconds, and it found a service ceiling of 15,000 feet.

The Spad was retired from replacement stores early in 1918, although several squadrons continued to operate right up to the Armistice. Several hundred S.VIIs were constructed in England for the RAF and they were supplied in large numbers to other Allied forces.

Ten Spad VII's still exist. □

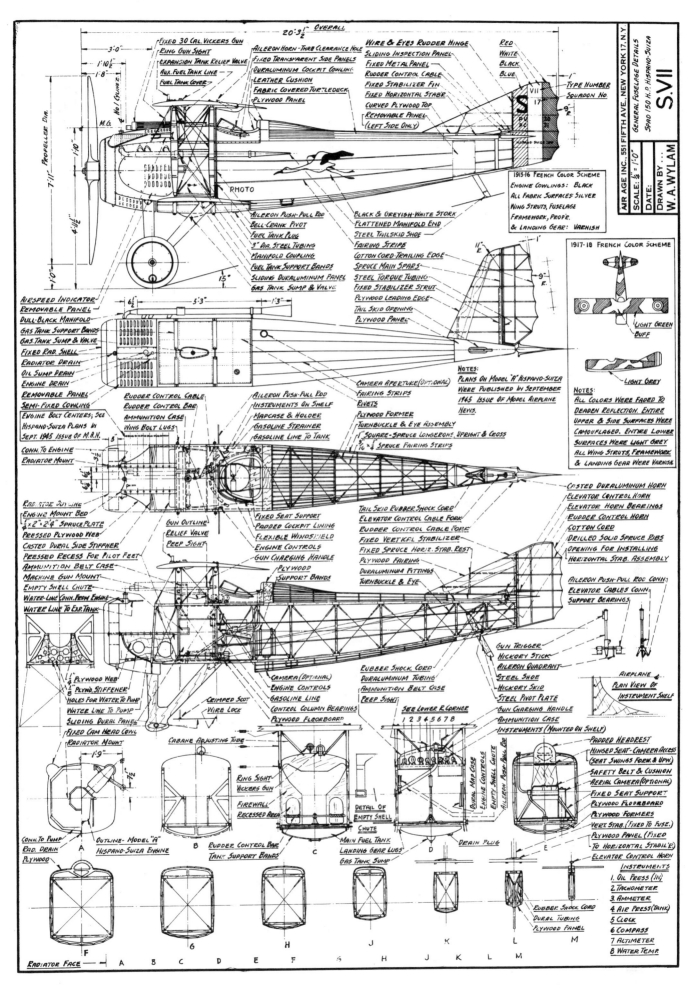

SPAD 150 H.P. HISPANO-SUIZA
GENERAL FUSELAGE DETAILS
S.VII

AIR AGE INC., 551 FIFTH AVE., NEW YORK 17, N.Y.
SCALE: ½ = 1'-0"
DATE:
DRAWN BY....
W. A. WYLAM

1915-16 FRENCH COLOR SCHEME
ENGINE COWLINGS: BLACK
ALL FABRIC SURFACES SILVER
WING STRUTS, FUSELAGE
FRAMEWORK, PROPE,
& LANDING GEAR: VARNISH

1917-18 FRENCH COLOR SCHEME
LIGHT GREEN
BUFF
LIGHT GREY

NOTES:
ALL COLORS WERE FADED TO
DEADEN REFLECTION. ENTIRE
UPPER & SIDE SURFACES WERE
CAMOUFLAGED. ENTIRE LOWER
SURFACES WERE LIGHT GREY.
ALL WING STRUTS, FRAMEWORK
& LANDING GEAR WERE VARNISH.

NOTES:
PLANS ON MODEL "A" HISPANO-SUIZA
WERE PUBLISHED IN SEPTEMBER
1945 ISSUE OF MODEL AIRPLANE
NEWS.

AIRPLANE
PLAN VIEW OF
INSTRUMENT SHELF

INSTRUMENTS
1. OIL PRESS (IN)
2. TACHOMETER
3. AMMETER
4. AIR PRESS (TANK)
5. CLOCK
6. COMPASS
7. ALTIMETER
8. WATER TEMP.

RADIATOR FACE

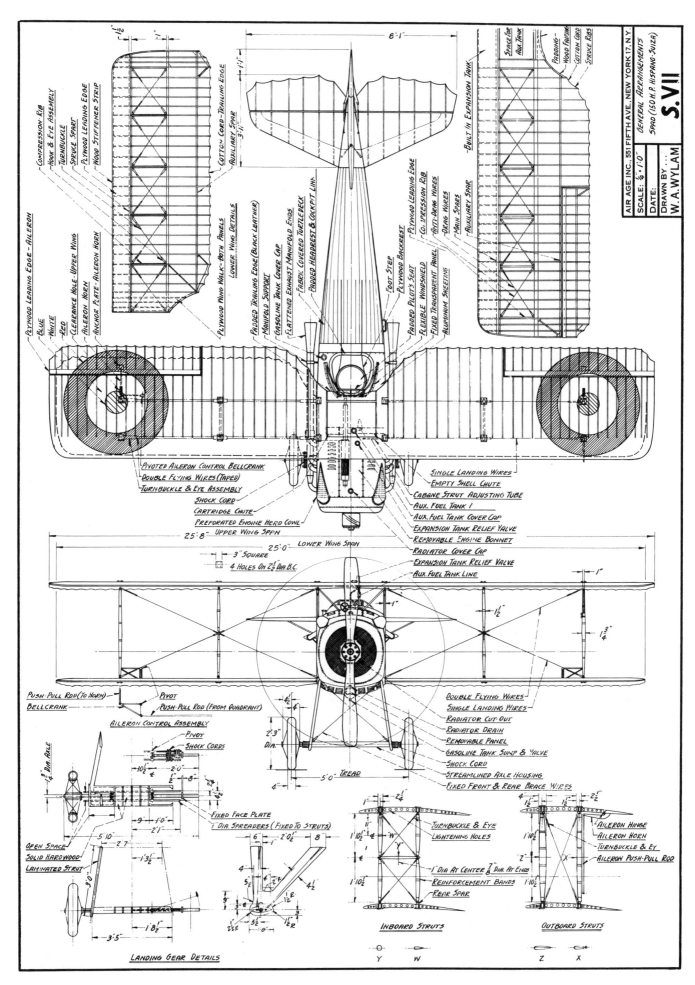

AIR AGE INC., 551 FIFTH AVE., NEW YORK 17, N.Y.

GENERAL ARRANGEMENTS

SPAD (150 H.P. HISPANO-SUIZA)

S.VII

SCALE: ¼=1'-0"

DATE:

DRAWN BY:
W. A. WYLAM

Compression Rib
Hook & Eye Assembly
Turnbuckle
Spruce Spar
Plywood Leading Edge
Wood Stiffener Strip
Cotton Cord-Trailing Edge
Auxiliary Spar

Space For Aux. Tank
Built In Expansion Tank
Padding
Wood Fairing
Cotton Cord
Spruce Ribs

Plywood Leading Edge-Aileron
Blue
White
Red
Clearance Hole-Upper Wing
Aileron Horn
Anchor Plate-Aileron Horn

Plywood Wing Walk-Both Panels
Lower Wing Details

Padded Trailing Edge(Black Leather)
Manifold Support
Gasoline Tank Cover Cap
Flattened Exhaust Manifold Ends
Fabric Covered Turtledeck
Padded Headrest & Cockpit Liner

Plywood Leading Edge
Compression Rib
Anti-Drag Wires
Drag Wires
Main Spars
Auxiliary Spar

Foot Step
Pilot's Seat
Padded Backrest
Flexible Windshield
Fixed Transparent Panel
Aluminum Sheeting

Pivoted Aileron Control Bellcrank
Double Flying Wires (Taped)
Turnbuckle & Eye Assembly
Shock Cord
Cartridge Chute
Preforated Engine Head Cowl
25'-8" Upper Wing Span

Single Landing Wires
Empty Shell Chute
Cabane Strut Adjusting Tube
Aux. Fuel Tank 1
Aux. Fuel Tank Cover Cap
Expansion Tank Relief Valve
Removable Engine Bonnet
Radiator Cover Cap
Expansion Tank Relief Valve
Aux. Fuel Tank Line

25'-0" Lower Wing Span
3" Square
4 Holes On 2½" Dia. B.C.

Push-Pull Rod (To Horn)
Bellcrank
Pivot
Push-Pull Rod (From Quadrant)
Aileron Control Assembly

Pivot
Shock Cords

Double Flying Wires
Single Landing Wires
Radiator Cut-Out
Radiator Drain
Removable Panel
Gasoline Tank Sump & Valve
Shock Cord
Streamlined Axle Housing
Fixed Front & Rear Brace Wires

2'-3" Dia.
TREAD
5'-0"

¾" Dia. Axle
Open Space
Solid Hardwood
Laminated Strut
Fixed Face Plate
1" Dia. Spreaders (Fixed To Struts)

LANDING GEAR DETAILS

Turnbuckle & Eye
Lightening Holes
1" Dia At Center ⅞" Dia. At Ends
Reinforcement Bands
Rear Spar

Aileron Hinge
Aileron Horn
Turnbuckle & Eye
Aileron Push-Pull Rod

INBOARD STRUTS

OUTBOARD STRUTS

Y   W

Z   X

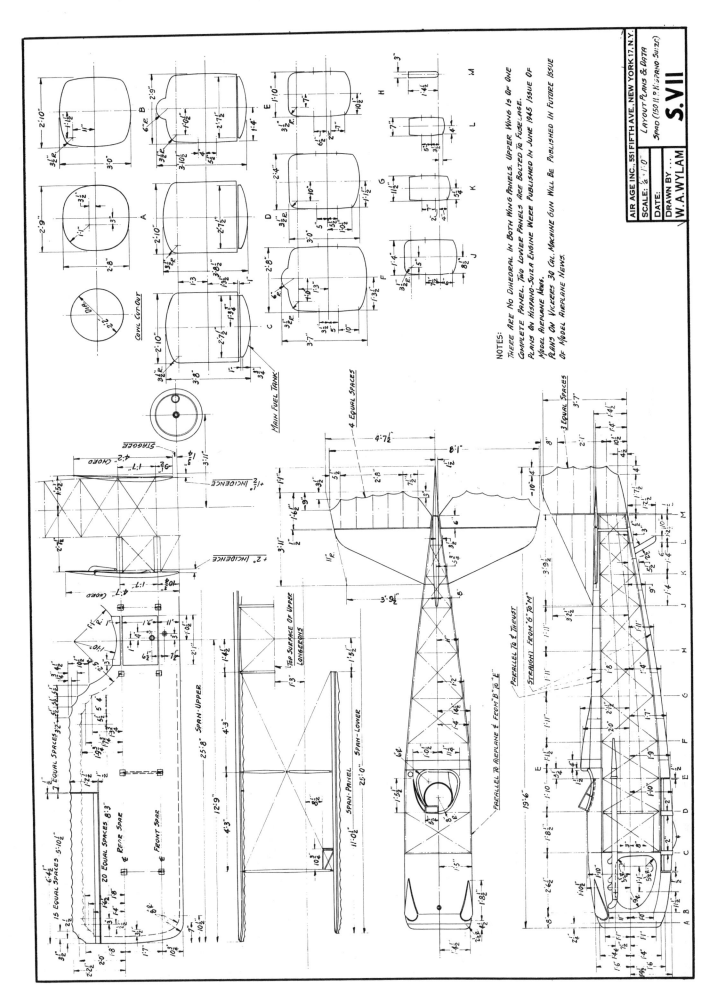

AIR AGE INC., 551 FIFTH AVE., NEW YORK 17, N.Y.

LAYOUT PLANS & DATA

SPAD (150 H.P. HISPANO SUIZA)

SCALE: ¾″=1′-0″

DATE:

DRAWN BY....
W. A. WYLAM

S.VII

NOTES:

THERE ARE NO DIHEDRAL IN BOTH WING PANELS. UPPER WING IS OF ONE
COMPLETE PANEL. TWO LOWER PANELS ARE BOLTED TO FUSELAGE.
PLANS ON HISPANO-SUIZA ENGINE WERE PUBLISHED IN JUNE 1945 ISSUE OF
MODEL AIRPLANE NEWS.
PLANS ON VICKERS 30 CAL. MACHINE GUN WILL BE PUBLISHED IN FUTURE ISSUE
OF MODEL AIRPLANE NEWS.

Spad S.XIA-2

drawings by WILLIAM WYLAM

FOLLOWING the great success of the Spad S.VII, French engineers developed from it a two-place reconnaisance version that was to fill a number of operational requirements, such as observation and light bombing. Powered by a 235-hp Hispano-Suiza engine, it entered service from 1917 with French, Belgian, and eventually AEF squadrons. Because of the additional weight gained with the increased size of the fuselage and the addition of bombs, more armament, etc., performance suffered. It was no match for the German fighters and was an easy target, leading to a re-evaluation of its use.

The Hispano-Suiza engine was changed to a more powerful Lorraine-Dietrich type 8Bb which delivered 250 hp at only 1,650 rpm and redesignated as Spad XVIA-2, but retained the same construction and appearance of the type XI.

Because it had a proven airframe, the uses and adaptations were many. Although generally disliked by pilots because of its vulnerability, the Spad XI and XVI gave good results in action.

Billy Mitchell's S.XVIA-2 is on show at the National Air & Space Museum in Washington, DC. □

The Spad S.XIA-2 was a two-place airplane used for observation and light bombing by the Allies. Air Age file photo.

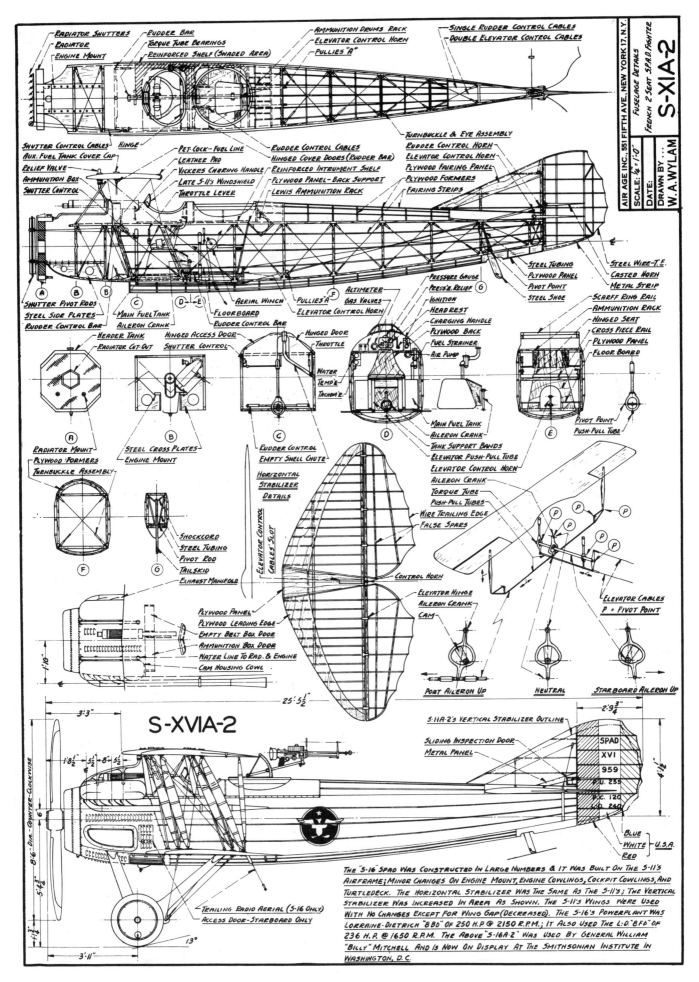

AIR AGE INC., 551 FIFTH AVE, NEW YORK 17, N.Y.

FRENCH 2 SEAT S.P.A.D. FIGHTER

FUSELAGE DETAILS

SCALE: ¼"=1'-0"

DATE:

DRAWN BY...
W. A. WYLAM

S-XIA-2

Radiator Shutters
Radiator
Engine Mount
Rudder Bar
Torque Tube Bearings
Reinforced Shelf (Shaded Area)
Ammunition Drums Rack
Elevator Control Horn
Pullies "A"
Single Rudder Control Cables
Double Elevator Control Cables

Shutter Control Cables
Aux. Fuel Tank Cover Cap
Relief Valve
Ammunition Box
Shutter Control
Hinge
Pet-Cock-Fuel Line
Leather Pad
Vickers Charing Handle
Late S-11's Windshield
Throttle Lever
Rudder Control Cables
Hinged Cover Doors (Rudder Bar)
Reinforced Intrument Shelf
Plywood Panel-Back Support
Lewis Ammunition Rack
Turnbuckle & Eye Assembly
Rudder Control Horn
Elevator Control Horn
Plywood Fairing Panel
Plywood Formers
Fairing Strips

Steel Tubing
Plywood Panel
Pivot Point
Steel Shoe
Steel Wire-T.E.
Casted Horn
Metal Strip

Shutter Pivot Rods
Steel Side Plates
Rudder Control Bar
Header Tank
Radiator Cut-Out
Main Fuel Tank
Aileron Crank
Hinged Access Door
Shutter Control
Aerial Winch
Floorboard
Elevator Control Bar
Pullies "A"
Altimeter
Gas Valves
Elevator Control Horn
Hinged Door
Throttle
Pressure Gauge
Press'e. Relief
Ignition
Headrest
Charging Handle
Plywood Back
Fuel Strainer
Air Pump
Scarff Ring Rail
Ammunition Rack
Hinged Seat
Cross Piece Rail
Plywood Panel
Floor Board

Water
Temp'e
Tachom'e
Main Fuel Tank
Aileron Crank
Tank Support Bands
Elevator Push-Pull Tube
Elevator Control Horn
Pivot Point
Push-Pull Tube

Radiator Mount
Plywood Formers
Turnbuckle Assembly
Steel Cross Plates
Engine Mount
Rudder Control
Empty Shell Chute
Horizontal
Stabilizer
Details
Aileron Crank
Torque Tube
Push-Pull Tubes
Wire Trailing Edge
False Spars

Shockcord
Steel Tubing
Pivot Rod
Tailskid
Exhaust Manifold
Control Horn
Elevator Hinge
Aileron Crank
Cam

Elevator Cables
P = Pivot Point

Elevator Control
Cables-Slot

1'10"

Plywood Panel
Plywood Leading Edge
Empty Belt Box Door
Ammunition Box Door
Water Line To Rad. & Engine
Cam Housing Cowl

Port Aileron Up
Neutral
Starboard Aileron Up

25'5½"

S-XVIA-2

3'3"

1'8½" 5½" 8" 5½"
6"

8'6" Dia. Counter-Clockwise

S-11A-2's Vertical Stabilizer Outline
Sliding Inspection Door
Metal Panel

2'9¾"

SPAD
XVI
959
U.255
C. 120
L-D 240

4'½"

BLUE
WHITE — U.S.A.
RED

Trailing Radio Aerial (S-16 Only)
Access Door-Starboard Only

3'11"
13°

THE "S-16" SPAD WAS CONSTRUCTED IN LARGE NUMBERS & IT WAS BUILT ON THE S-11'S AIRFRAME; MINOR CHANGES ON ENGINE MOUNT, ENGINE COWLINGS, COCKPIT COWLINGS, AND TURTLEDECK. THE HORIZONTAL STABILIZER WAS THE SAME AS THE S-11'S; THE VERTICAL STABILIZER WAS INCREASED IN AREA AS SHOWN. THE S-11'S WINGS WERE USED WITH NO CHANGES EXCEPT FOR WING GAP (DECREASED). THE S-16'S POWERPLANT WAS LORRAINE-DIETRICH "8Bd" OF 250 H.P. @ 2150 R.P.M.; IT ALSO USED THE L:D. "8Fb" OF 236 H.P. @ 1650 R.P.M. THE ABOVE "S-16A-2" WAS USED BY GENERAL WILLIAM "BILLY" MITCHELL AND IS NOW ON DISPLAY AT THE SMITHSONIAN INSTITUTE IN WASHINGTON, D.C.

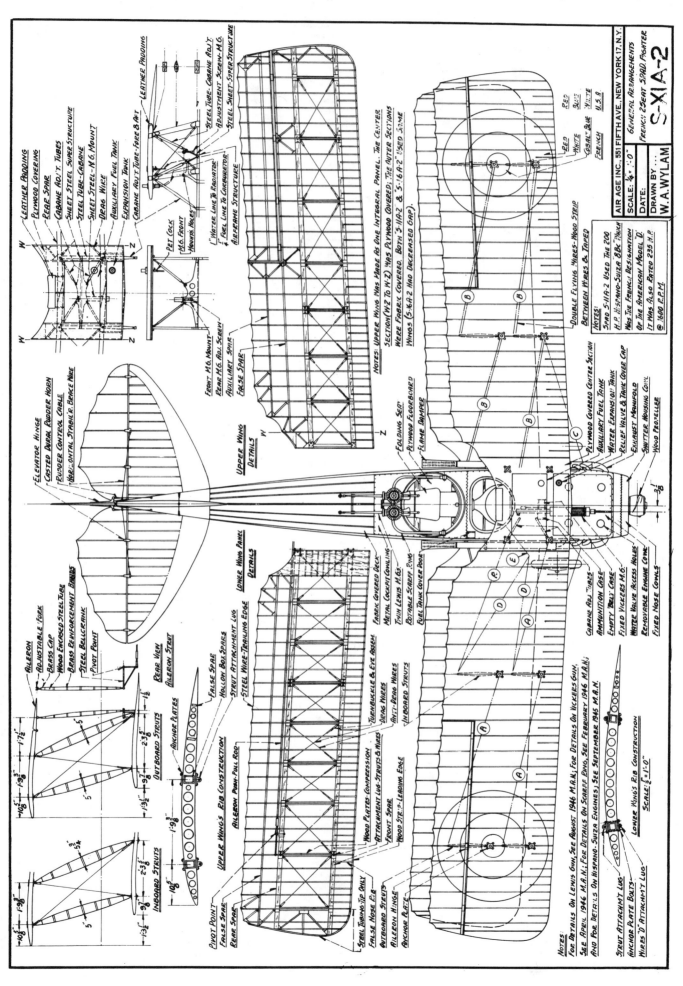

S-XIA-2

GENERAL ARRANGEMENTS

FRENCH 2-SEAT SPAD FIGHTER

DRAWN BY.... W. A. WYLAM

AIR AGE INC., 551 FIFTH AVE., NEW YORK 17, N.Y.

SCALE: 1/4" = 1'-0"

DATE:

RED
BLUE
WHITE
U.S.A.

RED
WHITE
COBALT BLUE
FRENCH

NOTES:
SPAD S-XIA-2 USED THE 200 H.P. HISPANO-SUIZA 8Bc ENGINE WAS THE FRENCH DESIGNATION OF THE AMERICAN MODEL "D". IT WAS ALSO RATED 235 H.P. @ 1600 R.P.M.

NOTES: UPPER WING WAS MADE AS ONE INTEGRAL PANEL. THE CENTER SECTION (W-Z TO W-Z) WAS PLYWOOD COVERED; THE OUTER SECTIONS WERE FABRIC COVERED, BOTH S-XIA-2 & S-XIA-2 USED SAME WINGS (S-XIA-2 HAD DECREASED GAP).

—DOUBLE FLYING WIRES-WOOD STRIP BETWEEN WIRES & TAPED

LEATHER PADDING
PLYWOOD COVERING
REAR SPAR
CABANE ADJ'T. TUBES
SHEET STEEL SUPER STRUCTURE
STEEL TUBE-CABANE
SHEET STEEL-N.6. MOUNT
DRAG WIRE
AUXILIARY FUEL TANK
EXPANSION TANK
CABANE ADJ'T TUBE-FORE & AFT

LEATHER PADDING
STEEL TUBE-CABANE ADJ'T.
ADJUSTMENT SCREW-M.G.
STEEL SHEET-SUPER STRUCTURE

1" WATER LINE TO RADIATOR
FUEL LINE TO CARBURETOR
AIRFRAME STRUCTURE

PET COCK
M.G. FRONT MOUNT'G HOLES

FRONT M.G. MOUNT
REAR M.G. ADJ. SCREW
AUXILIARY SPAR
FALSE SPAR

UPPER WINGS DETAILS

ELEVATOR HINGE
CASTED DURAL RUDDER HORN
RUDDER CONTROL CABLE
HORIZONTAL STABILR. BRACE WIRE

PLYWOOD COVERED CENTER SECTION
AUXILIARY FUEL TANK
WATER EXPANSION TANK
RELIEF VALVE & TANK COVER CAP
EXHAUST MANIFOLD
SHUTTER HOUSING COWL
WOOD PROPELLER

FOLDING SEAT
PLYWOOD FLOORBOARD
FLAME DAMPER

FABRIC COVERED DECK
METAL COCKPIT COWLING
TWIN LEWIS M.GS.
ROTABLE SCARFF RING
FUEL TANK COVER DOOR

CABANE ADJ. TUBES
AMMUNITION CASE
EMPTY BELT CASE
FIXED VICKERS M.G.
WATER VALVE ACCESS HOLES
REMOVABLE ENGINE COWL
FIXED NOSE COWLS

LOWER WING PANEL DETAILS

REAR VIEW

AILERON
ADJUSTABLE FORK
BRASS CAP
WOOD ENCASED STEEL TUBE
BRASS REINFORCEMENT BANDS
STEEL BELLCRANK
PIVOT POINT

AILERON STRUT

OUTBOARD STRUTS

INBOARD STRUTS

PIVOT POINT
FALSE NOSE RIB
REAR SPAR
OUTBOARD STRUTS
INBOARD STRUTS
ANCHOR PLATE

FALSE SPAR
HOLLOW BOX SPARS
STEEL ATTACHMENT LUG
STEEL WIRE-TRAILING EDGE

ANCHOR PLATES

WOOD PLATES (COMPRESSION)
ATTACHMENT LUG-STRUTS & WIRES
FRONT SPAR
WOOD STR. 1/2" LEADING EDGE

AILERON HINGE
ANCHOR PLATE

STRUT ATTACHM'T LUG
ANCHOR PLATE BOLTS
WIRES "D" ATTACHM'T LUG

UPPER WING'S RIB CONSTRUCTION
AILERON PUSH-PULL ROD

STEEL TUBING-TIP ONLY
FALSE NOSE RIB
OUTBOARD STRUTS
AILERON HINGE
ANCHOR PLATE

TURNBUCKLE & EYE ASSEM.
DRAG WIRES
ANTI-DRAG WIRES
INBOARD STRUTS

LOWER WING'S RIB CONSTRUCTION

SCALE: 1/2" = 1'-0"

NOTES:
FOR DETAILS ON LEWIS GUNS, SEE AUGUST 1946 M.A.N.; FOR DETAILS ON VICKERS GUN,
SEE APRIL 1946 M.A.N.; FOR DETAILS ON SCARFF RING, SEE FEBRUARY 1946 M.A.N.
AND FOR DETAILS ON HISPANO-SUIZA ENGINES, SEE SEPTEMBER 1945 M.A.N.

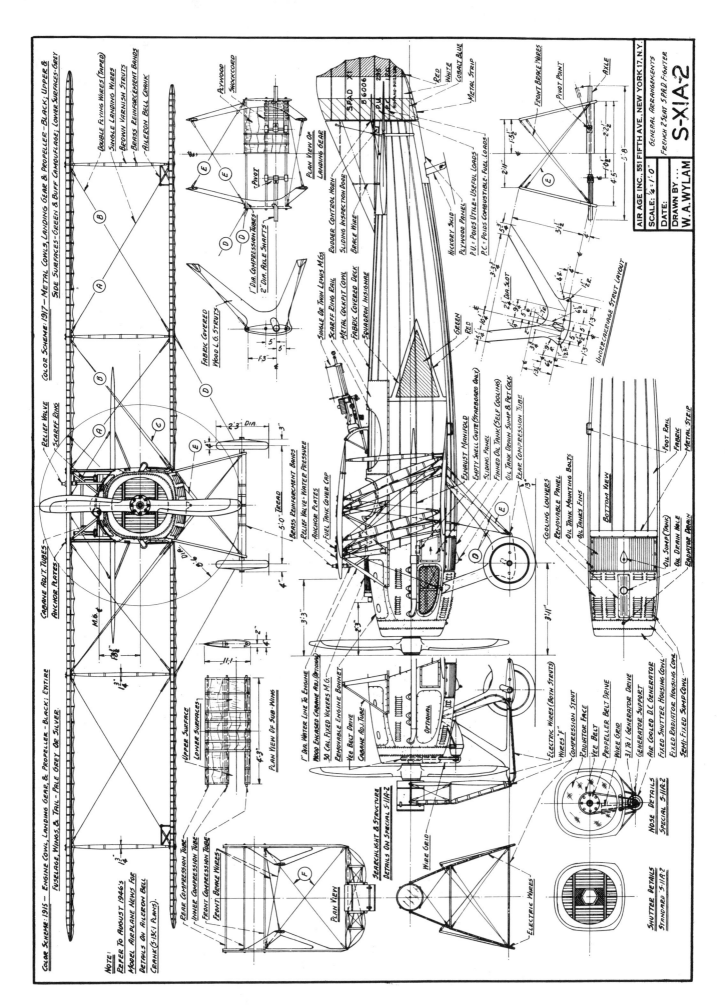

S-XIA-2

AIR AGE INC., 551 FIFTH AVE, NEW YORK 17, N.Y.
GENERAL ARRANGEMENTS
FRENCH 2-SEAT SPAD FIGHTER
SCALE: ¼"=1'-0"
DATE:
DRAWN BY ....
W. A. WYLAM

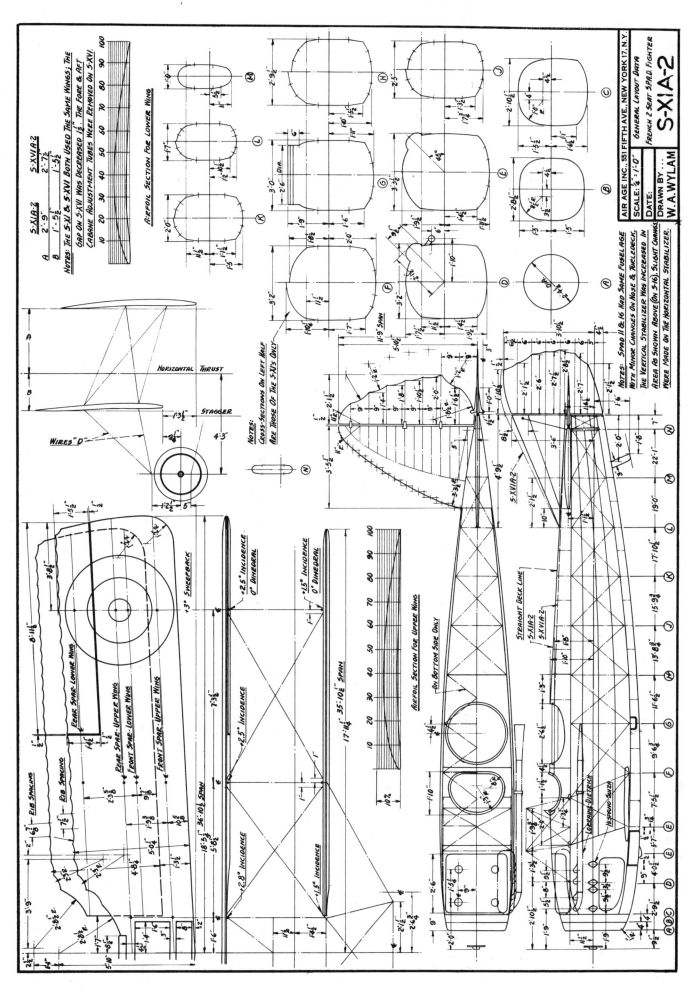

Airfoil Section For Lower Wing

Airfoil Section For Upper Wing

NOTES: The S-XI & S-XVI Both Used The Same Wings; The
Gap On S-XI Was Decreased 1½. The Fore & Aft
Cabane Adjustment Tubes Were Removed On S-XVI.

NOTES: S.PAD 11 & 16 Had Same Fuselage
With Minor Changes On Nose & Tuledeck.
The Vertical Stabilizer Was Increased In
Area As Shown Above (On S-16). Slight Changes
Were Made On The Horizontal Stabilizer.

AIR AGE INC., 551 FIFTH AVE., NEW YORK 17, N.Y.
GENERAL LAYOUT DATA
SCALE: ¼" = 1'-0"
FRENCH 2 SEAT S.P.A.D. FIGHTER
DATE:
DRAWN BY ....
W. A. WYLAM
S-XIA-2

Spad S.XIII C.1

drawings by WILLIAM WYLAM

MORE NOTED for its speed and strength than for its maneuverability or climb, the Spad XIII was a definite favorite because of one other very important characteristic—it was easy to fly. The Spad XIII was one of the best-liked Allied aircraft to see service in 1917-1918.

Like all other good fighting ships, it was a compromise between climb, speed, maneuverability, ease of construction, and maintenance. But the airplane proved itself over and over again where it counted—in the air and in battle. The first French squadron to be completely equipped with the new XIII was the Escadrille S.3 "Les Cigognes" (The Storks) of which the great French Ace Georges Guynemer was top ranking member. Killed in the XIII under mysterious circumstances, Guynemer never achieved a victory in the plane and an omen of bad luck was to prevail, although no basis in fact was ever established to substantiate it. In fact, the war records of the Spad XIII speak well for themselves.

The original models were powered by Hispano-Suiza type 8Ba eight-cylinder

V-type engines which at first delivered 200 hp and were soon improved to 220 hp at sea level. Among the most streamlined of WW I airplanes, it had a top speed of 134.5 mph. It could climb to 6,500 feet in 5 minutes 17 seconds and could reach a ceiling of slightly over 22,000 feet.

Six XIII C.1's still survive, one of them Guynemer's in Paris, another Ray Brooks' in Washington D.C. □

Considered easy to fly, the Spad S.XIII C.1 was a favorite mount for Allied pilots. It was a fighter that could take a hard punch and still remain air-worthy. Air Age file photos.

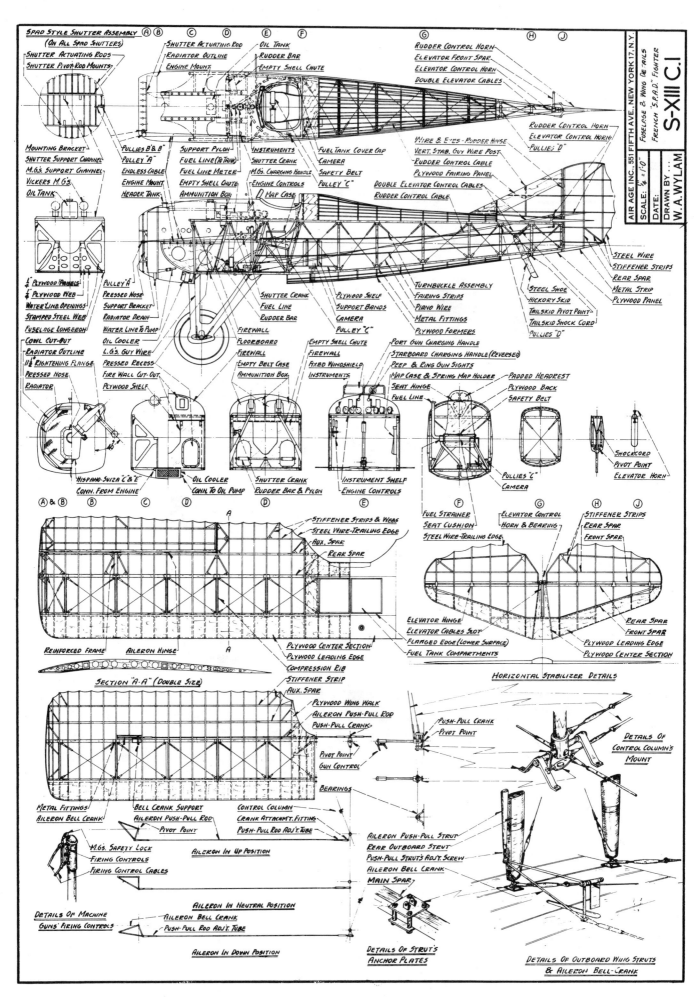

S-XIII C.I

French "S.P.A.D." Fighter
Fuselage & Wing Details

AIR AGE INC. 551 FIFTH AVE. NEW YORK 17, N.Y.

SCALE: ¾" = 1'-0"
DATE:
DRAWN BY ....
W. A. WYLAM

Spad Style Shutter Assembly (A)(B)
(On All Spad Shutters)
Shutter Actuating Rods
Shutter Pivot Rod Mounts

Shutter Actuating Rod
Radiator Outline
Engine Mount

Oil Tank
Rudder Bar
Empty Shell Chute

Rudder Control Horn
Elevator Front Spar
Elevator Control Horn
Double Elevator Cables

Mounting Bracket
Shutter Support Channel
M.G.'s. Support Channel
Vickers M.G.'s.
Oil Tank

Pullies "B" & "B"
Pulley "A"
Endless Cable
Engine Mount
Header Tank

Support Pylon
Fuel Line (To Tank)
Fuel Line Meter
Empty Shell Chute
Ammunition Box

Instruments
Shutter Crank
M.G.'s. Charging Handle
Engine Controls
Map Case

Fuel Tank Cover Cap
Camera
Safety Belt
Pulley "C"

Wire & Eyes - Rudder Hinge
Vert. Stab. Guy Wire Post
Rudder Control Cable
Plywood Fairing Panel
Double Elevator Control Cables
Rudder Control Cable

Rudder Control Horn
Elevator Control Horn
Pullies "D"

¾ Plywood Panels
⅛ Plywood Web
Water Line Openings
Stamped Steel Web
Fuselage Longeron
Cowl Cut-Out
Radiator Outline
11¾ Tightening Flange
Pressed Nose
Radiator

Pulley "A"
Pressed Nose
Support Bracket
Radiator Drain
Water Line To Pump
Oil Cooler
L.G.'s. Guy Wire
Pressed Recess
Fire Wall Cut-Out
Plywood Shelf

Shutter Crank
Fuel Line
Rudder Bar
Firewall
Floorboard
Firewall
Empty Belt Case
Ammunition Box

Plywood Shelf
Support Bands
Camera
Pulley "C"

Empty Shell Chute
Firewall
Fixed Windshield
Instruments

Turnbuckle Assembly
Fairing Strips
Piano Wire
Metal Fittings
Plywood Formers

Port Gun Charging Handle
Starboard Charging Handle (Reversed)
Peep & Ring Gun Sights
Map Case & Spring Map Holder
Seat Hinge
Fuel Line

Steel Wire
Stiffener Strips
Rear Spar
Metal Strip
Plywood Panel

Steel Shoe
Hickory Skid
Tailskid Pivot Point
Tailskid Shock Cord
Pullies "D"

Padded Headrest
Plywood Back
Safety Belt

Shockcord
Pivot Point
Elevator Horn

Hispano-Suiza "C & E"
Conn. From Engine

Oil Cooler
Conn. To Oil Pump

Shutter Crank
Rudder Bar & Pylon

Instrument Shelf
Engine Controls

Fuel Strainer
Seat Cushion
Steel Wire - Trailing Edge

Elevator Control
Horn & Bearing

Stiffener Strips
Rear Spar
Front Spar

Pullies "C"
Camera

(A) & (B) (B) (C) (D) (D) (E) (F) (G) (H) (J)

Stiffener Strips & Webs
Steel Wire - Trailing Edge
Aux. Spar
Rear Spar

Elevator Hinge
Elevator Cables Slot
Flanged Edge (Lower Surface)
Fuel Tank Compartments

Rear Spar
Front Spar
Plywood Leading Edge
Plywood Center Section

Horizontal Stabilizer Details

Reinforced Frame
Aileron Hinge

Plywood Center Section
Plywood Leading Edge
Compression Rib
Stiffener Strip
Aux. Spar

Plywood Wing Walk
Aileron Push-Pull Rod
Push-Pull Crank

Pivot Point
Gun Control

Push-Pull Crank
Pivot Point

Details Of
Control Column's
Mount

Section "A-A" (Double Size)

Bearings

Metal Fittings
Aileron Bell Crank

Bell Crank Support
Aileron Push-Pull Rod
Pivot Point

Control Column
Crank Attachmt. Fitting
Push-Pull Rod Adjt. Tube

Aileron Push-Pull Strut
Rear Outboard Strut
Push-Pull Strut's Adjt. Screw
Aileron Bell Crank
Main Spar

Aileron In Up Position

M.G.'s. Safety Lock
Firing Controls
Firing Control Cables

Aileron In Neutral Position
Aileron Bell Crank
Push-Pull Rod Adjt. Tube

**Details Of Machine
Guns' Firing Controls**

Aileron In Down Position

**Details Of Strut's
Anchor Plates**

**Details Of Outboard Wing Struts
& Aileron Bell-Crank**

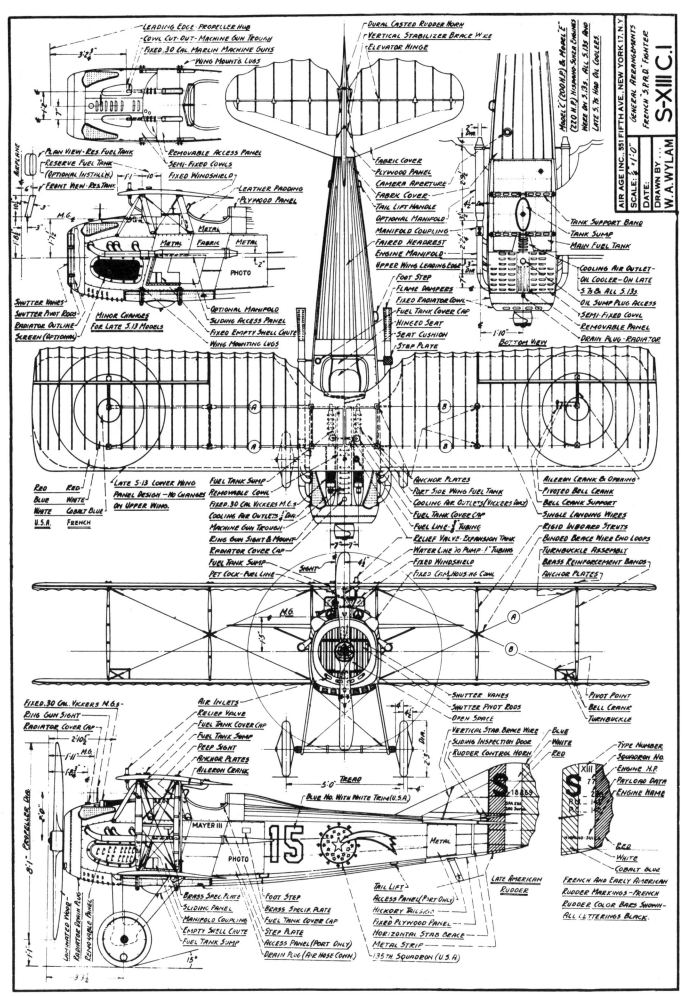

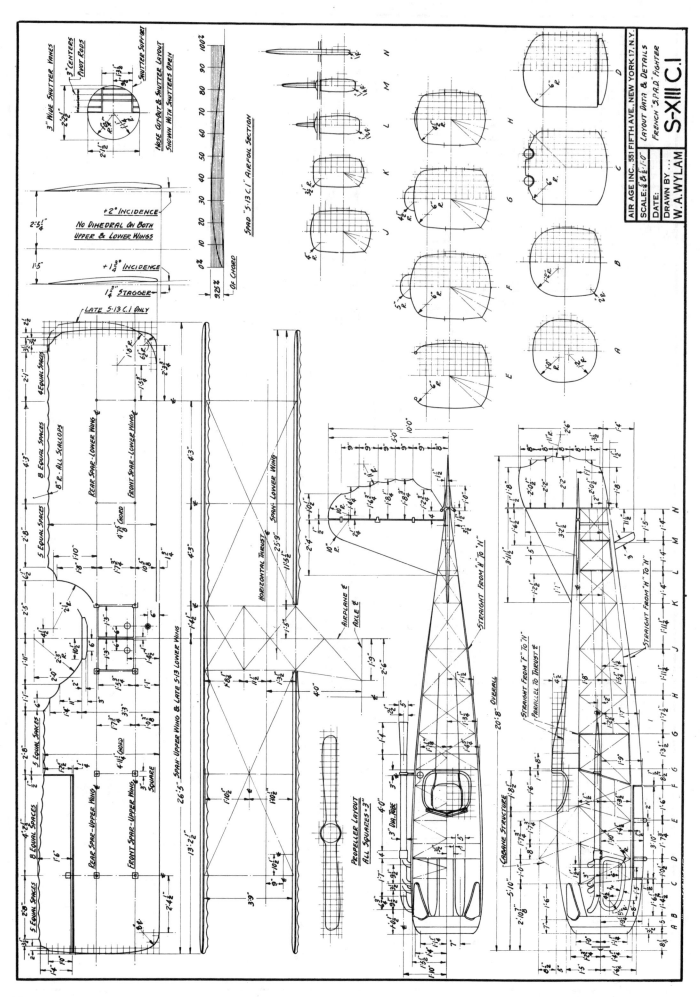

Standard Model J

drawings by WILLIS NYE

Standard J-1 with 180-hp Hisso engine.

DEVELOPED from the Standard H series biplanes designed in 1916, the J series aircraft were part of the USA's effort to produce machines as trainers for the war in Europe. A tandem two-seater, it was initially powered by the Hall-Scott 100-hp A-7A engine. It proved to be somewhat underpowered and so the J-1 was introduced, powered by a 175-hp engine, also from Hall-Scott. The H-S A-5A engine gave the airplane a maximum speed of 95 mph and was used for training and barnstorming as long after the war as the Jenny was.

Many J-1s are still flying or are in museums. ☐

Standard J-1 with Curtiss OX5 engine.
Photos courtesy of Leonard Opdycke, WW I Aeroplanes.

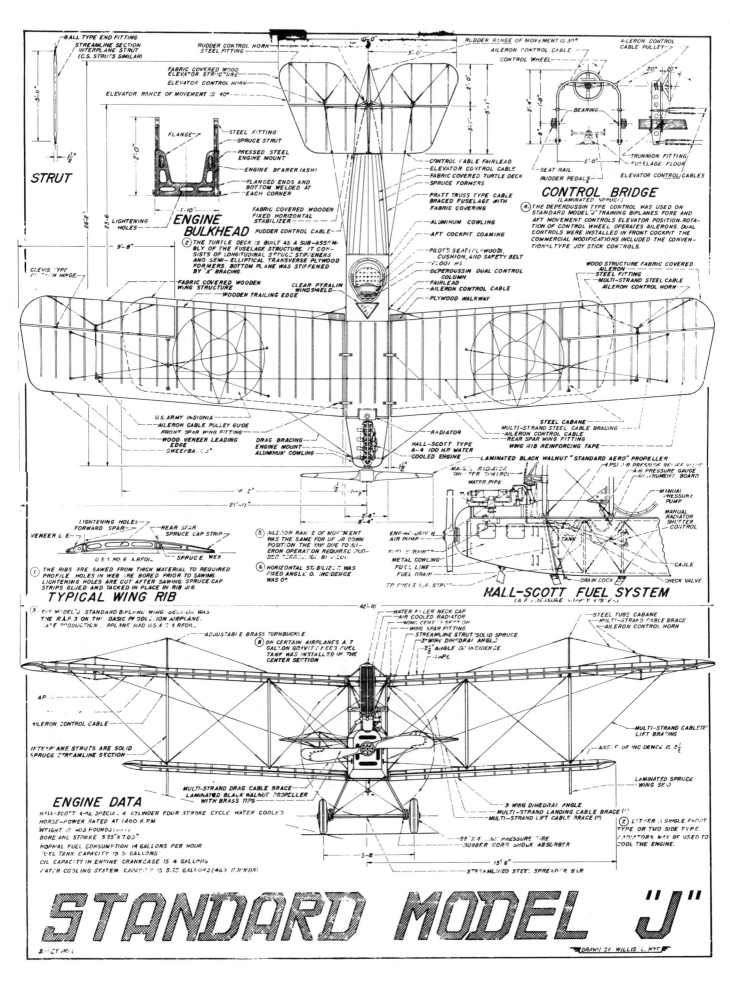

STANDARD MODEL "J"

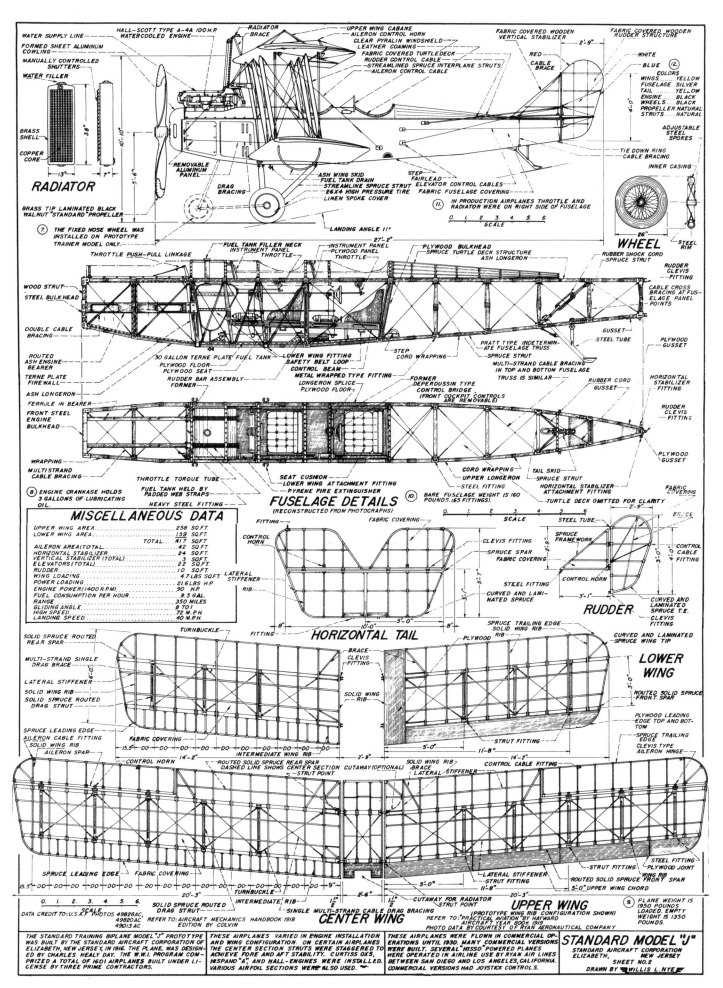

Thomas Morse S-4C &

drawings by WILLIS NYE

THE THOMAS Morse S-4C was a single-seat advanced trainer of which about 600 were built. Most went to the U.S. Army Air Service but a few also went to the U.S. Navy from 1917. They were powered by the 80-hp LeRhone rotary engine and also used the 100-hp Gnome rotary in some models.

Nicknamed "Tommy," the S-4C represented to student pursuit pilots all that was to be expected of a single-seat fighter by way of feel and appearance, plus a lot of gentleness that some combat types of WW I lacked. It was not considered

Designed as an advanced single-seat trainer for WW I fighter pilots, over 1,000 "Tommies" were built. This is the S-4B. Photo courtesy of Leonard Opdycke, WW I Aeroplanes.

The S-4E above and the S-4C below were to be seen by thousands of movie buffs when Hollywood used the airplane in their celluloid wars. "Jane's All the World's Aircraft" photos.

good enough, either in performance or handling qualities to be used as a fighter. It never went overseas and was relegated to training fields during WW I.

Over 1,000 were built and, following the Armistice, were declared surplus and purchased by sportsman pilots and barnstormers during the early '20s. The busy roar of its rotary engine that had echoed from dozens of training fields all over the country during the war continued to be heard until about 1930. The motion picture industry used a great many Tommys after that in Hollywood air epics.

Only one S-4B is left, at Cole Palen's Old Rhinebeck Aerodrome; four -C's are in museums, and there are no more -E's.   □

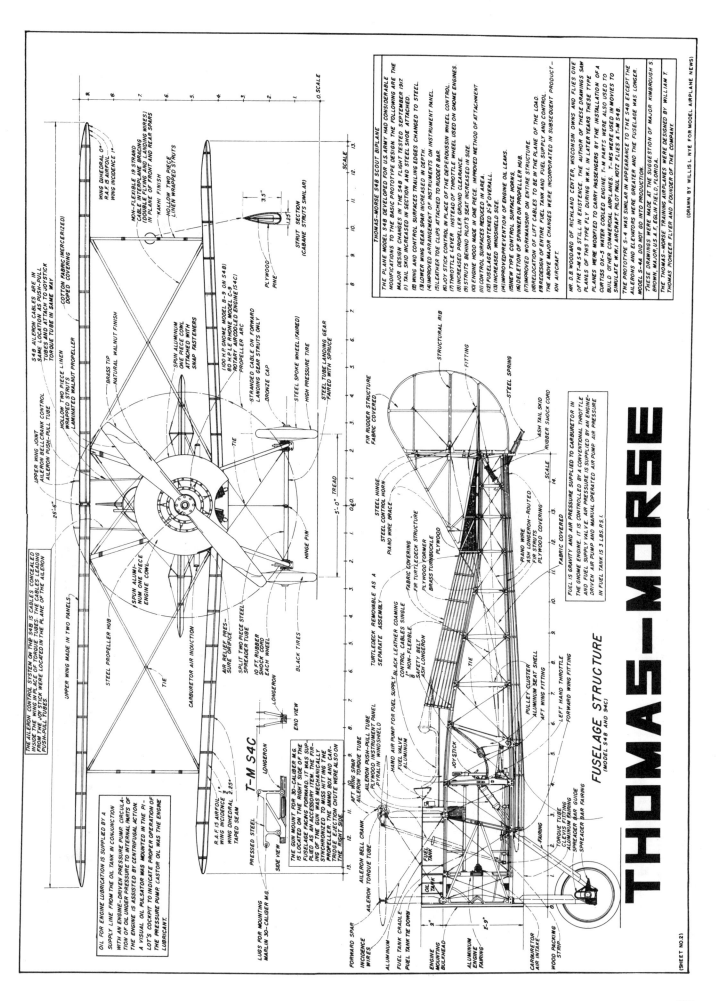

THOMAS-MORSE

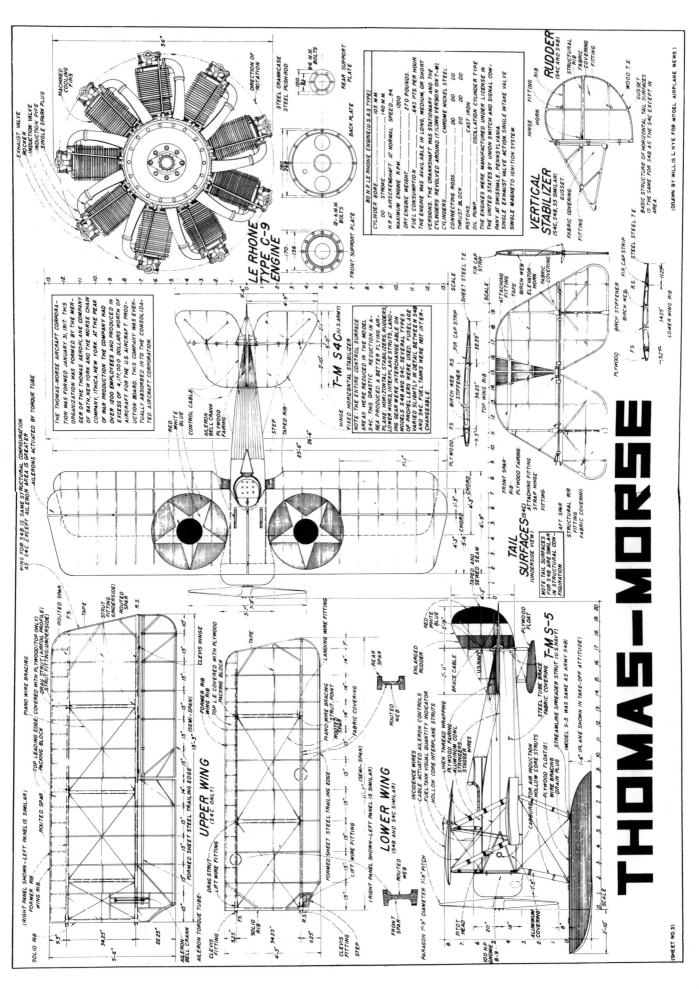

THOMAS-MORSE

LE RHONE TYPE C-9 ENGINE

RUDDER (S4C AND S4B)

VERTICAL STABILIZER (S4C, S4B, S5 SIMILAR)

TAIL SURFACES (S4C) (UNDERSIDE VIEW)

T-M S4C (U.S. ARMY)

T-M S-5 (U.S. NAVY)

UPPER WING (S4C ONLY)

LOWER WING (S4B AND S4C SIMILAR)

(DRAWN BY WILLIS L. NYE FOR MODEL AIRPLANE NEWS)

(SHEET NO. 3)

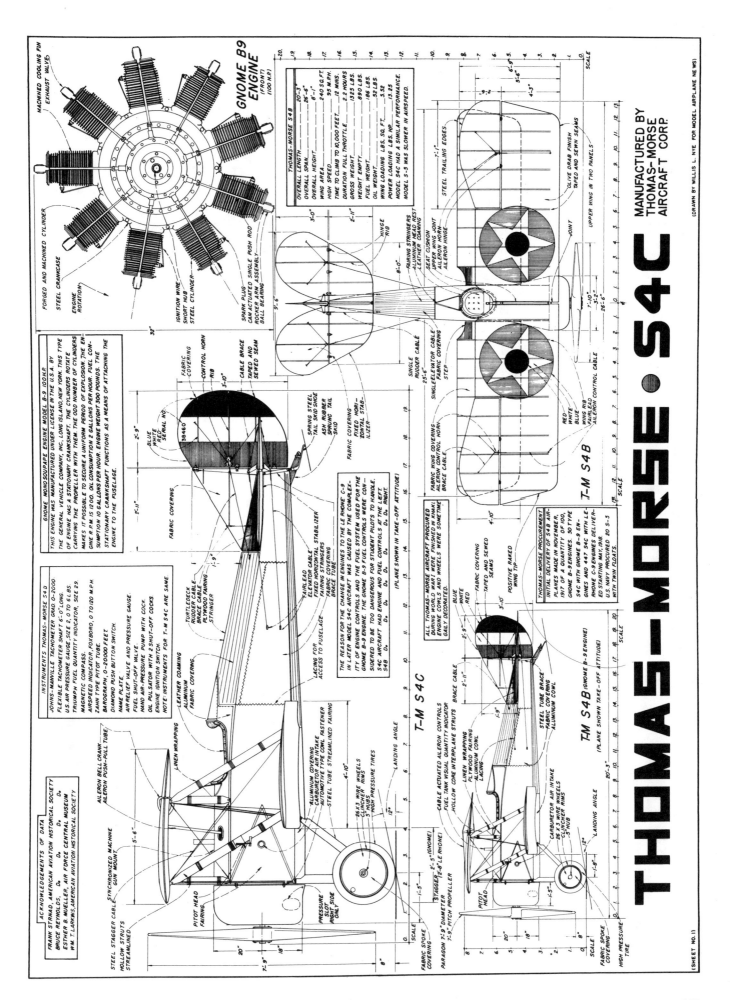

THOMAS-MORSE · S4C

MANUFACTURED BY THOMAS-MORSE AIRCRAFT CORP.

(DRAWN BY WILLIS L. NYE FOR MODEL AIRPLANE NEWS)

THOMAS-MORSE S4B	
OVERALL LENGTH	20'-3"
OVERALL SPAN	26'-6"
OVERALL HEIGHT	8'-1"
WING AREA	240 SQ.FT.
HIGH SPEED	95 M.P.H.
TIME TO CLIMB TO 10,000 FEET	12 MINS.
DURATION FULL THROTTLE	2 HOURS
GROSS WEIGHT	1325 LBS.
WEIGHT EMPTY	890 LBS.
FUEL WEIGHT	186 LBS.
OIL WEIGHT	52 LBS.
WING LOADING LBS. SQ. FT.	5.52
POWER LOADING LBS. H.P.	13.25
MODEL S4C HAD A SIMILAR PERFORMANCE. MODEL S-5 WAS SLOWER ON AIRSPEED.	

GNOME B9 ENGINE (FRONT) (100 H.P.)

GNOME MONO-SOUPAPE ENGINE MODEL B-9 100H.P. THIS ENGINE WAS MANUFACTURED UNDER LICENSE IN THE U.S.A. BY THE GENERAL VEHICLE COMPANY, INC., LONG ISLAND, NEW YORK. THIS TYPE OF ENGINE HAS A STATIONARY CRANKSHAFT. THE CYLINDERS ROTATE CARRYING THE PROPELLER WITH THEM. THE ODD NUMBER OF CYLINDERS MAKES IT POSSIBLE TO SECURE A UNIFORM PERIOD OF EXPLOSION. THE ENGINE R.P.M. IS 1200. OIL CONSUMPTION 2 GALLONS PER HOUR. FUEL CONSUMPTION 10 GALLONS PER HOUR. ENGINE WEIGHT 300 POUNDS. THE STATIONARY CRANKSHAFT FUNCTIONS AS A MEANS OF ATTACHING THE ENGINE TO THE FUSELAGE.

ACKNOWLEDGEMENTS OF DATA

FRANK STRNAD, AMERICAN AVIATION HISTORICAL SOCIETY
BRUCE REYNOLDS, D_0   D_0   D_0   D_0
ESTHER B. MUELLER, AIR FORCE CENTRAL MUSEUM
WM. T. LARKINS, AMERICAN AVIATION HISTORICAL SOCIETY

INSTRUMENTS THOMAS-MORSE S4B

JOHNS-MANVILLE TACHOMETER GRAD. 0-2000
FLEXIBLE TACHOMETER SHAFT 6'-0" LONG
U.S. AIR PRESSURE GAUGE, SIZE 2, 0 TO 6 LBS.
TRIUMPH FUEL QUANTITY INDICATOR, SIZE 29
MAGNETIC COMPASS
AIRSPEED INDICATOR, FOXBORO, 0 TO 120 M.P.H.
ZAHN TYPE PITOT TUBE.
BAROGRAPH, 0-20000 FEET
DIAMOND PUSH BUTTON SWITCH.
NAME PLATE.
AIR RELIEF VALVE AND PRESSURE GAUGE.
FUEL SHUT-OFF VALVE.
MANO AIR-PRESSURE PUMP WITH COCK.
OIL PULSATOR WITH 2 SHUT-OFF COCKS.
ENGINE IGNITION SWITCH.
NOTE INSTRUMENTS FOR T-M S4C ARE SAME.

THE REASON FOR THE CHANGE IN ENGINES TO THE LE RHONE C-9 IN LATER MODEL S4C AIRCRAFT WAS CAUSED BY THE COMPLEXITY OF ENGINE CONTROLS AND THE FUEL SYSTEM USED FOR THE GNOME B-9 ENGINE. THE GNOME B-9 FUEL CONTROLS WERE CONSIDERED TO BE TOO DANGEROUS FOR STUDENT PILOTS TO HANDLE. S4C AIRCRAFT HAD ENGINE AND FUEL CONTROLS AT THE LEFT.
S4B   D_0   D_0   D_0   D_0   D_0   RIGHT.

ALL THOMAS-MORSE AIRCRAFT PROCURED DURING WORLD WAR I WERE FINISHED IN KHAKI. ENGINE COWLS AND WHEELS WERE SOMETIME GAILY DECORATED.

THOMAS-MORSE PROCUREMENT
INITIAL DELIVERY OF S4B AIRPLANES MADE IN NOVEMBER, 1917 OF A QUANTITY OF 100, GNOME B-9 ENGINES. SO TYPE S4C WITH GNOME B-9 ENGINES AND 447 S4C WITH LE-RHONE C-9 ENGINES DELIVERED STARTING MAY, 1918. U.S. NAVY PROCURED 20 S-5 WITH TWIN FLOATS.

T-M S4C
(PLANE SHOWN IN TAKE-OFF ATTITUDE)

T-M S4B
(PLANE SHOWN TAKE-OFF ATTITUDE)

T-M S4C

T M S4B (GNOME B-9 ENGINE)
(PLANE SHOWN TAKE-OFF ATTITUDE)

(SHEET NO. 1)

129

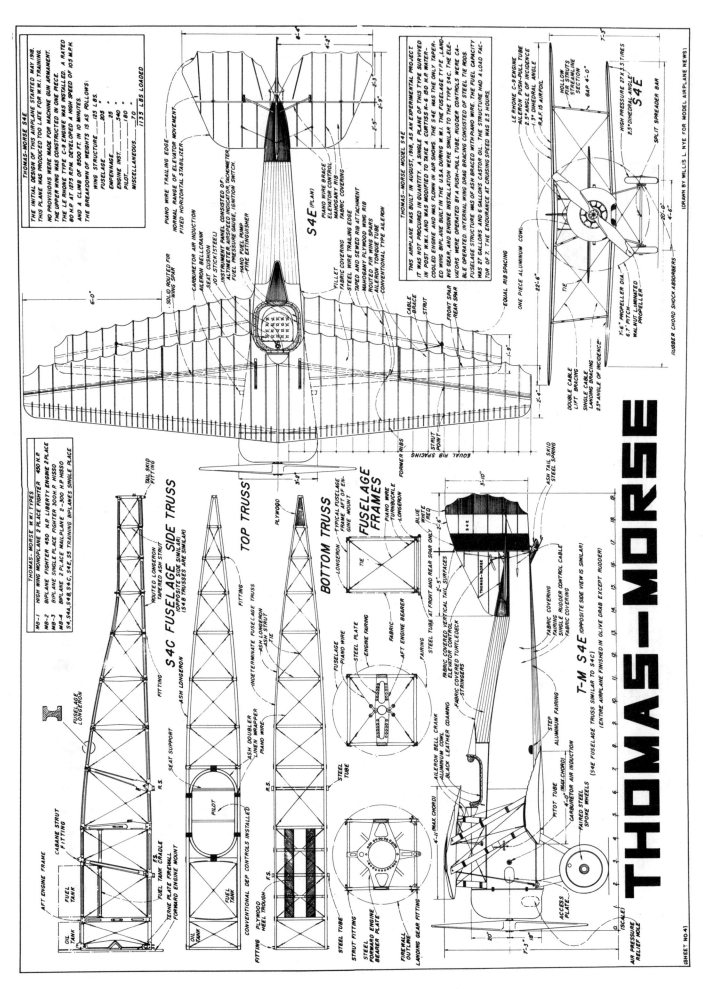

THOMAS-MORSE

S4E (PLAN)

S4C FUSELAGE SIDE TRUSS
(OPPOSITE SIDE SIMILAR)
(S4B TRUSSES ARE SIMILAR)

TOP TRUSS

BOTTOM TRUSS

FUSELAGE FRAMES

T-M S4E (OPPOSITE SIDE VIEW IS SIMILAR)
(S4E FUSELAGE TRUSS SIMILAR TO S4C)
(ENTIRE AIRPLANE FINISHED IN OLIVE DRAB EXCEPT RUDDER)

S4E

(DRAWN BY WILLIS L. NYE FOR MODEL AIRPLANE NEWS)

Wright Brothers

drawings by WILLIAM WYLAM

1903 Flyer, Model A, Model B

The Wright Brothers airplane was the first man-carrying aircraft in which the Army Signal Corp expressed an interest. Air Age file photo.

AT 10:35 a.m. on Thursday, December 17, 1903, at Kill Devil Hills in Kitty Hawk, North Carolina, Orville Wright piloted the Flyer on a flight that lasted just 12 seconds and covered about 120 feet. In doing so, the world's first powered, sustained, and controllable flight of a man-carrying airplane was recorded. The 12-hp engine and airframe were of Orville and Wilbur Wright's design and manufacture. The fourth and last flight that day—and of the Flyer ever—covered over 800 feet.

The use of wing warping, and the connection between it and the rudders, was the secret of the Flyer's controllability—the Wright's secret.

Not satisfied, the brothers set about modifying their design and thus developed the Wright Model A.

The Model A was similar to the original Flyer, the most noticeable dif-

Left: The Wright Brothers assembled their famous aircraft with little fanfare in this building. Smithsonian photo. Above: Side view of the original Wright airplane, 1903, at Kitty Hawk. Photo courtesy of Leonard Opdycke, WW I Aeroplanes.

ference being the addition of seats for pilot and passenger. This airplane paved the way for the Model B, which was accepted as a flying machine for the Army Signal Corps.

The 1903 Flyer has just been restored at the National Air & Space Museum in Washington, DC; seven other powered Wrights are on exhibit in various museums. □

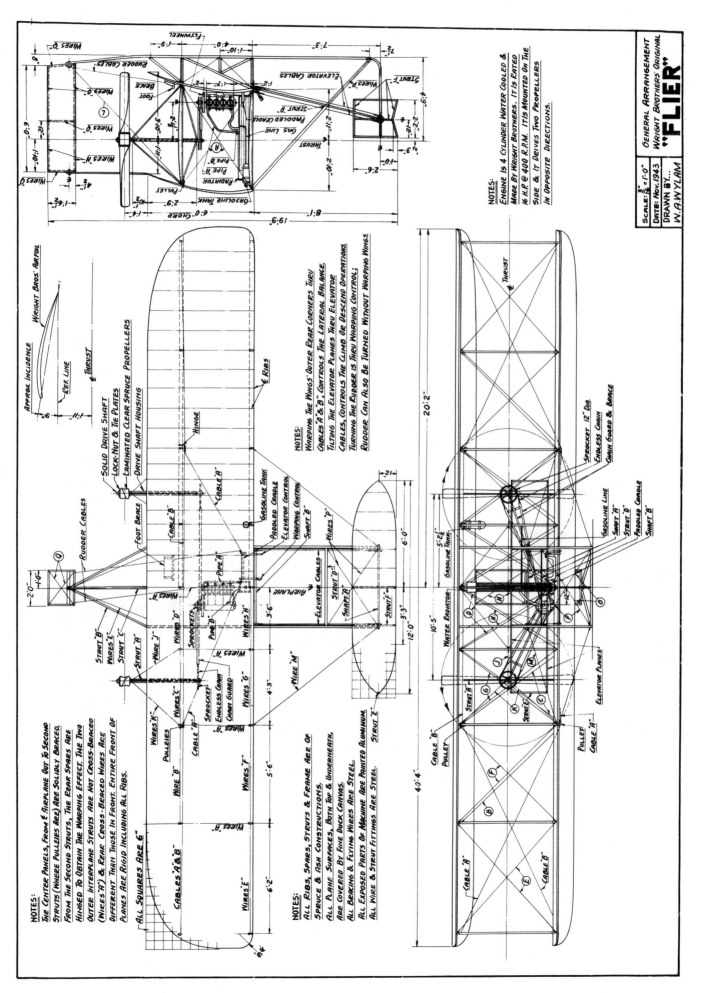

GENERAL ARRANGEMENT
WRIGHT BROTHERS' ORIGINAL
"FLIER"

SCALE: 3/16" = 1'-0"
DATE: Nov. 1943
DRAWN BY...
W. A. WYLAM

NOTES:
ENGINE IS 4 CYLINDER WATER COOLED & MADE BY WRIGHT BROTHERS. IT IS RATED 16 H.P. @ 400 R.P.M. IT IS MOUNTED ON THE SIDE & IT DRIVES TWO PROPELLERS IN OPPOSITE DIRECTIONS.

NOTES:
WARPING THE WINGS' OUTER REAR CORNERS THRU CABLES "A" & "B", CONTROLS THE LATERAL BALANCE. TILTING THE ELEVATOR PLANES THRU ELEVATOR CABLES, CONTROLS THE CLIMB OR DESCEND OPERATIONS. TURNING THE RUDDER IS THRU WARPING CONTROL; RUDDER CAN ALSO BE TURNED WITHOUT WARPING WINGS.

NOTES:
THE CENTER PANELS, FROM € AIRPLANE OUT TO SECOND STRUTS (WHERE PULLEYS ARE) ARE SOLIDLY BRACED. FROM THE SECOND STRUTS, THE REAR SPARS ARE HINGED TO OBTAIN THE WARPING EFFECT. THE TWO OUTER INTERPLANE STRUTS ARE NOT CROSS-BRACED (WIRES "R") & REAR CROSS-BRACED WIRES ARE DIFFERENT THAN THOSE IN FRONT. ENTIRE FRONT OF PLANES ARE RIGID INCLUDING ALL RIBS.

ALL SQUARES ARE 6"

NOTES:
ALL RIBS, SPARS, STRUTS & FRAME ARE OF SPRUCE & ASH CONSTRUCTIONS.
ALL PLANE SURFACES, BOTH TOP & UNDERNEATH, ARE COVERED BY FINE DUCK CANVAS.
ALL BRACING & FLYING WIRES ARE STEEL.
ALL EXPOSED PARTS OF MACHINE ARE PAINTED ALUMINUM.
ALL WIRE & STRUT FITTINGS ARE STEEL.

WRIGHT BROS. AIRFOIL
APPROX. INCIDENCE
REF. LINE
THRUST

SOLID DRIVE SHAFT
LOCK-NUT & TIE PLATES
LAMINATED CLEAR SPRUCE PROPELLERS
DRIVE SHAFT HOUSING

Wright Brothers 1908 Military. Orville Wright leaning over pilot's seat. Photo courtesy of the Smithsonian Institution.

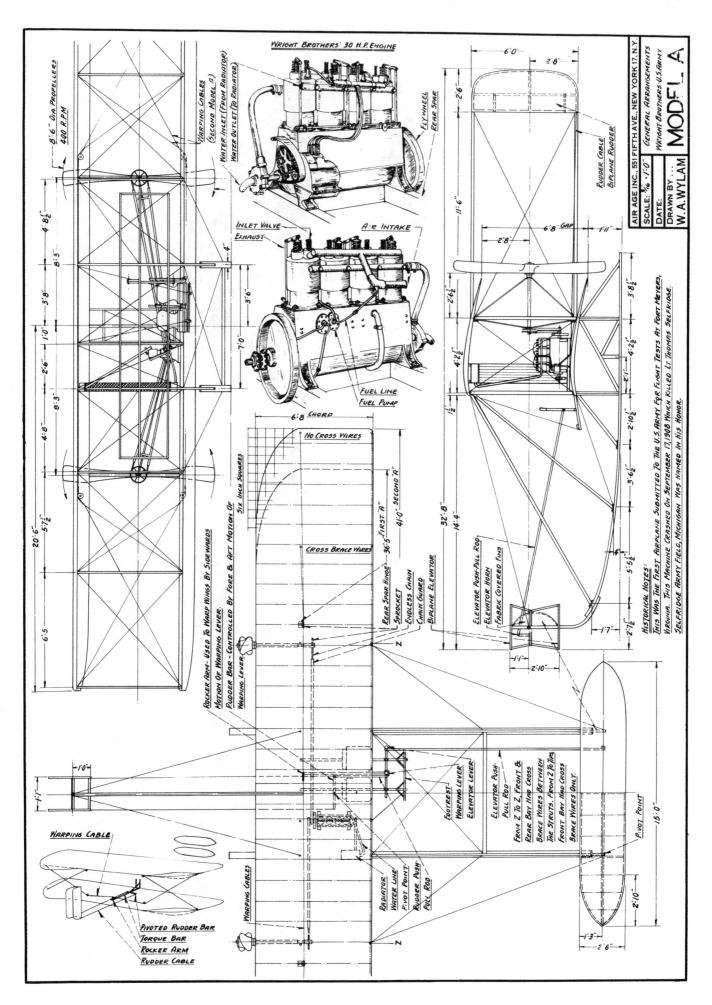

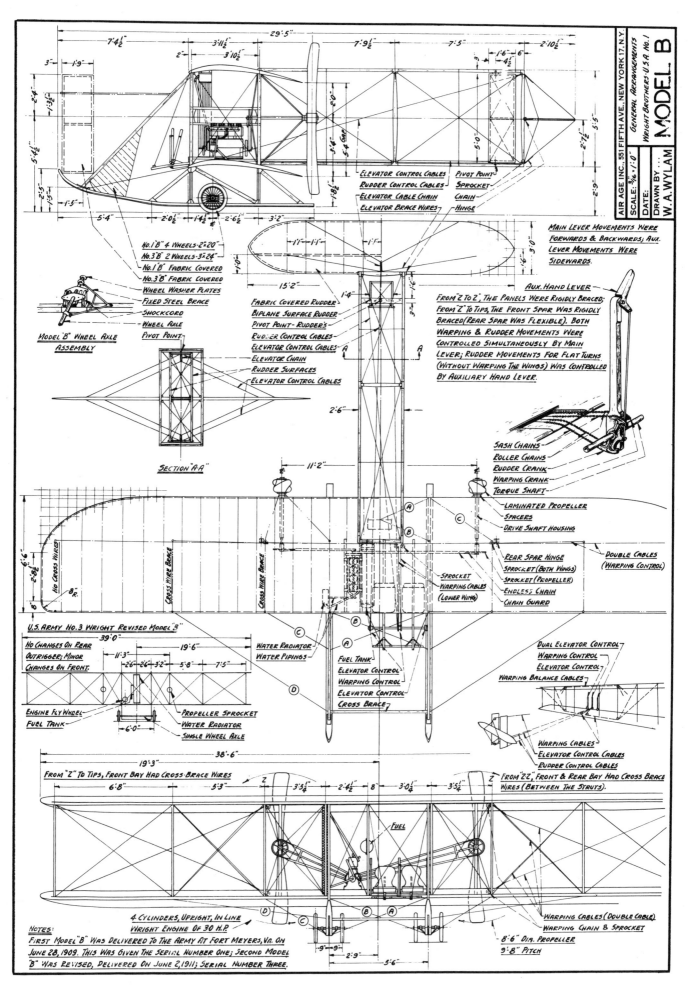

MODEL B

GENERAL ARRANGEMENTS
Wright Brothers-U.S.A. No.1

AIR AGE INC., 551 FIFTH AVE., NEW YORK 17, N.Y.
SCALE: 3/16 = 1'-0"
DATE: .....
DRAWN BY: W. A. WYLAM

ELEVATOR CONTROL CABLES
RUDDER CONTROL CABLES
ELEVATOR CABLE CHAIN
ELEVATOR BRACE WIRES
PIVOT POINT
SPROCKET
CHAIN
HINGE

No. 1 'B' 4 WHEELS-2"×20"
No. 3 'B' 2 WHEELS-3"×24"
No. 1 'B' FABRIC COVERED
No. 3 'B' FABRIC COVERED
WHEEL WASHER PLATES
FIXED STEEL BRACE
SHOCKCORD
WHEEL AXLE
PIVOT POINT

MODEL 'B' WHEEL AXLE
ASSEMBLY

FABRIC COVERED RUDDER
BIPLANE SURFACE RUDDER
PIVOT POINT-RUDDER'S
RUDDER CONTROL CABLES
ELEVATOR CONTROL CABLES
ELEVATOR CHAIN
RUDDER SURFACES
ELEVATOR CONTROL CABLES

SECTION "A-A"

MAIN LEVER MOVEMENTS WERE
FORWARDS & BACKWARDS; AUX.
LEVER MOVEMENTS WERE
SIDEWARDS.

AUX. HAND LEVER

FROM "Z" TO "Z", THE PANELS WERE RIGIDLY BRACED;
FROM "Z" TO TIPS, THE FRONT SPAR WAS RIGIDLY
BRACED (REAR SPAR WAS FLEXIBLE). BOTH
WARPING & RUDDER MOVEMENTS WERE
CONTROLLED SIMULTANEOUSLY BY MAIN
LEVER; RUDDER MOVEMENTS FOR FLAT TURNS
(WITHOUT WARPING THE WINGS) WAS CONTROLLED
BY AUXILIARY HAND LEVER.

SASH CHAINS
ROLLER CHAINS
RUDDER CRANK
WARPING CRANK
TORQUE SHAFT

LAMINATED PROPELLER
SPACERS
DRIVE SHAFT HOUSING

REAR SPAR HINGE
SPROCKET (BOTH WINGS)
SPROCKET (PROPELLER)
ENDLESS CHAIN
CHAIN GUARD

DOUBLE CABLES
(WARPING CONTROL)

NO CROSS WIRES
CROSS WIRE BRACE
CROSS WIRE BRACE

SPROCKET
WARPING CABLES
(LOWER WING)

WATER RADIATOR
WATER PIPINGS
FUEL TANK
ELEVATOR CONTROL
WARPING CONTROL
ELEVATOR CONTROL
CROSS BRACE

U.S. ARMY No.3 WRIGHT REVISED MODEL "B"

NO CHANGES ON REAR
OUTRIGGER; MINOR
CHANGES ON FRONT.

ENGINE FLY WHEEL
FUEL TANK
PROPELLER SPROCKET
WATER RADIATOR
SINGLE WHEEL AXLE

DUAL ELEVATOR CONTROL
WARPING CONTROL
ELEVATOR CONTROL
WARPING BALANCE CABLES

WARPING CABLES
ELEVATOR CONTROL CABLES
RUDDER CONTROL CABLES

FROM "Z" TO TIPS, FRONT BAY HAD CROSS-BRACE WIRES

FROM "ZZ", FRONT & REAR BAY HAD CROSS BRACE
WIRES (BETWEEN THE STRUTS).

FUEL

4 CYLINDERS, UPRIGHT, IN LINE
WRIGHT ENGINE OF 30 H.P.

WARPING CABLES (DOUBLE CABLE)
WARPING CHAIN & SPROCKET
8'-6" DIA. PROPELLER
9'-8" PITCH

NOTES:
FIRST MODEL "B" WAS DELIVERED TO THE ARMY AT FORT MEYERS, VA. ON
JUNE 28, 1909. THIS WAS GIVEN THE SERIAL NUMBER ONE; SECOND MODEL
"B" WAS REVISED, DELIVERED ON JUNE 2, 1911; SERIAL NUMBER THREE.

Engines

Clerget

drawing by WILLIAM WYLAM

ONE OF THE most successful engines of WW I was the rotary Clerget. The crankshaft remained fixed during operation and the entire engine rotated around it. This feature provided a number of advantages, one being easy maintenance. Another was the relatively light weight of the engines. Produced in 7- and 9-cylinder versions, the Clerget Company also produced limited quantities of 11- and even 16-cylinder rotary engines, the latter producing as much as 420 hp at 1,600 rpm with a weight of only 750 pounds. The Type 11EB of 11-cylinder configuration weighed 507 pounds and produced 210 hp at 1,300 rpm and the Type 9BF with 9 cylinders weighed 381 pounds and put out 153 hp at 1,250 rpm, according to *Jane's All the World's Aircraft* of 1919.

Manufactured in France by Clerget Blin Et Cie, it was also manufactured under a license agreement by Gwynnes Ltd. of London and was used in many different Allied aircraft, such as the Sopwith Camel, Beardmore, and others.

The rotary engine was little-used after WW I. Following the development of more powerful, liquid-cooled, rotating crankshaft style engines by Mercedes, Rolls Royce, Liberty, and Hispano-Suiza, the rotary engine became obsolete and production halted around 1925. A few were rebuilt as stationary radial engines after the war. □

Above: Type 11E.B. developed 200 hp at 1,300 rpm. Left: Type 9Z. was rated at 110 hp at 1,180 rpm.

The Type 9B.F. weighed 381 pounds and developed 140 hp at 1,250 rpm.

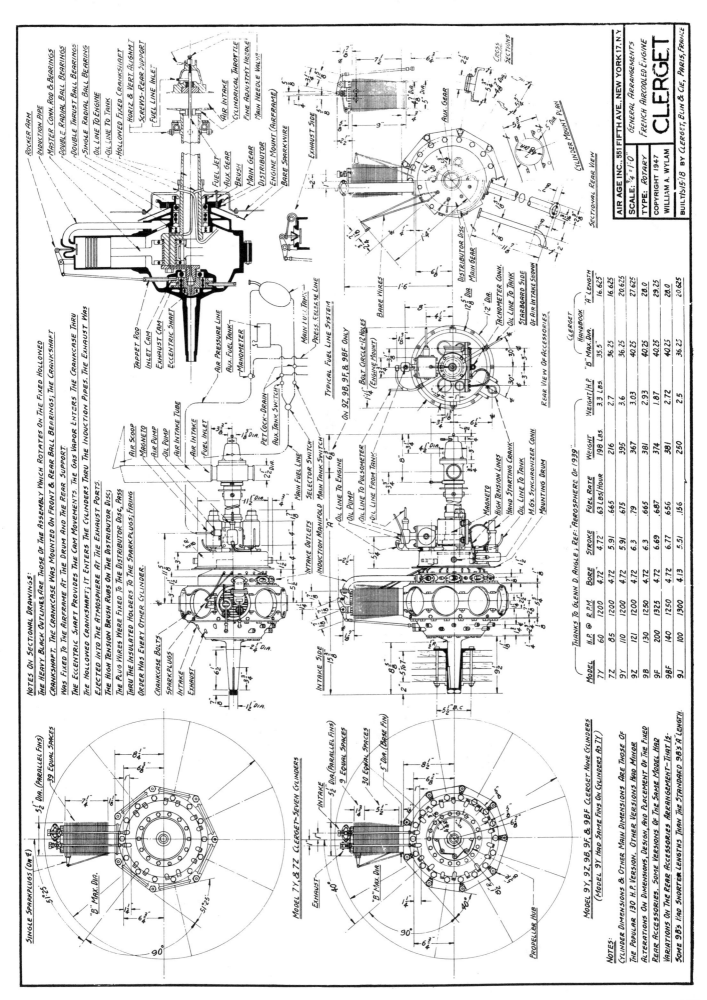

CLERGET

FRENCH AIRCOOLED ENGINE

GENERAL ARRANGEMENTS

AIR AGE INC. 551 FIFTH AVE., NEW YORK 17, N.Y.

SCALE: ¾" = 1'-0"

TYPE: ROTARY

COPYRIGHT 1947

WILLIAM A. WYLAM

BUILT 1915-18 by CLERGET, BLIN & CIE, PARIS, FRANCE

CYLINDER MOUNT PLAN

SECTIONAL REAR VIEW

CROSS SECTIONS

REAR VIEW OF ACCESSORIES

TYPICAL FUEL LINE SYSTEM

PRESS. RELEASE LINE

On 9Z, 9B, 9F, & 9BF ONLY

THANKS TO GLENN D. ANGLE; REF: "AEROSPHERE OF 1939"

MODEL	H.P. @ R.P.M.		BORE	STROKE	FUEL RATE	WEIGHT	WEIGHT/H.P.	"B" MAX. DIA.	CLERGET HANDBOOK "A" LENGTH
7Y	60	1200	4.72	4.72	63 Lbs/Hour	198 Lbs	3.3 Lbs	35.5"	16.625
7Z	85	1200	4.72	5.91	.665	216	2.7	36.25	16.625
9Y	110	1200	4.72	5.91	.675	395	3.6	36.25	20.625
9Z	121	1200	4.72	6.3	.79	367	3.03	40.25	27.625
9B	130	1250	4.72	6.3	.665	381	2.93	40.25	28.0
9F	200	1325	4.72	6.69	.687	374	1.87	40.25	29.25
98F	140	1250	4.72	6.77	.656	381	2.72	40.25	28.0
9J	100	1300	4.13	5.51	.156	250	2.5	36.25	20.625

NOTES ON SECTIONAL DRAWINGS:

THE HEAVY BLACK OUTLINES ARE THOSE OF THE ASSEMBLY WHICH ROTATES ON THE FIXED HOLLOWED CRANKSHAFT. THE CRANKCASE WAS MOUNTED ON FRONT & REAR BALL BEARINGS; THE CRANKSHAFT WAS FIXED TO THE AIRFRAME AT THE DRUM AND THE REAR SUPPORT.

THE ECCENTRIC SHAFT PROVIDES THE CAM MOVEMENTS. THE GAS VAPOR ENTERS THE CRANKCASE THRU THE HOLLOWED CRANKSHAFT; IT ENTERS THE CYLINDERS THRU THE INDUCTION PIPES. THE EXHAUST WAS EJECTED INTO THE ATMOSPHERE AT THE EXHAUST PORTS.

THE HIGH TENSION BRUSH RUBS ON THE DISTRIBUTOR DISC; THE PLUG WIRES WERE FIXED TO THE DISTRIBUTOR DISC, PASS THRU THE INSULATED HOLDERS TO THE SPARKPLUGS; FIRING ORDER WAS EVERY OTHER CYLINDER.

MODEL 7Y, & 7Z CLERGET-SEVEN CYLINDERS

MODEL 9Y, 9Z, 9B, 9F, & 9BF CLERGET NINE CYLINDERS
(MODEL 9Y HAD SAME FINS ON CYLINDERS AS 7Y)

NOTES:

CYLINDER DIMENSIONS & OTHER MAIN DIMENSIONS ARE THOSE OF THE POPULAR 130 H.P. VERSION. OTHER VERSIONS HAD MINOR ALTERATIONS ON DIMENSIONS, DESIGN, AND PLACEMENT OF THE FIXED REAR ACCESSORIES. SOME VERSIONS OF THE SAME MODEL HAD VARIATIONS ON THE REAR ACCESSORIES ARRANGEMENT—THAT IS SOME 9B's HAD SHORTER LENGTHS THAN THE STANDARD 9B's "A" LENGTH.

Hispano-Suiza

drawings by WILLIAM WYLAM

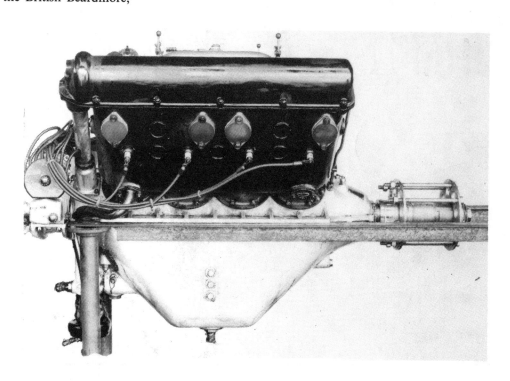

ONE OF THE MOST successful engines of its time, the Hispano-Suiza was a V-type 8 cylinder, liquid-cooled engine that was produced in both direct and geared drive configurations. With the main production facility in Barcelona, Spain, the engine was also manufactured in the United States by the Wright-Martin Company and versions were also produced in France and England. Eight models were made with the M version producing as much as 400 hp. Used in such aircraft as the British Beardmore,

S.E.5, Sage, Sopwith Dolphin, Supermarine, the French-built DeMarcay, and Nieuport variants, the engine probably achieved more recognition than any other by virtue of its use in the famous French-built Spad fighter plane.

The Hispano-Suiza engines, which were developed as early as 1916, had a reliable design and provided a sound basis for the company which is still in business producing jet engines under the name of SNECMA in Paris, France. □

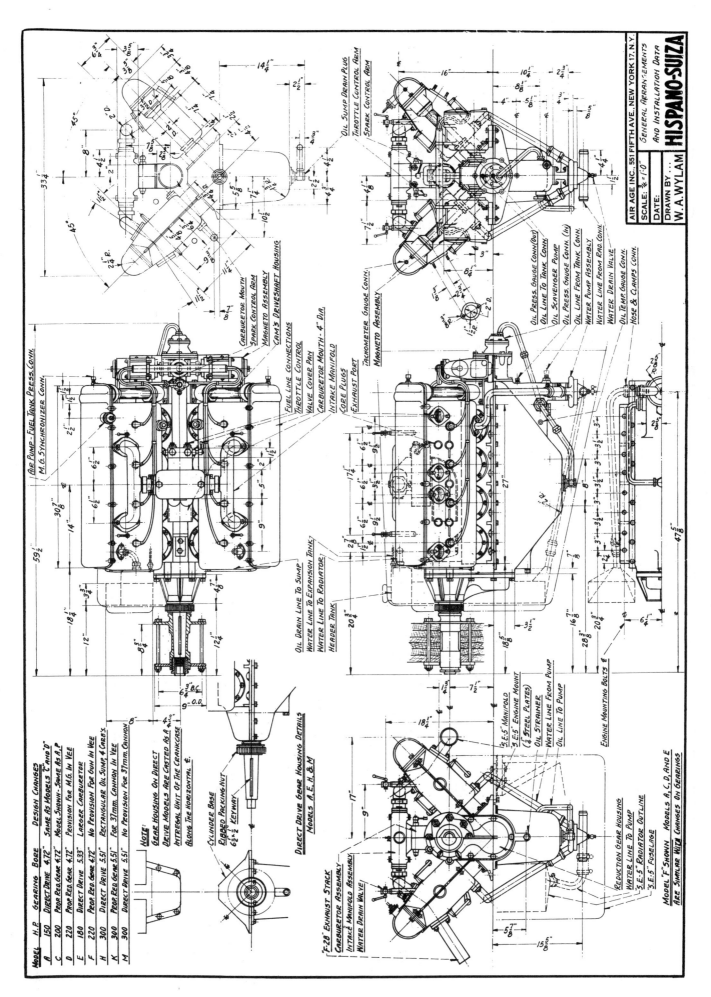

MODEL	H.P.	GEARING	BORE	DESIGN CHANGES
A	150	DIRECT DRIVE	4.72"	SAME AS MODELS "C" AND "D"
C	200	PROP RED GEAR	4.72"	MODEL SHOWN – SAME AS A.P.
D	220	PROP RED GEAR	4.72"	PROVISION FOR M.G. IN VEE
E	180	DIRECT DRIVE	5.33"	LARGER CARBURETOR
F	220	PROP RED GEAR	4.72"	NO PROVISION FOR GUN IN VEE
H	300	DIRECT DRIVE	5.51"	RECTANGULAR OIL SUMP 4 CROSS.
K	300	PROP RED GEAR	5.51"	FOR 37mm CANNON IN VEE
M	300	DIRECT DRIVE	5.51"	NO PROVISION FOR 37mm CANNON

NOTE:
GEAR HOUSING ON DIRECT
DRIVE MODELS ARE CASTED AS A
INTEGRAL UNIT OF THE CRANKCASE
ALONG THE HORIZONTAL ℄.

DIRECT DRIVE GEAR HOUSING DETAILS
MODELS A, E, H, & M

CYLINDER BASE
RIBBED PACKING NUT
6½ x 2 KEYWAY

AIR PUMP - FUEL TANK PRESS. CONN.
M.G. SYNCHRONIZER CONN.

CARBURETOR MOUTH
SPARK CONTROL ARM
MAGNETO ASSEMBLY
CAM'S DRIVESHAFT HOUSING

FUEL LINE CONNECTIONS
THROTTLE CONTROL
VALVE COVER PAN
CARBURETOR MOUTH - 4" DIA.
INTAKE MANIFOLD
CORE PLUGS
EXHAUST PORT

OIL DRAIN LINE TO SUMP
WATER LINE TO EXPANSION TANK
WATER LINE TO RADIATOR
HEADER TANK

OIL SUMP DRAIN PLUG
THROTTLE CONTROL ARM
SPARK CONTROL ARM

TACHOMETER GAUGE CONN.
MAGNETO ASSEMBLY

OIL PRESS. GAUGE CONN. (OUT)
OIL LINE TO TANK CONN.
OIL SCAVENGER PUMP
OIL PRESS. GAUGE CONN. (IN)
OIL LINE FROM TANK CONN.
WATER PUMP ASSEMBLY
WATER LINE FROM RAD. CONN.
WATER DRAIN VALVE
OIL TEMP GAUGE CONN.
HOSE & CLAMPS CONN.

"F-28" EXHAUST STACK
CARBURETOR ASSEMBLY
INTAKE MANIFOLD ASSEMBLY
WATER DRAIN VALVE

"S.E.5" MANIFOLD
"S.E.5" ENGINE MOUNT
(2 STEEL PLATES)
OIL STRAINER
WATER LINE FROM PUMP
OIL LINE TO PUMP
ENGINE MOUNTING BOLTS ℄

REDUCTION GEAR HOUSING
WATER LINE TO PUMP
"S.E.5" RADIATOR OUTLINE
"S.E.5" FUSELAGE

MODEL "F" SHOWN - MODELS A, C, D, AND E
ARE SIMILAR WITH CHANGES ON GEARINGS

AIR AGE INC., 551 FIFTH AVE., NEW YORK 17, N.Y.
GENERAL ARRANGEMENTS
AND INSTALLATION DATA
SCALE: 3/8" = 1'-0"
DATE:
DRAWN BY ...
W. A. WYLAM
HISPANO-SUIZA

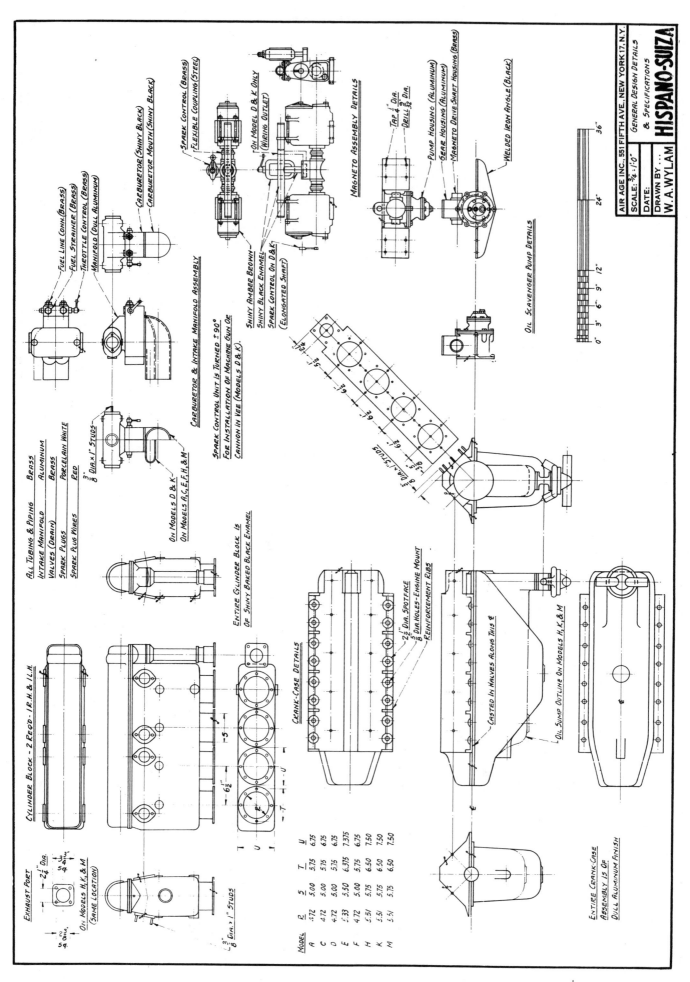

SPARK CONTROL (BRASS)

FLEXIBLE COUPLING (STEEL)

CARBURETOR (SHINY BLACK)

CARBURETOR MOUTH (SHINY BLACK)

THROTTLE CONTROL (BRASS)

MANIFOLD (DULL ALUMINUM)

FUEL STRAINER (BRASS)

FUEL LINE CONN. (BRASS)

ON MODEL D & K ONLY (WIRING OUTLET)

SHINY AMBER BROWN
SHINY BLACK ENAMEL
SPARK CONTROL ON D & K (ELONGATED SHAFT)

MAGNETO ASSEMBLY DETAILS

TAP ¼" DIA.
DRILL 9⁄32" DIA.

PUMP HOUSING (ALUMINUM)

GEAR HOUSING (ALUMINUM)

MAGNETO DRIVE SHAFT HOUSING (BRASS)

WELDED IRON ANGLE (BLACK)

OIL SCAVENGER PUMP DETAILS

AIR AGE INC., 551 FIFTH AVE., NEW YORK 17, N.Y.
GENERAL DESIGN DETAILS & SPECIFICATIONS
HISPANO-SUIZA
SCALE: ¾"=1'-0"
DATE:
DRAWN BY ....
W. A. WYLAM

36"
24"
12" 9" 6" 3" 0"

CARBURETOR & INTAKE MANIFOLD ASSEMBLY

SPARK CONTROL UNIT IS TURNED ±90°
FOR INSTALLATION OF MACHINE GUN OR
CANNON IN VEE (MODELS D & K)

3⁄8" DIA. x 1" STUDS

ON MODELS D & K
ON MODELS A, C, E, F, H, & M

ALL TUBING & PIPING .... BRASS
INTAKE MANIFOLD .... ALUMINUM
VALVES (DRAIN) .... BRASS
SPARK PLUGS .... PORCELAIN WHITE
SPARK PLUG WIRES .... RED

ENTIRE CYLINDER BLOCK IS
OF SHINY BAKED BLACK ENAMEL

CRANK-CASE DETAILS

2½" DIA. SPOTFACE
5⁄8" DIA. HOLES-ENGINE MOUNT
REINFORCEMENT RIBS

CASTED IN HALVES ALONG THIS ₵

OIL SUMP OUTLINE ON MODELS H, K, & M

CYLINDER BLOCK - 2 REQD - 1 R.H. & 1 L.H.

5"
6½"

Model	R	S	T	U
A	4.72	5.00	5.75	6.75
C	4.72	5.00	5.75	6.75
D	4.72	5.00	5.75	6.75
E	5.33	5.50	6.375	7.375
F	4.72	5.00	5.75	6.75
H	5.51	5.75	6.50	7.50
K	5.51	5.75	6.50	7.50
M	5.51	5.75	6.50	7.50

EXHAUST PORT

2¼" DIA.
¾" DIA.

ON MODELS H, K, & M
(SAME LOCATION)

2⅛" DIA.
SQ.

3⁄8" DIA. x 1" STUDS

ENTIRE CRANK-CASE
ASSEMBLY IS OF
DULL ALUMINUM FINISH

Mercedes 160 hp & 180 hp

drawings by WILLIAM WYLAM

DESCRIBED as very reliable, the Mercedes engine was developed for the Automobile Technical Society prize of 5,000 pounds sterling during 1911. The 100-hp model won the chief prize in the Kaiser engine competition in 1912 and the Mercedes-Daimler Motoren Gesellschaft, Stuttgart, Germany, firm went on to produce even larger engines and automobiles. Produced between 1914 and 1918, the 160- and 180-hp versions were used in a wide variety of German aircraft, such as the Albatros D.III and the Fokker D.VII. The F-1466 engine had a rating of 160 hp at 1,400 rpm and the F-1466D-3A was rated at 180 hp at 1,400 rpm. These were liquid-cooled engines and were known for their reliability and excellent durability due to the fine craftsmanship insisted upon by the company, a feature that is still held to modern times.□

Left and below: Mercedes engines were known for their ruggedness and low maintenance requirements.

Above: Front and rear views of the Mercedes demonstrate the thin profile which allowed for streamlining of the airframe design. "Jane's All the World's Aircraft" photos.

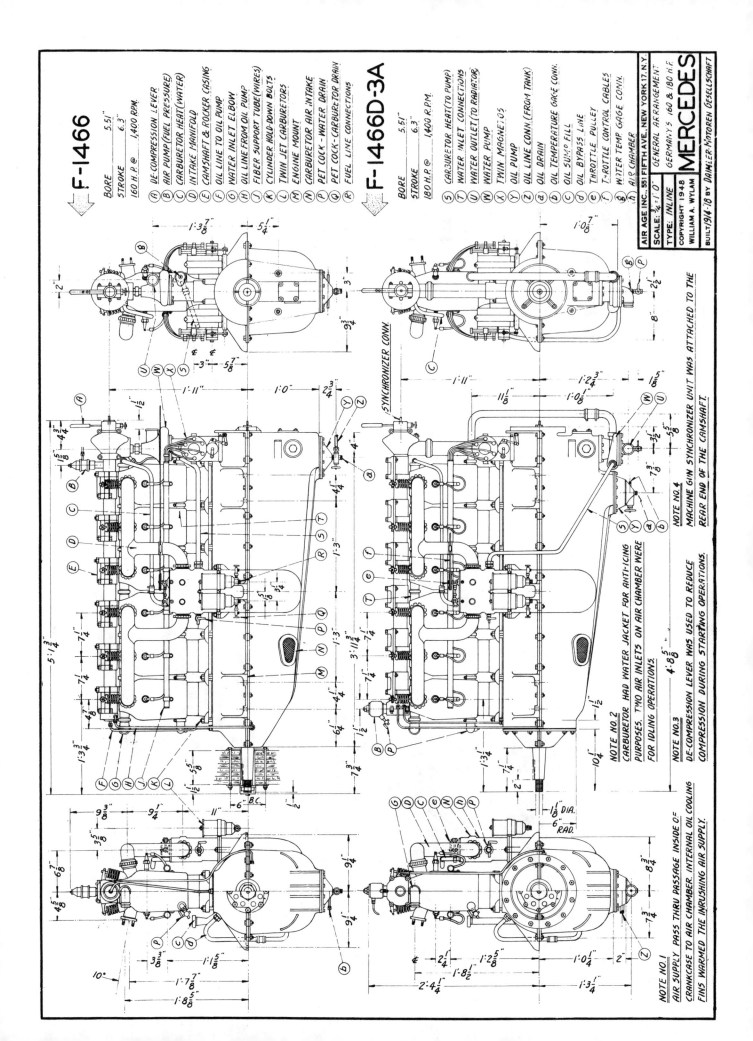

F-1466

BORE 5.51"
STROKE 6.3"
160 H.P. @ 1,400 R.P.M.

(A) DE-COMPRESSION LEVER
(B) AIR PUMP (FUEL PRESSURE)
(C) CARBURETOR HEAT (WATER)
(D) INTAKE MANIFOLD
(E) CAMSHAFT & ROCKER CASING
(F) OIL LINE TO OIL PUMP
(G) WATER INLET ELBOW
(H) OIL LINE FROM OIL PUMP
(J) FIBER SUPPORT TUBE (WIRES)
(K) CYLINDER HOLD-DOWN BOLTS
(L) TWIN JET CARBURETORS
(M) ENGINE MOUNT
(N) CARBURETOR AIR INTAKE
(P) PET COCK - WATER DRAIN
(Q) PET COCK - CARBURETOR DRAIN
(R) FUEL LINE CONNECTIONS

F-1466D-3A

BORE 5.51"
STROKE 6.3"
180 H.P. @ 1,400 R.P.M.

(S) CARBURETOR HEAT (TO PUMP)
(T) WATER INLET CONNECTIONS
(U) WATER OUTLET (TO RADIATOR)
(W) WATER PUMP
(X) TWIN MAGNETOS
(Y) OIL PUMP
(Z) OIL LINE CONN. (FROM TANK)
(a) OIL DRAIN
(b) OIL TEMPERATURE GAGE CONN.
(c) OIL SUMP FILL
(d) OIL BYPASS LINE
(e) THROTTLE PULLEY
(f) T-ROTTLE CONTROL CABLES
(g) WATER TEMP GAGE CONN.
(h) AIR CHAMBER

AIR AGE INC., 551 FIFTH AVE, NEW YORK 17, N.Y.

GENERAL ARRANGEMENT

MERCEDES

GERMANY'S 160 & 180 n.f.

SCALE: 3/4":1'-0"	
TYPE: INLINE	COPYRIGHT 1948
	WILLIAM A. WYLAM
BUILT 1914-'18 BY DAIMLER-MOTOREN GESELLSCHAFT	

SYNCHRONIZER CONN.

NOTE NO.4
MACHINE GUN SYNCHRONIZER UNIT WAS ATTACHED TO THE
REAR END OF THE CAMSHAFT.

NOTE NO.2
CARBURETOR HAD WATER JACKET FOR ANTI-ICING
PURPOSES. TWO AIR INLETS ON AIR CHAMBER WERE
FOR IDLING OPERATIONS.

NOTE NO.3
DE-COMPRESSION LEVER WAS USED TO REDUCE
COMPRESSION DURING STARTING OPERATIONS.

NOTE NO.1
AIR SUPPLY PASS THRU PASSAGE INSIDE OF
CRANKCASE TO AIR CHAMBER. INTERNAL OIL COOLING
FINS WARMED THE INRUSHING AIR SUPPLY.

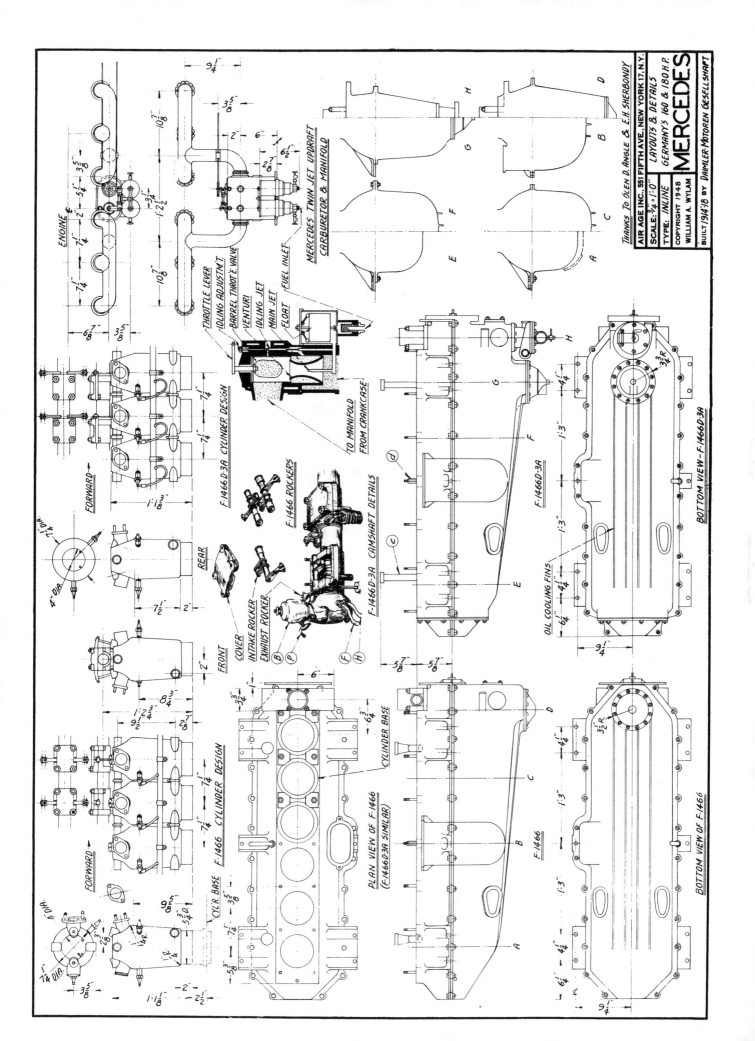

MERCEDES

THANKS TO GLEN D. ANGLE & E.H. SHERBONDY
AIR AGE INC., 551 FIFTH AVE., NEW YORK 17, N.Y.
LAYOUTS & DETAILS
GERMANY'S 160 & 180 H.P.
SCALE: 3/4" = 1'-0"
TYPE: INLINE
COPYRIGHT 1948
WILLIAM A. WYLAM
BUILT 1914-18 BY DAIMLER-MOTOREN GESELLSHAFT

ENGINE

MERCEDES TWIN JET UPDRAFT
CARBURETOR & MANIFOLD

THROTTLE LEVER
IDLING ADJUST'M'T.
BARREL THROT'E VALVE
VENTURI
IDLING JET
MAIN JET
FLOAT
FUEL INLET

TO MANIFOLD
FROM CRANKCASE

F-1466D-3A CYLINDER DESIGN

FORWARD

REAR

FRONT

F-1466 ROCKERS

F-1466D-3A CAMSHAFT DETAILS

COVER
INTAKE ROCKER
EXHAUST ROCKER

CYLR. BASE   F-1466 CYLINDER DESIGN

FORWARD

PLAN VIEW OF F-1466
(F-1466D-3A SIMILAR)

CYLINDER BASE

F-1466D-3A

F-1466

BOTTOM VIEW-F-1466D-3A

OIL COOLING FINS

BOTTOM VIEW OF F-1466

Siemens-Halske

drawing by WILLIAM WYLAM

THE SIEMENS & HALSKE Aero Engine Department, Berliner Chausse, Berlin-Spandau, engaged in the manufacturing of aero-engines before WW I. Toward the end of the war, they designed and manufactured rotary engines in which the crankcase and the crankshaft were geared together, so that each rotated at half-engine speed in opposite directions. For the time, this engine made some very remarkable climbs to high altitudes. For high-altitude performance, the engine was fitted with high-compression cylinders. Used in such airplanes as the Roland Parasol and the Siemens-Schuckert biplanes, the engine had the capability of turning huge, four-bladed props due to the unique nature of the engine gearing, giving the aircraft equipped with them some very powerful and maneuverable machines. □

The Siemens-Halske Sh.III contra-rotary, on exhibit at the Science Museum in S. Kensington, England. Science Museum photo.

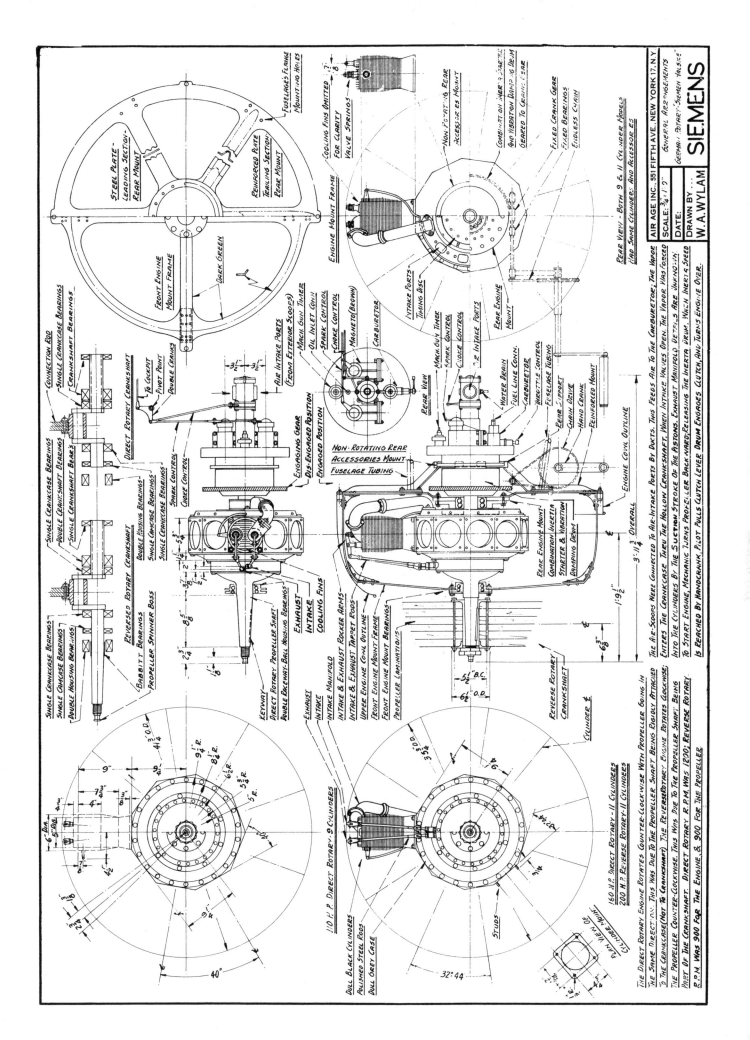

SIEMENS

AIR AGE INC., 551 FIFTH AVE. NEW YORK 17, N.Y.

GENERAL ARRANGEMENTS

GERMAN ROTARY: SIEMENS HALSKE

SCALE: 3/4" = 1' 0"

DATE:

DRAWN BY ...
W. A. WYLAM

Lewis Machine Gun

drawing by WILLIAM WYLAM

AS IN ANY WAR, the unfortunate method of force comes from firepower or killing power. Early pilots of WW I observation aircraft soon discovered that they were sitting ducks for ground fire. Following a number of casualties, pilots began to carry side-arm weapons and even rifles. The concept of fixed guns on aircraft came as a result of the pilot's inability to fly his aircraft and fire his weapon with any authority by leaning over the side of his airplane. As this approach to aircraft weaponry developed, so did the need for faster firing guns. The Lewis Machine Gun, Model 1918, was an outgrowth of the infantry type machine gun used by ground personnel, and was attached with a flexible mount atop the wings of many Allied aircraft, as well as being located in the rear of the aircraft for use by an aerial gunner. Being fully automatic and gas-operated, the Lewis provided a formidable new fighting tool for the Allies in the air. □

A pair of Lewises mounted on a Scarff ring in the rear cockpit. It is the same mounting as the one in the drawing.

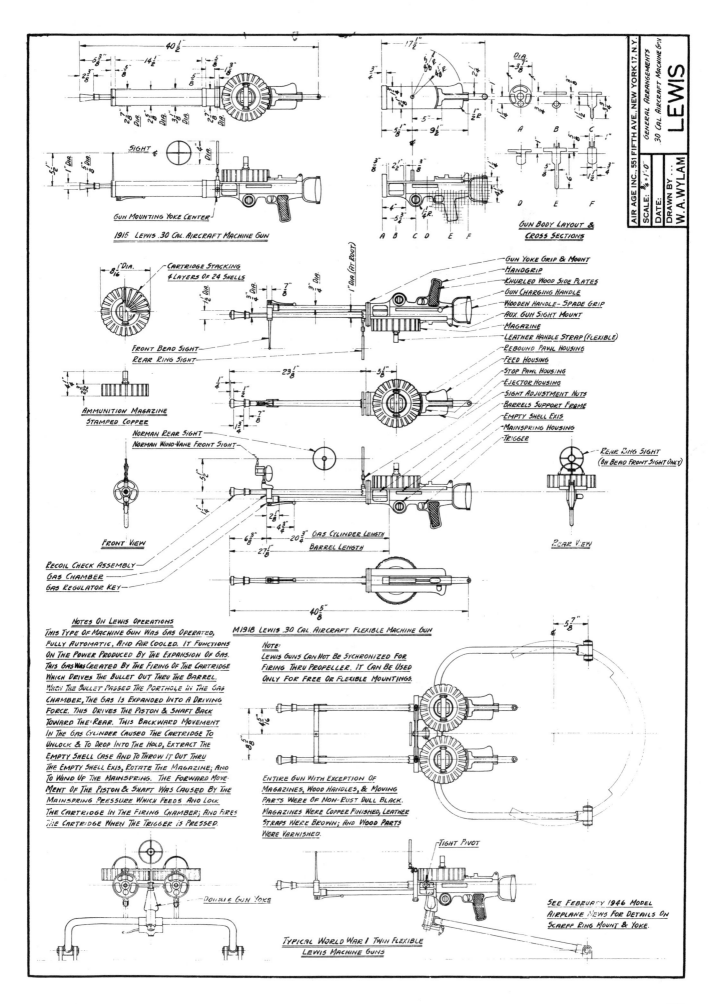

AIR AGE INC., 551 FIFTH AVE., NEW YORK 17, N.Y.
GENERAL ARRANGEMENTS
30 CAL. AIRCRAFT MACHINE GUN
LEWIS
SCALE: 3/4=1'-0"
DATE:
DRAWN BY —
W. A. WYLAM

Gun Body Layout & Cross Sections

1915 Lewis .30 Cal. Aircraft Machine Gun

Gun Mounting Yoke Center

SIGHT

Cartridge Stacking 4 Layers of 24 Shells

Front Bead Sight
Rear Ring Sight

Ammunition Magazine Stamped Copper

Norman Rear Sight
Norman Wind-Vane Front Sight

Gun Yoke Grip & Mount
Handgrip
Knurled Wood Side Plates
Gun Charging Handle
Wooden Handle - Spade Grip
Aux. Gun Sight Mount
Magazine
Leather Handle Strap (Flexible)
Rebound Pawl Housing
Feed Housing
Stop Pawl Housing
Ejector Housing
Sight Adjustment Nuts
Barrels Support Frame
Empty Shell Exis
Mainspring Housing
Trigger

Rear Ring Sight (On Bead Front Sight Only)

Front View

Recoil Check Assembly
Gas Chamber
Gas Regulator Key

Gas Cylinder Length
Barrel Length

Rear View

Notes On Lewis Operations

This Type Of Machine Gun Was Gas Operated, Fully Automatic, And Air Cooled. It Functions On The Power Produced By The Expansion Of Gas. This Gas Was Created By The Firing Of The Cartridge Which Drives The Bullet Out Thru The Barrel. When The Bullet Passed The Porthole In The Gas Chamber, The Gas Is Expanded Into A Driving Force. This Drives The Piston & Shaft Back Toward The Rear. This Backward Movement In The Gas Cylinder Caused The Cartridge To Unlock & To Drop Into The Hold, Extract The Empty Shell Case And To Throw It Out Thru The Empty Shell Exis, Rotate The Magazine; And To Wind Up The Mainspring. The Forward Movement Of The Piston & Shaft Was Caused By The Mainspring Pressure Which Feeds And Lock The Cartridge In The Firing Chamber; And Fires The Cartridge When The Trigger Is Pressed.

M1918 Lewis .30 Cal. Aircraft Flexible Machine Gun

Note:
Lewis Guns Can Not Be Sychronized For Firing Thru Propeller. It Can Be Used Only For Free Or Flexible Mountings.

Entire Gun With Exception Of Magazines, Wood Handles, & Moving Parts Were Of Non-Rust Dull Black. Magazines Were Copper Finished, Leather Straps Were Brown; And Wood Parts Were Varnished.

Double Gun Yoke

Tight Pivot

See February 1946 Model Airplane News For Details On Scarff Ring Mount & Yoke.

Typical World War I Twin Flexible Lewis Machine Guns

Vickers Machine Gun

drawing by WILLIAM WYLAM

THE FIRST experiments in arming an aircraft consisted of firing hand-held pistols and carbines. Machine guns were attached to the upper wings of scout biplanes, mounted at angles on the sides, pivoting on mountings in rear cockpits, or on pusher scouts like the D.H.2, fixed in front of the pilot. All these were awkward or dangerous: the obvious best location was in front of the pilot firing through the propeller of a tractor design.

At first, pilots tried mounting a single gun on the cowling and firing through the turning propeller, making holes in it occasionally. A surprising number of holes could be made before the propeller disintegrated!

Roland Garros put iron wedges around the base of his blades to deflect the bullets, but the vibration eventually destroyed the propeller. Fokker developed a mechanical synchronizer which interrupted the operation of the gun when the blade was in front of it, and soon after a better hydraulic system appeared. The Vickers took its place, first one only and then in pairs, on the cowls of most Allied aircraft. ☐

The Vickers, like the Lewis and the German Spandau, was developed from the earlier gun designed by Hiram Maxim.

<figure>
VICKERS 1915 .30 CAL. AIRCRAFT FIXED MACHINE GUN

COOLING AIR OUTLETS — FLUTED CYLINDER

GUN CHARGING HANDLE
AUX. CHARGING HANDLE
FIRING CONTROL

CANVAS BELT
FRONT COVER
REAR COVER

ALUMINUM COOLING BARREL
GUN SYNCHRONIZER (MECHANICAL)
FRONT GUN MOUNT
CARTRIDGE FEED SECTION
EMPTY SHELL CASES EXIS
</figure>

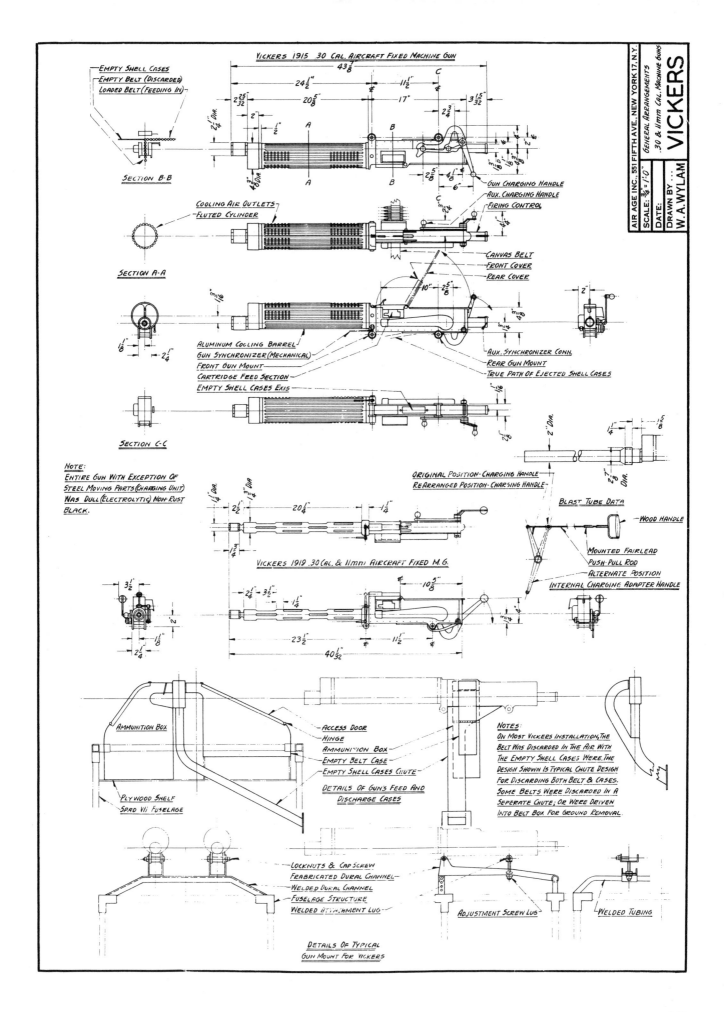

AIR AGE INC., 551 FIFTH AVE., NEW YORK 17, N.Y.

GENERAL ARRANGEMENTS
.30 & 11mm CAL. MACHINE GUNS

SCALE: ¾" = 1'-0"
DATE:
DRAWN BY ....
W. A. WYLAM

VICKERS

VICKERS 1915 .30 CAL. AIRCRAFT FIXED MACHINE GUN

EMPTY SHELL CASES
EMPTY BELT (DISCARDED)
LOADED BELT (FEEDING IN)

SECTION B-B

COOLING AIR OUTLETS
FLUTED CYLINDER

SECTION A-A

GUN CHARGING HANDLE
AUX. CHARGING HANDLE
FIRING CONTROL

CANVAS BELT
FRONT COVER
REAR COVER

ALUMINUM COOLING BARREL
GUN SYNCHRONIZER (MECHANICAL)
FRONT GUN MOUNT
CARTRIDGE FEED SECTION
EMPTY SHELL CASES EXIS

AUX. SYNCHRONIZER CONN.
REAR GUN MOUNT
TRUE PATH OF EJECTED SHELL CASES

SECTION C-C

NOTE:
ENTIRE GUN WITH EXCEPTION OF
STEEL MOVING PARTS (CHARGING UNIT)
WAS DULL (ELECTROLYTIC) NON-RUST
BLACK.

ORIGINAL POSITION - CHARGING HANDLE
REARRANGED POSITION - CHARGING HANDLE

BLAST TUBE DATA

WOOD HANDLE

MOUNTED FAIRLEAD
PUSH-PULL ROD
ALTERNATE POSITION
INTERNAL CHARGING ADAPTER HANDLE

VICKERS 1919 .30 CAL. & 11mm AIRCRAFT FIXED M.G.

AMMUNITION BOX

PLYWOOD SHELF
SPAD VII FUSELAGE

ACCESS DOOR
HINGE
AMMUNITION BOX
EMPTY BELT CASE
EMPTY SHELL CASES CHUTE

DETAILS OF GUN'S FEED AND
DISCHARGE CASES

NOTES:
ON MOST VICKERS INSTALLATION, THE
BELT WAS DISCARDED IN THE AIR WITH
THE EMPTY SHELL CASES WERE. THE
DESIGN SHOWN IS TYPICAL CHUTE DESIGN
FOR DISCARDING BOTH BELT & CASES.
SOME BELTS WERE DISCARDED IN A
SEPERATE CHUTE; OR WERE DRIVEN
INTO BELT BOX FOR GROUND REMOVAL.

LOCKNUTS & CAP SCREW
FABRICATED DURAL CHANNEL
WELDED DURAL CHANNEL
FUSELAGE STRUCTURE
WELDED ATTACHMENT LUG

ADJUSTMENT SCREW LUG

WELDED TUBING

DETAILS OF TYPICAL
GUN MOUNT FOR VICKERS

Air Bombs

drawing by WILLIAM WYLAM

Bombs being loaded into German Halberstadt CL.II light bombers.

ONE OF THE FIRST bombs to fall from an aircraft on an enemy was a glass jar filled with petrol, nails, and powder. The airplane in war was seen as providing a better vantage point in observing enemy troop movements.

The first bombing equipment was nothing more than a pilot with a satchel with a few lightweight bombs made from artillery shells or hand grenades that he simply tossed over the side. Encouraged with this new way of creating havoc on the ground, aircraft were soon equipped with racks under the aircraft, a release mechanism in the cockpit for the pilot to activate, and even additional crew members to assume the tasks of gunner and bombardier.

Shortly after the end of WW I, General Billy Mitchell managed to sink a battleship in a test for the Navy using only bombs. □

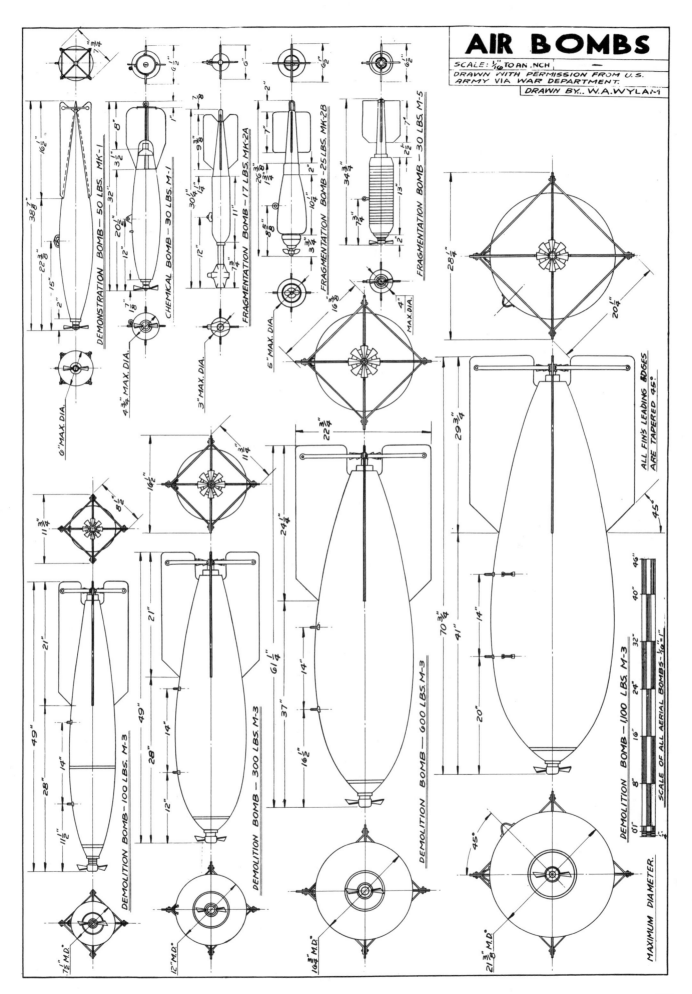

AIR BOMBS

SCALE: 1/10" TO AN INCH

DRAWN WITH PERMISSION FROM U.S. ARMY VIA WAR DEPARTMENT.

DRAWN BY.. W.A.WYLAM

DEMONSTRATION BOMB — 50 LBS. MK-1

CHEMICAL BOMB — 30 LBS. M-1

FRAGMENTATION BOMB — 17 LBS. MK-2A

FRAGMENTATION BOMB — 25 LBS. MK-2B

FRAGMENTATION BOMB — 30 LBS. M-5

DEMOLITION BOMB — 100 LBS. M-3

DEMOLITION BOMB — 300 LBS. M-3

DEMOLITION BOMB — 600 LBS. M-3

DEMOLITION BOMB — 1,100 LBS. M-3

ALL FINS LEADING EDGES ARE TAPERED 45°

SCALE OF ALL AERIAL BOMBS — 1/10" = 1"

MAXIMUM DIAMETER.